1000
HEALTH AND BEAUTY
HINTS

1000 HEALTH AND BEAUTY HINTS

Consultant editor
Pat Baikie

Exeter Books

NEW YORK

CONTENTS

Top to Toe Tips by Pat Baikie 7

Eyes 8 Hair 14
Mouth 22 Ears 24
Skin 26 Feet 33 Hands 35
Legs 38 Arms 45 Midriff 47

Starting Afresh by Pat Baikie 49

Hints on bathing 50
Cleansing preparations 56
Perfumes 69

Maximising on Make-up by Jean McGlone 75

Facts on foundation 76
Pretty lips 85
Light and bright highlighters 88
The eyes have it 93 Face shaping 101
Neat nails 106 Fake tan 108
Make-up moneysavers 111

Dress Sense by Angela Kennedy 117

The right foundations 118
Best foot forward 127 Working wardrobes 129
Shopping strategy 131
Packing to perfection 136
Figure fitting facts 139
Quick instant updates 145

Daily Difficulties by Pat Baikie 153

How to remain cool   154
How to keep warm   162
Short cuts   166

Colourwise by Jean McGlone and Angela Kennedy

Looking on the bright side   I
Eyes right for colour   IV
The well-shaped eye   VI
Lip shapes   IX   Nice nails   X
Wardrobe winners   XI
Versatility and variety   XII
Colour co-ordination   XIV
Looks in harmony   XVI

Natural Alternatives by Jean McGlone 173

Fruit   174   Dairy products   179
Eggs   181   Vegetables   183
Plants and herbs   186   Honey   200

Health on the Spot by Catherine Mackwood 201

Stress factors   202   No Smoking   209
Sleep and relaxation   210
Food   217   Which diet?   228

Health on the Run by Catherine Mackwood 233

Exercise for pleasure   234
What to wear   243
From unfit to fit   244
Essential exercise   252
For aches and pains   263
20 minutes a day   267
Exercise aids   270
Jogging and running   274

© 1983 Hennerwood Publications Limited

First published in USA 1984
by Exeter Books
Distributed by Bookthrift
Exeter is a trademark of Simon & Schuster, Inc.
Bookthrift is a registered trademark of Simon & Schuster, Inc.
New York, New York.

ALL RIGHTS RESERVED

ISBN 0-671-07397-4

Printed and bound in Great Britain by
Collins Glasgow

TOP TO TOE TIPS

Eyes right, healthy and bright

Be lavish with light: Tired, watering eyes could be a sign of eye-strain, caused by reading, sewing or other close work. Have lights brighter than you **think** you need them, or use a reading lamp shining over your shoulder on to whatever you're looking or working at. Take into account whether you are left or right-handed to avoid shadows.

Never neglect puffiness: Puffy eyes may be caused by a kidney complaint, so a medical check is a good idea. Puffiness could also be due to a cold or using a night cream or moisturizer that's too rich to be absorbed by the delicate skin around your eyes. One solution is to dot on a minute amount of light-textured cream or oil to your browbone only. This will melt and be absorbed all around your eyes. While the puffiness lasts, avoid pearly eyeshadow, which only emphasizes the problem. See Puffy eyes, page 167.

Dark looks: Dark rings under your eyes may simply mean lack of sleep, exercise or fresh air but could be due to an internal disorder, such as anaemia or even to depression, so check with your doctor if the condition persists. Dark rings are, however, a normal feature in some dark-skinned people. Meanwhile, try a daily walk or, preferably, a gentle jog – don't be too energetic the first time around, build up your fitness gradually. The effect of dark shadows can be temporarily lessened by using a cube of ice wrapped in a clean handkerchief to gently massage the area; then camouflage with a concealer before applying your usual eye make-up.

Delicate areas: Wrinkles and lines around eyes are the first to form on a face. They are not only due to age but are there, in fact, from about 20 onwards. The skin around your eyes is very fine and delicate and tends to dry out quickly, which is why lines form so readily. To counteract dryness, use a moisturizer or an eye cream under your make-up, fingerprinting it in so gently that you can't see the skin move beneath your finger. (See Chapter 3 Care with fine lines page 83.)

Relieving tension: Superficial signs of tension (e.g. wrinkles and lines) around your eyes can be banished quickly by massage. One of the most beneficial movements is eyebrow pinching. Begin near your nose, take your eyebrows between finger and thumb and pinch lightly, moving outwards towards your temples.

Take a pair of sparkling eyes: To make your eyes look young and sparkling before a special occasion, massage the back of your neck for two or three minutes by taking up the skin between your fingers and pinching or kneading it as you would dough. Then lie down for 10 minutes with your feet 30 cm (12 inches) above your head, your thighs and legs supported on cushions and cold compresses over your eyes.

Specs before the eyes

Accentuate the positive: If you need glasses don't settle for a mediocre style, in the hope that they won't be noticed. Choose a pair that will make the most of your good features and play down your bad ones. If your eyes are your strong point, for instance, choose large lenses to accentuate them; if you have a well-shaped nose, make sure the glasses do not detract from it.

Facing up: If you can't decide on your face shape, use a lipstick or soft eye pencil to draw around the outline of your face as you see it in your mirror, then select a spectacle shape, according to the guidelines which follow.

For a round face: Create an illusion of more length below the eyes with a horizontal frame, fairly straight across the browline. Avoid styles which become narrower towards the temples.

For a square face: Avoid obvious horizontals and angular oblong frames, go for rounded shapes. Choose a fairly wide frame which is not too shallow.

For a long face: Go for a deep frame, with the nose bridge low-set but slender. Metal frames are a good idea.

For a heart-shaped face: Choose a shape that is angular but not too deep, with emphasis at the browline and temples. The frame shouldn't be too heavy.

round   square   long   heart shaped

Colour co-ordination: If you choose a coloured frame, wherever possible aim for a tone that complements your hair colour and your choice of eyeshadows. For instance a blue-green frame would team well with light brown hair and hazel eyeshadows.

A question of application: If you wear glasses don't look down or close your lids when applying eye colour. After all, you don't normally go round with your eyes closed. Instead, look straight ahead, into the mirror, and you're much more likely to put all the shades in just the right places and with a lighter touch. (See Chapter 3 Special Spectacles page 94.)

If you wear bi-focals: Applying fiddly products like eyeshadow may present problems if you wear bi-focals. Go for a monochromatic effect by using different shades of one colour. Always put on your make-up under a really bright light (the pupil of the eye becomes smaller under bright light and this has the effect of increasing the range of focusing).

If you wear contact lenses: Lash building formulas with filaments can make your eyes water and smart if you wear contact lenses. So avoid these and restrict yourself to one light coat of the old-style block and brush type or learn to use eye pencils, rather than shadows containing fibres which can work loose on the lid. If you prefer to steer clear of mascara altogether, one possibility is to curl lashes with an eyelash curler.

Specs for noses

If you have a long or large nose: Select a frame with the bridge in a solid colour, set fairly low down on the frame. A heavy frame helps to create the illusion of a smaller nose.

If you have a short nose: Choose a frame with a transparent bridge set fairly high. Spectacles without lower rims help, as do gradient frames darker at the top, paling towards the bottom.

If you have a shiny nose: First make up your nose so that it has a good matt surface. Choose a frame with as slim a bridge as possible and make sure that the fit is good, otherwise you'll wear away the benefits of foundation.

Avoid blinking in the sun: Sunglasses are a must, if only because screwing up eyes against the sun causes premature wrinkling of facial skin. To be effective, sunglasses should filter 85% to 90% of transmitted light. If you can see your eyes clearly reflected in a mirror while wearing your sunglasses, they are too light. The ideal lens colour is grey, with green and brown equal second. You can now buy lenses which are sensitive to light. They lighten or darken according to the sun's brightness.

Into shape: When choosing sunglasses, take your face shape into consideration, as for choosing spectacles (see above).

A lens for every purpose: It's a good idea to choose plastic lenses for sports, because of their greater resistance to impact. For skiing or water skiing, choose glasses designed particularly to absorb ultra-violet light. In a very hot climate, go for sunglasses that do cut out ultra-violet light but absorb more infra-red. Polarized lenses are good for glare conditions when sailing and driving. However, they will also show up the toughening patterns on the car windscreen, which can be distracting.

Quality check: To check on the quality of the lens on sunglasses, hold them out at arm's length. Look through each lens separately at a slim vertical object such as a door post or window frame. Then rotate the lens slightly, either by twisting your wrist to and fro or rotating your hand and arm in a small circle. If the lens is of an acceptable quality, the vertical image will remain true. If it seems to move or waver, the quality is poor.

For the children: If your children are going to wear sunglasses, it's important to buy them the same quality as you would buy for yourself and select safety lenses made of either plastic or toughened glass. However, sunglasses are not usually necessary for young eyes because a child's eye is quick to adapt to changing conditions of light and so does not require glare protection to the same extent as an adult.

Making up your eyes according to your skin type

Oily skin: If your skin is oily and eye make-up tends to crease and then float off, avoid cream shadows. Carry your foundation over your eyelid and blot with translucent face powder before applying shadow in powder consistency.

Dark pigment: If your skin is darkly pigmented, blot out any natural drabness with a pale eyeshadow colour, in creamy consistency and then build up your chosen eye colour scheme. The bonus is that with the muddy tone cancelled out, you can get away with a lighter application and brighter shadow colours.

Fair and fine: If your skin is fair and very thin, you may suffer from red-rimmed eyelids. The most effective camouflage is to use a blue eye pencil to outline inside your lower lid. Using blue as part of shadow pattern will also accentuate the whites of your eyes.

For the mature: As skin ages it becomes crêpey on the eyelid. If this is your problem, go for a moisturized cream shadow that smoothes on easily and which doesn't lodge in your wrinkles and make them more noticeable. Waterproof formulae shadows are a good idea.

Don't be brow beaten

Away with strays: Keep brows in trim by tweezing out any stray hairs from beneath the natural arch. Tweeze sharply in the direction in which the hair grows and pat on some soothing antiseptic cream afterwards if the area becomes slightly reddened. Always tweeze at least fifteen minutes before you apply make-up, in order to give time for the flush to die down. (See Chapter 3 Unruly eyebrows page 96.)

The perfect brow: If you hold a pencil upright against your nose with the blunt end close to the outer edge of your nostril, the tip of the pencil will point to where your browline should begin. Now slowly swivel the pencil until the tip crosses to the extreme outer edge of your eye. This is the point where your brow should end. (See Chapter 3 Eyebrow shaping page 96.)

Coming to grips with tweezers: It is important to choose the right type of tweezer for your purpose. They come in various designs, ordinary-grip and scissor-grip with three types of tip – straight-across, diagonal and spoon-shaped. The straight-across design seems to get a better hold on the hair; the diagonal copes with really obstinate stubble.

The gentle touch: If your eyebrows are sparse, don't be too heavy-handed with eyebrow pencils as nothing looks harsher and more unnatural. If your brows are thin, or need colour, try this trick instead: blot your mascara brush (the wand type is best) on a tissue until it feels dry; stroke it across your brows in the opposite direction to which they grow, and then use it to brush your brows back into shape.

Closing in: For wide-apart brows the secret is to create an illusion of closeness by shading in eyeshadow right up to the sides of your nose, thereby compensating for a lack of brow.

Home rules for gloriously healthy hair

Don't break your hair: All sorts of conditions can affect hair health and, as always, condition is easier than cure. Try to avoid these: washing too frequently with too-harsh shampoos; drying by rubbing too hard with a towel or overheating with a dryer, tongs or rollers – all of which can break the hair.

Watch out for split ends: Even something as simple as constantly pushing your hair back off your face, or pushing clips in at the same place, can result in injury to the hair shaft and the ends will eventually split and open up like a Y. These splits can travel right up the hair leaving a series of broken wisps all over the head. Never neglect split ends, have them trimmed at once.

The best of brushes and combs: Beware of spiky hair brushes and combs as these can easily damage your hair. The best brushes are either natural bristle or a mixture of bristle and nylon. Ideally, use a bone comb. Next best are good quality vulcanite or the best nylon. Check the teeth for any rough edges and if there are some, file them with the fine surface of an emery board.

Hair exercise: To keep your hair in tip-top condition, it needs daily brushing, massage and fresh air. Try to brush your hair in front of an open window with your head down to stimulate circulation. Brush upwards starting at the base of your neck and continuing the stroke over your head. Dry massage helps relieve scalp tension. Place your hands on each side of your head and massage your scalp all over with your palms.

Keeping in condition: Choose your shampoo according to the condition of your scalp. If your scalp is dry, remember that over-shampooing can remove all trace of natural oils. Dilute your shampoo with water before applying it to your hair. If you have a normal scalp, concentrate on your scalp during the first application of shampoo, then with the second, massage the suds into the bulk of your hair. If you have a dandruff-prone scalp, make sure you rinse off every speck of shampoo. Wash combs and brushes at the same time.

A brush to match your hair: Choose your brush shape to suit your hair texture, which falls into three categories – fine, average or coarse. Choose a bristle consistency according to the quality, which will be either thick or thin. For coarse hair, use a semi-radial shape, one with a half-moon of bristles. For average hair, try a complete radial one with bristles all round and for fine hair, choose a flat paddle shape or a radial. As regards the type of bristle, for thick hair, a mixture of nylon and bristle is the best. All-bristle is good for thin hair.

The right conditioner: Choose your conditioner for the state of your hair, whether it's dry, dull or normal. For dry unmanageable hair, after applying conditioner, blot your hair with a towel but don't rub it. Lank dull hair also needs conditioning to give it body. Even if your hair is normal, it's still wise to take precautions against splitting/brittle ends, so make a concentrated effort to massage conditioner into hair tips.

Getting the colour right

Making the most of your hair colour: Your hair should radiate colour and vitality. The hair experts say that a good test for hair colour is to focus a 150W bulb over your head. It should pick out lots of highlights.

Colour harmony: If you do colour your hair, then don't overlook the rules of colour harmony. **Skin tone**: if you cool your hair colour (e.g. to ash tones), then warm the colour of your foundation (e.g. to pink or peach) and vice versa. **Eyes and lips**: if you lighten and soften your hair colour, then lighten and soften your eye make-up and lipstick. If you darken and strengthen your hair colour, strengthen the eye make-up and lipstick. **Blusher**: if you lighten and cool your hair colour, then lighten and cool your blusher. If you strengthen and darken your hair colour, strengthen your blusher.

Hair growth

Steady rate: Hair grows at a reasonably steady rate, averaging 1 cm (½ inch) a month. So 12.5–15 cm (5–6 inches) a year equals uniform shoulder length hair in about two years. A hair stays in the head for an average of three years.

Short and healthy: Healthiest hair is usually shortish hair because it never grows long enough and old enough to be damaged. Long hair can be healthy if it's looked after well and trimmed regularly.

The long and short of it: The secret when growing hair from short to long is to have your hair trimmed often, even if you can hardly bear to part with the smallest fraction of an inch. Hair never grows evenly all over the scalp, so you can't keep a clean shape-holding edge unless it's scissored regularly, which should be about every six weeks to two months.

Halfway stage: It's not easy to survive the half way stage when a fringe is growing out especially when the rest of your hair is long. Here's how to make lighter work of waiting. At first, brush your fringe back and keep it there under a headband or scarf. Once the fringe is slightly longer, you can catch it back in a long slide or a

comb, blending in the sides with the crown hair. After a month or so, try brushing the fringe to one side and blend it in with the side hair, backcombing slightly if necessary; hold again with a comb or slide. When two months have passed and your fringe is long enough, try parting your hair in the centre and secure the fringe ends under the side hair with kirby grips. Finally, as the ends grow, you can either start to tuck them behind your ears and forget them, or see the advantages of keeping the slightly shorter side bits of hair, framing your face and curling up prettily.

Hair styling

The right proportions: Your head should be in proportion to the rest of you. Try to make your head and hairstyle about an eighth of your total height. If you are very tall, choose a longish hairstyle and if you are very short, avoid wearing your hair long or at shoulder length.

A question of balance: Take your vital statistics into consideration before creating a hairstyle. If you have large hips, for instance, they will only look bigger if your hair is scraped right back or screwed up on top of your head. A soft, full chignon would be a better choice.

All one length: Let age be the yardstick when deciding on which length to wear your hair. A good general rule for the over fifties is an all-one short length maintained by regular cutting.

Thirty plus: For most women aged about 30, long hair hanging straight starts to get in the way. If you want to keep your hair long try putting it up. Tie it in a pony tail on top, at the back or on either side of your head and then twist the tail into a tight roll that can then be wrapped around your head in any direction. Another idea is to try plaiting which is easier on wet hair. Make three big plaits and intertwine them to form a woven-look chignon.

Cutting curls: Curly hair needs as strong an outline as straight hair and, therefore, needs regular styling. By cutting a seemingly uncontrollable mass of curls into a definite shape, a stylist can strengthen up the frame of a hairdo and the natural curl then becomes of secondary importance.

Ring the changes: No need to get bored with a short cut. Ring the changes with partings. Tuck your hair behind one ear and hold it in position with a comb. Wear a circlet of beads, or thread a few beads through your hair.

The waiting game: The best hairdos during pregnancy are either one that's long and easy to manage, softly permed perhaps, or a short style that's well cut and looks good with the minimum of upkeep. A light perm on long hair is particularly versatile; you can take up the sides for evening and leave the back hanging free.

Fringe plus: Consider the advantages of a fringe – a short, serrated fringe breaks up a round face; a smooth diagonal sweep of fringe shortens a long face; a fringe parted in the middle tends to soften a square face.

Your hairdo should complement your face shape

The diamond-shaped face: If your cheekbones are very wide, your chin pointed and your forehead and jawline narrow, the hairdo for you has height and width at the top to balance the width of your cheeks. Brush your hair close to your head at the cheekline and let it stop there or widen again below. A full fringe helps to make your forehead seem broader.

The triangular-shaped face: If your jaw is as wide as or wider than your cheekbones and you have a narrow, usually low, forehead, your hairdo should be wide at the temples, with a fairly full crown to balance the heavy jawline. If you wear a fringe, start it high on the crown to extend a low forehead.

The heart-shaped face: The most flattering hairdo for you is one that adds width and fullness to the lower part of your face. A medium to long cut is best.

The square face: If you have a square face with angular lines, the hairdo for you is one with soft, rounded lines. The length should be medium rather than short. Try a wave over your brow, or a curved fringe and curl the ends of the hair to soften any harsh angles.

The oblong face: If your face is long and thin, with forehead, cheekbones and jawline all narrow, forming a long oval, your best choice is a hairdo that makes a wide, pretty frame around your face. The crown should be rounded but not too high, the sides quite full and the ends flicked up.

The round face: If your face is fairly short and broad, with rounded contours and full, plump cheeks, you need a hairdo with high, narrow lines. The crown should be fairly high to lengthen your face and the sides close to your head and as smooth as possible. A diagonal fringe breaks up circular lines. Bring your side hair forward on to your cheeks to cut their width.

heart shaped   *square*   *oblong*   *round*

Blow drying

The basic blow-dry technique: You will need a full radial hairbrush (one with bristles all round) and a dryer with a blow-wave nozzle. The dryer needs to be in tune with what you want to achieve: 900 watts is ideal for random blow-drying and 450 watts is better for controlled styling, that is concentrating on one section of hair at a time. Hold the dryer at least 10 cm (4 inches) from hair and angle it so that the air always flows down the length of the hair shaft, away from the scalp, to smooth down any short ends.

A sleek pageboy effect: By straightening curly/wavy hair or by lifting flat, fine hair you can achieve a pageboy effect. Hold the brush in your left hand and dryer in right (reverse order if you're left-handed). Gradually work through hair, section by section, making sure that one section is completely dry before moving on to the next. Work from the crown down the back, and then do the sides, finishing with a swept-back effect. Lift hair and brush it thoroughly from root to just short of tip.

For a fuller style: You can give hair extra body by rolling it round the brush as though you are fixing a roller in place. Play the dryer on the rolled up hair and then release it.

Lightly permed hair: When hair is lightly permed, it can be blown dry into a full curly style. Lift it, brushing under each section of hair from root to just short of tip. Work from the crown down the back of the head, then from the parting down either side.

To curb the curl: If you wish to straighten naturally curly hair, concentrate on straightening out the curl in the roots. That way the ends will become much more manageable.

Holiday hair

Cap it: It takes time to fit long hair under a swimming cap, so that the shape fits the contours of the cap. Make a centre parting and, handling one side at a time, twist your hair from the front, rolling it along your scalp to centre back. Then pin to hold it temporarily. Repeat on the other side. Cross the twists over each other, tucking up the ends and securing with pins. This way the hair is even all the way round and the cap clings like a glove.

Sans cap: If you don't swim in a cap and have long hair, put it up in such a way that it will stay put even if you are pushed under the water. Part your hair across from ear to ear, comb both sections up into ponytails on top of your head. Twist them round each other, tuck in the ends and secure with chignon pins.

Tails up: Another way to cope with long hair while swimming is to comb it up into a ponytail. Secure it with a ponytail clip which is better than an elastic band which might leave marks in your hair. Comb through the length of the ponytail, tuck in the ends and anchor firmly with a few pins.

Finger short hair after a swim: One of the best quick-setting methods for short hair, is to pat your head with a towel and mop up any excess moisture. Then start to finger dry, running your fingers through the hair and your palms along the scalp.

Under the sun: Hair bleaches a shade or two in the sun, a plus fact if you have mousy or fair hair. If you have blonde hair which is artificially coloured, remember that chemicals in swimming pools can damage your hair, so wear a cap.

Combing damp hair: If you swim a great deal and your hair is consistently damp, use the right comb, one with widely spaced blunt teeth, which slides easily through the hair. Tugging and pulling at wet hair can cause split ends and breakages.

Take a test: If you're considering colouring your hair after a sunny holiday, your hair will be more porous than normal, due to the effect of sun and sea, which means that dyes penetrate easily and colours take with a vengeance. Always do a strand test as recommended by the product manufacturer, before applying a product overall.

Moist hair: In a humid climate, all hair types pick up moisture from the atmosphere which means that naturally curly hair becomes fuller and frizzier and permed hair plumper and heavier. It's advisable to have a perm three weeks before going away to give it time to settle down.

Dry air: In hot, dry air, hair does exactly what you want it to in double quick time. You can forget about packing heated rollers and curling tongs and rely on sponge rollers. Within an hour you'll have a set with as much spring and bounce as you could wish for.

Cold, dry mountain air: This type of air often causes static build up and fly-away hair. If you're skiing and wearing woolly caps, the problem is aggravated. A conditioner is a necessity.

For a prettier smile

Avoid smudges: If you have an oily skin, choose a lipstick with a low fat content as anything greasy in consistency will tend to smudge and smear.

Smooth protection: If you have dry skin, choose a greasy, moist type of lipstick which will give more protection on your lips and you will be able to smooth it on easily.

Make teeth look whiter: If your teeth have a yellow cast, choose coral, brick tones in lipstick to make your teeth look whiter.

Nose to mouth lines: To counteract nose to mouth lines, pull down your upper lip to cover your upper teeth. At the same time, cover your lower teeth with your lower lip. Hold for a count of six, then relax. Repeat four or five times.

Droopy corners: To counteract droopy lines at the corner of your mouth, try to smile as broadly as possible while keeping your lips firmly pressed together (see chapter 3 'Livening up lips', page 85).

Healthy gums and teeth

Clean after every meal: Try to brush your teeth after every meal, or at least sluice out your mouth with fresh water. The correct brushing technique is to rest the bristles of your toothbrush along your gums and brush away from your gums on to your teeth. Never brush towards your gums. Start at the back of your mouth and work round to your front teeth. Replace your toothbrush as soon as the bristles start to bend (every three or four months).

Gum exercise: Gums need stimulation – brushing helps; so does eating plenty of hard raw fruits and vegetables.

Clear spaces: Keep the spaces between your teeth clear by using tooth picks or unwaxed dental floss. Remember the idea is to clean between your teeth and not to saw relentlessly into your gums. Use it preferably at night before brushing.

Regular check-ups: Everyone should have a dental check-up every six months. Even if your teeth are hard and pain-free and your gums are pink and firm, do visit the dentist regularly.

Wash and brush-up: After use, run your toothbrush under a fast-running cold tap to remove dentifrice and any particles of food between the bristles, then hang the brush, head up, to dry. Do not let it nestle with other toothbrushes in a glass or container.

Warm water: If you have sensitive teeth and gums, it is best to brush your teeth using warm water.

Banishing hair (See also sections on arms and legs pages 44–45).

The permanent way: Electrolysis is the only permanent way of removing hair (see page 45).

Waxing is wise: Waxing is effective for three to six weeks. Wax, mostly bees or paraffin variety, is used to rip out hair at the roots. It has a double bonus: no dark shadow remains and regrowth is not usually stubbly. (See also page 44.)

Chemical hair removers: Depilatories are effective for three to seven days. These chemical hair removers achieve good results on facial hair. A minor disadvantage with this method is the tell-tale smell.

Quick tweeze: Tweezing is effective for one to four days. This method is fine for isolated hairs. A caution however, when a hair is pulled, it often splits at the root and, with the next growth, you get two for one.

Bleach with care: Bleaching is effective for up to four weeks but a patch test first is advisable. That means you should apply the product to the skin of your wrist or elbow and wait for 24 hours to see if any reaction occurs.

Taking care

Earache: Always seek medical advice if earache lasts for more than a few hours or is severe. The cause may be as varied as inflammation of the middle ear, a build-up of wax or a boil. Don't attempt self diagnosis.

Cleaning: To clean your outer ear, use a flexible stick, the tip bound in cotton wool and dipped in soap suds or cleansing lotion. To remove cleanser, or dry the ear, rewind fresh cotton wool around the tip of the stick. **Do not poke it into your inner ear,** or you will damage it.

Pressurization: When flying, it's quite usual to feel discomfort in your ears because as you fly higher, the pressure outside falls. Suck a sweet or keep swallowing; anything which makes you open your mouth (e.g. yawning) and helps equalize the outside and inside pressure.

Swimmers take note: If you swim a lot, especially underwater, always take care to shake the water out of your ears afterwards and to dry them carefully. It's a good idea to protect your ears with wax plugs.

The art of camouflage

No lobes: If you have virtually no lobes, choose earrings in a shape that circles each ear, thereby following the natural curve.

Irregular shape: If you have irregular shaped ears, cover them with your hair and wear drop earrings, so that your ears appear longer than they are.

Large ears – large lobes: Be wary of extra heavy earrings which could, with a lot of wear, stretch your lobes.

'Ivory shells': If you have small ears, you can show them off to great effect by wearing off-the-ear hairdos and pretty earrings. Avoid an untidy hairline which could mar your profile.

Pronounced rim and lobe: If you have large ears with protruding inner rims, choose simple shapes in earrings, such as studs or pearls, which help detract from a pronounced rim and lobe.

No make-up: Don't make up your ears unless they are too red or glaringly shiny, in which case you might want to cover the outer rim with foundation. Otherwise be content with a dab of blusher on the lobes, a good trick for evening as it helps brighten the face as well as detracting from the size of the lobes.

Pierced ears

The professionals: Beauty therapists and jewellers who pierce ears use sterile sophisticated equipment. In the most widely practised method an operator gives a local anaesthetic and uses a syringe-shaped plunger to pierce the lobe. Once the holes are made they must be kept open. For this reason sleepers are usually inserted straight away and should be kept in place for the specified time. Never pierce your own ears.

Go for gold: Sleepers can be rings or studs. Most operators prefer the latter. The best metal to choose is 9-carat gold. It's not advisable to wear silver earrings until six months after your ears have been pierced, because silver goes through an oxidation process which could cause irritation.

An even match: How can you be sure that your pierced ears will be evenly matched? For a start no one has absolutely identical ears. One ear is always closer to the corner of the mouth, or higher or lower than the other. Most operators rely on their eye. Avoid holes that are too low. The rim of the lobe should always show below an earring.

Not for the children: There are no hard and fast rules, but most operators do not like to pierce the ears of children under seven.

A change of mind: If by any chance you are not happy with pierced ears, you can let the holes fill in again, quite naturally. You'll be left with a mild form of scar tissue. The lining of the puncture feels like a little hard bead but you can't see it.

Know your skin type

Dry skin: This type of skin roughens easily, it may even flake, and feels taut and dry after washing. It needs plenty of thorough but gentle cleansing, regular stimulation with massage and generous quantities of oil and moisture. It also needs extra careful protection (see also Chapter 2, page 64).

Oily skin: When a skin is shiny on waking in the morning this indicates an excess of oil. It is hard to maintain a matt make-up on oily skin which needs plenty of washing with soap and hot water, an application of astringent lotion before making up and a shine-proof foundation lotion.

Combination or patchy skin: This type of skin should be treated as if it were two different types of skin: the dry part to be gently cleansed and regularly lubricated and the oily part deeply cleansed and toned. The ideal consistency of foundation is one which is not too drying for the cheeks and yet keeps the central panel of the face matt (see also Chapter 2, page 66).

Sensitive skin: This should be washed, if at all, with softened water and skin care products for sensitive skin should be used. Care must be taken to prevent thread veins on the cheeks. Protective creams should be used to guard this type of skin from all weathers (see also Chapter 2, page 67).

Blemished skin: A skin with a tendency to recurrent spots is classified as a blemished skin. The general circulation should be stimulated and ordinary fatty creams should be avoided. The face should always be washed with the hands only, as sponges and face cloths spread infection. A clean towel should be used every time the face is dried and a fresh blob of cotton wool for each application of face powder (see also Chapter 2, page 67).

Acne: This condition can be treated by special preparations. If these do not help it is wise to consult a doctor. The skin should never be touched as this is a certain way of spreading infection.

Water works wonders for your skin

Water is good for you: Your body needs to drink in a certain amount of water daily in order to function properly; if you don't take in your quota then your body draws on all its water reservoirs, including those of your skin. To help avoid dehydrated skin drink between six and eight glasses of water a day.

On the surface: Your skin can be protected against water loss by the use of moisturizing products. These add extra moisture as well as preventing it from escaping.

A question of timing: The best time to apply moisturizers is after washing or bathing while your skin is at its most receptive.

Getting a boost: There's nothing quite like a moisturizing face mask to give your skin a boost – especially if it's applied over an ordinary moisturizer. Apply both before you get into a hot steamy bath and you can enjoy all the benefits of a facial sauna. The mask acts as an occlusive layer, so there's only one way for moisture to go and that's inwards. The real benefit is that the concentration of steam causes perspiration which, in turn, creates pressure and helps soften and force out any sebum that may be blocking your pores.

Rinsing is important: Soap and water washing has always been popular because it is the only cleansing treatment that leaves your face feeling really fresh. However, to keep your skin supple and moist all the soap must be washed off. Some beauty experts recommend as many as thirty rinses, others settle for twenty splashes. Whatever you do, make sure that every little scrap of soap residue is removed or the soap will dry your skin.

Water quality: Consider the quality of the water you use. In the formulation of skin care products most beauty houses automatically use de-ionized or soft water because it is better for the skin. At home, the softer your tap water the better.

Improve texture and tone: A simple warm water splash aided by lots of brisk patting with your fingertips, will help to improve your skin texture and tone.

Under pressure: In excessively dry conditions, such as pressurized cabins on long-haul flights, bottled mineral water makes the best facial refresher. Either spray it on or apply on cotton wool at frequent intervals. (See Chapter 3 Make-up freshener routine page 82.)

In the heat: Whenever you are subjecting your skin to a lot of heat, such as a hairstyling session with a powerful blow dryer or a prolonged cooking session when your face is exposed to blasts of hot air every time you open the oven door, apply an extra application of moisturizer prior to or during the session to help prevent water loss.

Water plus: A dash of water helps your skin to get the best from proprietary moisturizers. Wet your face, pat with a clean towel to remove excess water only. Then, while your skin is still damp, dot on moisturizer and spread smoothly and gently.

Getting deep-down clean

Really clean: All sorts of dirt collects on the exposed skin of a face. There's perspiration, excess oil from your skin, everyday dust and grime, dead skin cells and make-up. Most pore-clogging debris can be washed off with soap and water but make-up should be removed with a make-up remover before you go into the soap and water stage.

A good cleansing: All skin types respond to a really good cleansing massage. Use an emollient (creamy) cleanser and proceed as follows. Begin with the left hand side. Start massaging from the base of the front of your neck, moving up to jawline from left side of your neck to right. Next, go along left to jawline from chin to ear, from chin to the outer corner of your eye, overlapping your strokes to cover the whole cheek area. Repeat the above movements on the right side of your face. For the forehead, using both hands, stroke from your brows upwards into your hairline. For the eyes, glide from the inner corner of each eye across upper lids and then from outer corners along lower lids (be extra gentle around the eye area). Finally stroke down the bridge of your nose and across your upper lip.

Make time for in-depth massage

The correct touch: Whereas a salon expert devotes 20–25 minutes to a facial massage, the simple upward and outward movements of a home routine need less time. However, the time you take and the degree of pressure used should vary according to your type of skin. For a dry or sensitive skin type, movements should be very light and take 7–10 minutes; for combination or oily skins, 5 minutes is ideal and the movements can be more brisk as these complexion types need more stimulation.

The right type of massage creams: Choose a fluffy light consistency of cleansing cream and moisturizer as a massage cream. All you need is as much as you can load on the two middle fingers of your hand. The trick is to warm the cream slightly in the palm of your hand, then apply it first to the lower part of your face, working the cream until it is soft and warm before touching the tender skin around your eyes.

Get a friend to help: A face massage is easier to do on someone else rather than on yourself, so get together with a friend. Use a chair which enables the 'client' to lie with her head well supported and her feet up (a canvas garden lounger is good). The chair should be at the right height for the 'beautician' to reach the head and neck comfortably. Place a clean towel around the client's chest, leaving the throat and tops of shoulders bare. Keep hair out of the way in a bandeau or bath cap.

Early warnings in skin care

Late teens – early twenties: A normal skin is smooth, soft and firm with a clear healthy colour, which could be likened to the skin of an apple. Even at this age moisturizing is essential as the natural moisture cells can begin to deflate. Use a moisturizer under make-up.

Mid-twenties: The ideal skin tone now resembles that of a peach – more soft and smooth, less glowing than an apple. Moisturizer helps counteract the appearance of fine expression lines around the eyes.

Mid-thirties: The average skin becomes more dry and parched looking with a tendency to a pale sallowness (not a jaundiced colour – more creamy). Main danger spots to watch are around eyes and mouth. Fine criss-cross lines indicate dryness and really dry patches on cheeks and forehead show up in reddish colour. Remember, laughter is not the only emotion your face registers. You could develop your share of frown and disapproval lines, so watch your habitual expression. At this age, switch to a richer day and night moisturizer and stimulate your skin with massage, as described on page 29, and masks to boost circulation and revive flagging colour.

Early forties: Watch out for deepening of lines under the eye and a tendency for the throat to become crêpey. Continue the skin care pattern of the thirties and think in terms of 24 hours' nourishment for your skin. Look at moisture-based make-up ranges and eye and throat creams for daytime use.

Mid-forties and over: Without a good skin care routine, your skin will become extra dry and lax, with deeply-etched lines around mouth and eyes and on the forehead. Sallow tones could become greyer and dull; tiny surface capillaries could rupture, leaving small purple-red blotches. Sagging muscles often make the jaw-line heavier and the corners of the mouth might drop. The neck becomes more lined and the throat muscles sag a bit. Gentle massage with appropriate creams can bring good results in all danger areas. Remember that skin care need not only be a bedtime routine. Follow appropriate tips given above and try to spare a little more time each day for essential maintenance.

Banish blemishes

Allergies: Cosmetic allergies have a lot to do with the individual's susceptibility to an ingredient. Often it is difficult to pinpoint the offending substance. Someone who has been using a product for weeks, or years, will suddenly develop a reaction, such as red patches and itching. Once allergic to an ingredient you will go on being allergic to it. Major manufacturers take care to screen out the worst offenders. If you suspect a cosmetic, stop using it and if the reaction persists see your doctor who may recommend a visit to a dermatologist who will, in turn, carry out patch tests to help identify the culprit.

Birthmarks: Most prevalent in young babies, these usually disappear by the age of five but if they persist, they very often change colour and become less noticeable. Birthmarks can be disguised with one of the opaque camouflage creams made specially for this purpose. (See Chapter 3 Covering slight imperfections page 76.)

Bruises: Applying cold compresses or rubbing frequently with ice will help speed the recovery of bruised areas.

Chloasma: This is the name given to the darkening of skin pigment caused by exposure to sunlight in conjunction with taking contraceptive pills or being pregnant. There are complete sun block products which aim to deflect the sun completely and thereby offer a respite to anyone who needs to shun the sun – albeit temporarily. (See Chapter 3 Go for maximum protection page 109.)

Freckles:　Prevention is easier than cure. Constant use of a make-up base and sun deflectant cream will keep freckles in hibernation. Lemon juice will temporarily fade freckles a bit. Here's the routine: apply the juice on a pad of cotton wool or a soft complexion brush. Leave on for 10–15 minutes, then rinse off with lukewarm water. As lemon can be drying, use a moisturizer after treatment. (See Chapter 3 Too many freckles page 77.)

Moles:　These can vary in size from a pinhead to something the size of a 50 pence piece. They often appear in childhood or early teens. Small moles, described as beauty spots, can be a positive asset, helping to draw attention to dimpled cheeks or pretty eyes. If a mole suddenly changes appearance or more hairs sprout, consult a doctor. Moles do sometimes change during pregnancy but always ask your doctor to check them for you. Moles you'd rather be without can be removed by minor plastic surgery.

Warts:　These are contagious and it is possible to catch them from someone else. They occur most often on the skin of young teenagers. Warts often disappear of their own accord. When they are disfiguring and need treatment, it is advisable to see a doctor.

Summing up skin care (See also Chapter 2 for further information on skin care)

Don't touch:　Beware of mannerisms like continually toying with a fringe or strand of hair framing the side of your face. That's the sort of thing which can lead to spots or skin blemishes.

The neck is important:　Remember that your face includes your neck and the area under your chin and that the sides of your face are just as important as the portion you can see full face in the mirror.

The first to age:　The oiliest part of the face is at the nostrils, the driest about the eyes. Treat these two areas with special care as they are the first to show signs of ageing with nose-to-mouth lines and around-the-eye lines.

Go gently: Eyes deserve the gentlest of care. The skin around your eyes is so thin and fragile, so unprotected by basic bone structure and supporting tissue, that it is extremely vulnerable. When applying moisturizer or eye cream to the surrounding area, use fingertips only in a patting action. Never rub or scrub.

Making amends: There is always time to make amends in skin care. Although you can't put back the clock, you can slow up the effect of ageing by using preparations correctly and regularly. You must care for your skin on a daily basis. *Most important of all*, if you treat yourself to a skin care preparation make sure you treat your skin accordingly, reading every word of the accompanying instructions, before you start applying the product haphazardly.

Foot care

Aching feet: Nothing is more ageing than the walk of a woman whose feet hurt. Aching, tired feet cause a halting walk, which has no spring or lift, simply because you can't stand the pain of the weight pressing on your arches. The pain increases with each pound above the normal weight for your age and height, so watch your weight.

Daily routine: Aim for a daily bath or foot soak. With a soak, start by wiggling your toes in warm water, then add hot and finally cold water. This simple routine, especially at the end of a day, draws the blood to the feet and closes the pores, leaving the feet refreshed and feeling lighter than they have done all day. Add bathsalts – or even table salts – to foot baths to help diminish the tired feeling in aching joints.

Regular maintenance: Daily, or several times a week, tackle minor blemishes. Use a pumice stone to get rid of dried hard skin. Foot creams and oils, applied regularly, help to reduce the horny pads on the heel and ball of the foot. Toe nails need regular trimming. Cut them straight across and use an emery board for filing at the corners.

Foot exercises: Strengthen arches by walking about on the outside of your feet or on tiptoes. Swimming is also great exercise, although nothing beats walking barefoot. Children especially should be allowed to run about barefoot as much as possible in warm weather.

Daily massage: Massage feet once a day after your bath or shower, using a body lotion or moisturizer. When your feet ache, rub them briskly with cologne. (See Chapter 7 Feet, page 207.)

Hot foot: If perspiration is your problem, splash on astringent, let it dry, then dust your feet with talc.

Banish bunions: If you want to discourage bunions, try this exercise – hold your foot in one hand and your big toe in the other. Gently pull it apart from the other toes and rotate it, again with a gentle movement.

Pedicure routine: Soak your feet in warm, soapy water (while you bathe or shower). Smooth any rough spots by rubbing them with a pumice stone or abrasive lotion. Clip nails straight across, using nail nippers. File smooth using a nail file or emery board. Push back cuticles using a cuticle pusher.

When to seek professional help

Foot infections: These are quite common and are usually caused by fungi living on the sole between the toes and under the nails. If you suspect trouble of that sort, see your doctor. It's important that these conditions are cleared up speedily or they soon spread.

Ingrown toenails: See your doctor or a chiropodist if your nails start to grow inwards. Don't try to resolve the problem yourself.

Stubborn corns: Go to a chiropodist if you have stubborn corns or a build up of hard skin.

HANDS

Reviving routines

Smooth nails: Whenever you use moisturizer on your face or body, apply a little to your nails too.

Cuticle care: Push back cuticles with a towel every time you dry your hands.

First aid for hands and nails

Quick repair: In just a few hours you can see results from hand care. Resolve, for a day at least, to keep your hands out of water as far as possible and wear rubber gloves for all wet jobs.

Wipe not wash: Instead of washing your hands during the day, wipe them clean with cleansing cream, or lotion and tissues, or paper towels.

Restoration: If your hands are at the rough and sore stage, then you're caught up in that vicious circle where hands collect dirt more easily and so need extra washing which makes them rougher still. The solution is to soak them for a few minutes in warm water, pat dry and then apply a coat of petroleum jelly, rubbing well into cuticles too. Tissue off any excess jelly after a few minutes. Repeat up to three times a day.

Putting up a barrier: It pays to wear a barrier cream for all jobs where gloves are not practical, including gardening. When handling soil, take the extra precaution of working some white soap under your fingernails before you begin. This will prevent the soil becoming ingrained underneath.

Lemon to the rescue: If your fingers are stained with nicotine or discoloured, scrub them with a soapy nail brush and rub over with half a lemon.

Age spots: When hands look dingy, with age spots much in evidence, soak them in the juice of lemon with enough oil – kitchen or beauty variety – added to cover them. Treat age spots once a week.

Hand exercises

For supple fingers: Try piano playing to make your fingers supple. Rest the tips (the balls not the nail tips) lightly on a table. Then tap the little finger 10 times, keeping all the other tips down. Repeat with each finger. Drum your fingers as though you're being impatient, then raise your hands above your head and keep them there for a minute or two.

For hand circulation: Clench each fist in turn and open and stretch the fingers, clench again, then throw fingers out really vigorously and with strength. Repeat several times.

To apply hand cream

The best way: Rest one elbow on a table and apply hand cream from your finger tips to your wrist. Smooth it on, finger by finger, as though drawing on tight gloves. Finish by shaking your hand from the wrist, until it flops like a rag doll. Repeat with your other hand. Another good method is to massage hands back and front. Work in hand cream, using squeezing, circling and pinching movements from base to fingertip. Manipulate each finger separately and don't hurry the routine.

Nail care

Gently does it: Don't dig at your nails or scrub them aggressively with a brush, as you will lift the nail plate away from the flesh.

All together now: Poor quality nails look better short. Certainly don't save the odd long one, which will only bear the brunt of any pressure and eventually split, probably low down where it hurts.

Problems grow out: Bruise marks on fingernails usually grow out. Horizontal ridges, similar on all the nails, often indicate past illness and usually disappear in time.

Time heals: It takes about six months for a fingernail to grow, so it takes a correspondingly long time for any treatment to produce results. Injury, illness, nail disorder and brittleness need a cure and/or appropriate convalescence. Don't be discouraged if results are slow.

Restrict removers: Touch up your nail polish rather than removing it every day. Removers do more harm than good.

A common problem: One of the most common nail disorders is pain and swelling in the area where the nail and the skin join. Contributory causes include a too fierce manicure or repeatedly putting hands in very hot water. Treat by wearing rubber gloves – interlined with cotton if wearing for longer than fifteen minutes – drying hands thoroughly and manicuring carefully.

Hangnails: Slits along the side of the nails are called hangnails and are a common occurrence. For causes see above.

Feed those nails: A high protein diet rich in iron, calcium potassium, vitamin B and iodine, often helps to keep nails in good condition. Foods such as yogurt, apricots, peanut butter, celery, carrots, soya, eggs and seafood are all excellent.

Cider vinegar for strength: Soaking nails in cider vinegar sometimes helps to strengthen them.

Gelatine is great: An envelope of gelatine or three level teaspoonfuls taken every day, either in fruit juice or dissolved in a cup of soup, can help maintain good, strong nails.

Toughen them up: Paint your nails with white iodine before polishing them; use one of the proprietary nail hardeners once or twice a week if you want to toughen them up.

Taking the shine: Add a teaspoonful of ordinary salt to half a glass of cold water and dip your fingernails in this holding them there for two minutes. The salt helps strengthen the nails. Always buff your nails to stimulate the circulation of the blood which feeds the nailbed. Buff in one direction only or nails may become overheated.

Manicure routine: File nails to a good oval shape using a nail file or emery board. Insert the file or emery board just under your nail, so that you're holding the file on a slant. Holding it straight against the tip of the nail can encourage the sides to peel. File from sides to centre, using short one-way strokes, not back and forth. Massage in cuticle cream. Soak fingernails for a few minutes in warm soapy (or shampoo) water. Scrub gently with nail brush to remove dirt. Gently push back cuticles using a cuticle pusher, rubber-end hoof stick or orange stick with its tip wrapped in cotton wool. Gently scrape away the fine film around cuticles using a cuticle knife. Cut back any waste skin around the nails using cuticle or skin nipper. Buff nails using a nail buffer or go on to apply polish. (See also pages 106–108, Chapter 3.)

Don'ts

Don't cut cuticles: You may create hangnails if you cut your cuticles.

Don't use a steel nail file: If you have problem nails a steel file will be too harsh. An emery board is much kinder.

Don't file nails right down to their corners: You may cause calluses if you file nails down to their corners.

Don't bite your nails: If you find it difficult to kick the habit of nail biting, consider painting on one of the special polishes available from the chemist.

Show a leg

Measure up: Ideally, thighs should be 15 cm (6 inches) less than waist, calves 15–17 cm (6–7 inches) less than the thighs and ankles 12.5–15 cm (5–6 inches) less than the calves.

Thread veins: These occur mostly on the upper leg and are not veins in the true sense but stretch cracks under the surface layer of skin, into which there is a leakage of tiny traces of blood. They can be caused by hormonal changes during pregnancy, or if you take the pill, and tight girdles or boots may aggravate the problem. They can be camouflaged by a masking cream.

All-round beauty treatment: The skin on legs tends to be very dry and dead cell debris which accumulates needs to be sloughed off. Massage and towelling are the best all-round beauty treatments. Just rub your legs with a friction pad or mitt and then dry them, towelling vigorously. Finish off with an application of body lotion.

Rough skin and goose pimples

Daily routine: Treat rough skin and goose pimples to a daily dose of body or hand lotion. Smooth it in before an exercise routine, so that the lotion can work more effectively with the warmth of your circulation.

Improve circulation: When you are having your bath, massage rough skin with a loofah to improve circulation and break down the accumulation of thickened cells.

Use a moisturizer: Morning and night knead a moisturizing lotion into rough skin with a rotary movement, using the knuckles of both hands and working up from your ankles.

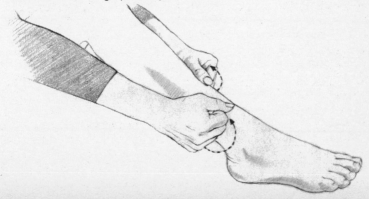

Problem: Wobbly thighs

Sensible diet: Soft, loose tissue on thighs is usually the result of overeating coupled with lack of exercise. Keep to a sensible diet, go for long walks, use an exercise bike and you'll lose weight. The bulges will also begin to decrease.

Salon massage: Spot reducing with salon massage, either the manual or machine variety, helps to firm thighs. The deeper the massage technique, the better.

Massage is helpful: Try this every night for a month. Use body lotion to smooth the way and make massage movements on your thighs towards the heart, never down. Use both hands and wring and twist as though you are wringing wet cloths, then knuckle the flesh using your fist knuckles upward to pummel gently.

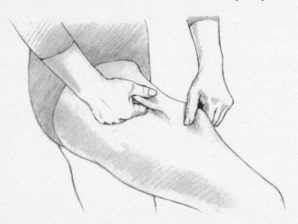

For inner thighs: Knead excess flesh as you would pastry, then smooth out. You can also carry out this routine in the bath, in which case use rough kitchen salt or oatmeal in your hand as you knead and then shower off.

Beware hot water: Experts stress that if your thighs are a potential danger area and show signs of flab, never take a hot bath for too long; 37°C/98°F and a maximum of seven minutes should be your rule.

Problem: Heavy or slight calves

Treatments: Hard muscles, built up by years of exercise such as skating or dancing, cannot be altered to any extent even with professional massage and electrical treatments. However, slack calves can be slimmed successfully (see Chapter 8 Backs of calves, page 242). Suction cup massage, in a salon, helps to get rid of subcutaneous fat, i.e. the fat just under the skin.

Day by day: Pummelling and massaging your calves every day will help to reduce them. Use a body lotion or cream for 'wet' massage or massage dry using a finely-milled talc.

Problem: Fleshy knees

Coming to grips: One of the most effective ways of coming to grips with the fat on knees is to stand and rub your knees together; or grip a bath towel between your knees grab an end with each hand and 'saw' away for a really good friction rub.

Speedy results: Wet massage helps to speed up results. Every day massage in a body lotion holding your knee steady with your thumb; with your fingers, make small circular movements all over.

For smooth knees: Scrub your knees during a bath or shower using upward strokes towards your heart. Follow with a nourishing massage, using a good emollient body lotion.

For summer camouflage: Heavy knees can be made more attractive by using blusher, or a tinted sun lotion, to shade away heaviness around the sides of your knees. This trick is effective too on the inside of knees.

Problem: Varicose veins

Over stretched: Too much standing or sitting allows blood in leg veins to become stagnant and sluggish due to lack of contractions in leg muscles to aid the blood in its return to the heart. The veins become over-stretched, their valves cannot close properly and the vein walls thicken and lose their elasticity, becoming curled and controlled.

A family trait: People with a family tendency to varicose veins should try to avoid too much standing and should rest with the legs propped. Gentle daily walking will also help to keep leg muscles firm and the support of a fine elastic stocking or tights may be all that is required in mild cases.

During pregnancy: It is especially important to rest your legs when you are pregnant. If you stand for too long, your legs may swell and the fluid in your blood will seep out from your veins and arteries into the surrounding tissues. This happens particularly in pregnant women who are overweight. Wearing support tights during pregnancy is a great help towards preventing varicose veins.

A simple disguise: If varicose veins are very slight, they can be disguised by make-up.

Problem: Thick ankles

Fat is one thing, puffiness is another: Which are you tackling? If you can't tell the difference, press the bulge with your thumb; if a 'hole' appears, that usually indicates a fatty base. There may be a medical reason for puffiness and you should consult your doctor.

Strengthen the muscles: Exercises can't perform miracles but they can trim as much as 2.5 cm (1 inch) of fat off your ankles. (See Chapter 8, page 261.)

Impaired circulation: Lack of correct exercise can cause ankles to become thick and puffy because of impaired circulation. Prolonged standing has the same result and tight shoes don't help either.

Massage: Take a soft cloth, hold the ends tightly in each hand and pull hard forwards and back across the front of your ankles and then across the back.

A heavy book: Thick ankles can often be reduced by placing a heavy book on the floor and standing tip-toe on its edge. Then sink your heels on to the floor, with your toes gripping the book. Do this a few times daily with a sturdy chair to hold on to.

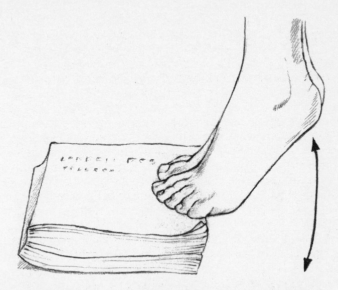

Good habits: Learn good habits when you are sitting down which will help prevent swollen ankles. Don't habitually cross your legs or sit with one foot hooked behind the rungs of a chair as both will cut off your circulation. Sit correctly with both feet on the floor in front of you.

Long standing: When you are standing for long periods whether as part of your job or during a long wait for a bus, relieve the pressure on your ankles by balancing on one foot, raise the other slightly and circle your ankle from right to left, left to right. Change to your other foot and repeat.

Reduce swelling: After a day's shopping or a lot of standing about, you may have some temporary swellings. Immerse your feet, up to the ankles, in hot and then cold water, which will do wonders to reduce swollen ankles. (For details on foot baths for aching feet, see Daily routine, page 33.)

Relaxation: Aim to relax for 10 minutes or so every day with your feet, legs and thighs supported, so that they slope gently upwards; ideally your feet should be 30 cm (12 inches) higher than your head. Lie on a tip-back chair, the floor or your bed, with cushions adjusting the height.

For a smooth finish

Waxing: This method removes hair from the roots and is one of
the best ways to remove hair. Would-be waxers often panic: it's
the thought of applying hot, burning wax and ripping it off. In fact,
the conventional wax need only be warm and there are cold
applications too. Be prepared for post-waxing tingle, especially in
areas where wax strips have overlapped. Skin can also appear
pink and tender, so allow at least a day between waxing and a
special occasion or sun-bathing. The only real disadvantage is
that before tackling repetitive treatments hair must be long
enough for the wax to get a good grip.

Bikini hair: For strong bikini hair, which sometimes becomes
'ingrown', rub with a loofah before waxing or think about getting
rid of the unruly edges altogether with electrolysis (see page 45).

Shaving: This is another popular method of removing hair on
legs. It cuts the hair across at skin level and the cost is minimal.
When using an electric razor, apply a pre-shave lotion or talcum
powder first, which dries the skin thoroughly and gives a close
shave. To wet shave, use warm water and soap (not shaving
cream, the skin is too soft for that). The technique is to shave with
long smooth strokes, from ankle upwards.

Removing light hair growth: Pumice or hair-removing gloves
are ideal for removing a light hair growth and for dealing with
specific areas like front of legs only, if you want to fade out at the
sides and ignore the backs. Do remember that pumice has quite a
rasp to it. Used in the bath, the weight of the water doubles its
effectiveness and it is only too easy to rub your skin until it is sore.

Bleach away: The appearance of hair can be minimized by using
a special bleaching preparation. You can make your own as
follows: mix two tablespoons of 20-volume peroxide with five or six
drops of ammonia. Add enough mild soapflakes to make a paste.
(This is enough for the fronts of both legs.) Apply immediately and
leave on for about 10 minutes. Rinse off well. If the results aren't
light enough, or the hair has a reddish tinge, mix more fresh paste
in a day or so and re-apply. Caution: a patch test is advisable with
all bleaching, (see Bleach with care page 24).

Gone forever: Electrolysis will remove hairs permanently but only after several treatments. Salons don't like being committed to a time, but an approximate estimate for 'half leg' electrolysis would be half-hourly appointments twice a week for about six months. Discomfort, during treatment, can be anything from a slight tingle to a short sharp pain, depending on the sensitivity of your skin and the operator's skill.

For a smooth effect: Depilatories, chemical hair-removers in cream, lotion or mousse consistencies, give a smoother effect than shaving with slightly longer lasting results. Clean the hairy area with warm water, no soap; apply depilatory with a spatula, or something similar, to a thickness of 3 mm (⅛th inch). Leave on for suggested number of minutes. In practice, it's not easy to completely cover curly hair, so try stroking against the lie of the hairs, then with them. For speed, most users wipe off the first application with a damp cloth and re-apply blobs of depilatory to stubborn hairs. After two to three minutes these usually come away.

The hair you don't want

Downwards first: To shave underarms, use warm water and soap, then shave first with downwards strokes, then re-lather and shave in the opposite direction.

The sting: Deodorants don't work properly even on two-day old fuzz. Conversely, if you apply a strong anti-perspirant immediately after shaving it will sting. So apply a finely milled deodorant talc as soon as you have shaved.

Leave alone: Fine down on arms is quite normal and best left alone. If your arm hair is very dark or particularly heavy, bleach it rather than remove it. Never ever shave.

Getting rid of goose pimples

Bad circulation: Goose pimples are the direct result of bad circulation. The best cure is a daily circulation booster treatment. In your bath use a loofah, coarse bath mitt, pumice stone or stiff circulation brush and a good lathering soap. Rub up and down your arms. This treatment also helps to remove dead cells.

Nourish well: Lubricate problem areas on your upper arms with a good nourishing cream and knuckle it in, working up from your wrist to your shoulder line. Then smooth on hand or body lotion, stroking it on until it is completely absorbed.

Vitamin A: Goose flesh can also be a sign that your diet lacks vitamin A. This is found in margarine, peanut butter, carrots, milk and cheese, egg yolks, herrings and sardines.

Sea fresh salt

Body rub down: Sea salt can work wonders for tired and blemished skin, when used to give a brisk rub down before bathing. It also makes you feel very good, much as the sea salty air of the seaside does. Take one average-sized household cup of sea salt and gradually add warm water to make a paste. To check the consistency, spread it on the back of your hand, and when it is right, stand in the bath or shower and rub the paste all over your body. You can do the rub down with your finger tips or you can use a coarse-textured face cloth. It will make your skin tingle. Massage for a few minutes only but over every part of your body, then take a bath or shower to wash off the salt mixture.

Elbows: Something to lean on

Regeneration: Elbows wrinkle fast because they are leaned on and this hardens and dries the skin. The gradual loss of the skin's elasticity is also a natural part of the ageing process, which affects elbows as well as the rest of your body. With a tough spot like elbows, the main objective is to break down the accumulation of thickened cells, so that regenerating lotions can really pour into your skin instead of trickling through the dead cell deposits. Don't be afraid to scrub elbows with a good stiff brush to remove dead cell deposits before applying lotion.

Friction wash: If your elbows are discoloured and flaky, give them a friction wash with a loofah or towelling mitt, then rinse, dry and apply a rich lubricating cream.

Double action: Whenever you use a lotion on your hands rub some into your elbows at the same time.

Elbow saver: When you are wearing a short-sleeved dress, check that your elbows are smooth. A rub over with concentrated bath oil, or even oil from the kitchen cupboard, will work wonders, provided you give the oil time to soak in.

Rough treatment: For any really rough patches of skin, perhaps around your heels or elbows, you can afford to be quite rough in your treatment. Use sea salt straight on these areas, rubbing it into the skin with something rough in texture, such as a loofah. A few minutes of this massage treatment (repeated regularly at bathtime if required) will be sufficient to flake away the layers of dry skin. Always rinse off the salt thoroughly as any left will only cause further dryness. Rinse first with warm water and then cool.

MIDRIFF

Minimizing your middle

The big bulge: Midriff is the name loosely applied to one big bulge or a concertina of three – the actual midriff, the waist and the tummy. Lie flat on your back with a ruler on your front. If your weight is normal, the ruler can touch both your ribs and your pelvis. If one end sticks up in the air, it means that something (like fat!) is pushing it out.

Pinch test: Take a deep pinch of skin on your side, just over the lower ribs. If the distance between thumb and finger is greater than 2.5 cm (1 inch), you are probably too fat.

Instant reduction: You can achieve instant midriff reduction with good posture and correct deep breathing. (See pages 245–248.)

Cover up: Stretch marks on the tummy which usually identify fresh or old areas of flab, are the results of actual scarring of the skin and are not just associated with pregnancy. They can occur in puberty (from fast growth), obesity and after prolonged use of steroid ointments containing cortisone or hydro-cortisone. What happens is that the skin's elasticity becomes impaired and the skin has become thinner allowing blood vessels to dilate. This is the reason why stretch marks are often angry looking in the early stages. Later on, they become bluish and then, after pregnancy, with tension removed, take on the white and silvery tone of a scar. At the latter stage marks can be camouflaged with a concealer cream.

Skin under tension: Keep stretch marks at bay by applying oil, or a good emollient cream, and rubbing it in gently, but thoroughly, to the area of skin under tension.

STARTING AFRESH

HINTS ON BATHING

Preparations and paraphernalia

Bath salts: As well as having a fresh fragrance, bath salts soften water without clouding it or preventing soap from lathering.

Bath cubes: Bath salts and bath cubes contain the same salts but the cubes are in powdered form: they effervesce in water and disintegrate quickly.

Bath oils and emulsions: To coat your skin with minuscule globules of nourishment, which are then polished in with a towel, use bath oils or emulsions. There are floating oils for dry skin, but they have no water-softening or cleansing properties and leave an oily scum around the bath.

Capsules: Bath oils in gelatine capsule form usually contain a high perfume concentration. They release their contents as they dissolve.

Foam and bubble baths: It is not frivolous to fill your bath with creamy gleaming lather. Foam and bubble baths contain detergent to cleanse the skin. They are also ideal for young children who are reluctant to wash and for old people who lack the agility to soap themselves. They leave no tell-tale ring around the bath.

Powder for polish: Talcum powder contains similar components to face powder and provides a pleasant smooth surface on your skin. This helps to keep you cool and to absorb perspiration. Some are extra emollient and, when buffed on with a puff, will polish your skin to a satiny sheen.

Loofahs: To remove dead cells and keep your skin healthy use a loofah. A natural loofah is anything from 25–40 cm (10–16 inches) long: the longer ones are ideal for reaching neglected areas, such as between your shoulder blades: the short ones, or loofah mitts, are fine for underwater massage on flabby areas such as tops of your legs.

Massage gloves: Give yourself a treat with massage gloves. They can be used wet, or dry, with a light circular movement all over your body. They are available in a variety of textures: jute ones give a gentle massage; polypropylene, more scratchy, gives a firmer massage; towelling is mildly stimulating.

Friction straps: Help slough off dead skin with friction straps that are specially designed for reaching right round to your back. They come in a combination of towelling and sponge.

Body brushes: Whip up your circulation and deep cleanse your skin with a body brush. The 'heads' are made of stiff natural bristle or soft sponge.

Before a bath

Remove make-up: Always remove all your make-up. Steam is a wonderful cleanser; it opens your pores so they can exude the dirt.

Bathtime set: Remember that steam 'fixes' waves, so pin your hair into shape and put on a net or cap for a quick bathtime set.

Test the water: Place your elbow in your bath water before you step in. It should feel pleasantly warm. Adjust hot or cold water if necessary.

After a bath

Cool finish: While the warm bath water is running away, and the air still comfortably warm, turn on the cold tap to cool the escaping water, than scoop up handfuls and splash it over yourself. Even better, invest in a shower spray for your bath taps. The cold water quickens the circulation and gives you an added spurt of energy.

Closing thought: Always pat your face with skin tonic to close the pores.

Return to normal: Kneiff, the famous herbalist and innovator of bath treatments, recommended that, after a bath, a person should slip on a towelling robe, or moisture-absorbent garment, and walk round or exercise until their body temperature had returned to normal.

While still damp: The best time to apply moisturizing products to your face is after washing or bathing while your skin is still damp and at its most receptive.

Body lotion: Apply body lotion to your skin while it is still damp after a bath and massage it in lightly with a circular movement. Use different degrees of pressure and/or applicators for the different areas – gently on trunk, legs and arms but firmly on tarnished patches, where there is a real accumulation of dead cells, such as elbows, heels and knees.

Powder dust: If you find a talcum powder shaker messy, use a talcum pad. You can make your own and refill it when necessary from a giant family pack of talcum. Just fill a purchased towelling mitt with talcum powder or make your own mitt from cotton or open-weave towelling fabric.

Special baths

Sauna: The first effect of a sauna is complete relaxation of body and mind and, through a drop in blood pressure, mental strain disappears and the muscles relax. The usual pattern is: shower, sauna, shower, sauna, shower and relax.

Steam or dry heat: According to the method of heating and the degree of humidity, the sauna can be a steam bath or dry-heat bath. Perspiration usually starts in about eight minutes, during the first sauna. After 10–20 minutes in the sauna, you take a quick shower, starting warm and gradually getting cooler. Then you repeat the sauna session. Perspiration breaks out very quickly the second time. After this, you take a cold shower and then relax for at least half an hour.

Weight loss: A sauna helps weight loss, because it eliminates toxins and surplus water from the tissues and these can produce obesity. The mistake some would-be slimmers make is to stay in the sauna for too long which can cause over fatigue and even fainting. Most of the weight loss will return after a drink.

The benefits: The purpose of treatments, such as the sauna or Turkish baths, is to draw off excess fluid from your body which reduces weight, sometimes quite drastically, but always only temporarily – and to draw deep-seated grime and accumulated debris out of your pores. Your pores are opened by the action of the 'bath' and perspiration follows, which reduces your body's water content and pushes out any clogging matter.

The follow on: When the treatment is followed by a toning massage and a plunge in cold water, or a rub with skin tonic to close the pores, you will, most likely, feel gloriously refreshed though tired.

Beauty baths

A mock turkish bath: This special sort of deep-cleansing treatment is ideal if your skin is showing signs of winter neglect. Allow at least an hour and a half during the evening and be prepared to go straight to bed afterwards.

The components: You'll need bath salts, soap, a loofah or bath mitts for friction, a nail brush, pumice stone for any areas of hard skin and a large thick towel.

The method: Run a hot bath and pour in two generous handfuls of the salts. Stretch out and lie in this for 10 minutes, not soaping. Then, for the next 10 minutes or so, using soap, rub and scrub every inch of you. Start by brushing your fingernails, then use the loofah or mitt to rub your hands, arms, elbows, (pumice will come in handy here too), and upper arms. All this helps to speed up the blood circulation and remove the invisible layer of cast-off cells that dull the skin's surface. Repeat the treatment on toenails, feet, ankles, calves, knees and thighs. Then lie back, bend your knees and go round your tummy, in a clockwise direction, with the loofah or mitt or, if you are tender in that area, use a sponge. Massaging like this helps to encourage your blood circulation and to keep your waist small. Finally, sit upright and repeat that first massage around your tummy before moving on to your shoulders and back.

After the bath: When you get out of the bath, wrap yourself in a towel and lie down. After about half an hour, run another bath but this time use soap and lather well all over, paying particular attention to the back of your neck, the backs of your arms and elbows, the backs of your legs and heels. Finally, shower or rinse off in clean water, towel dry and go to bed for the night.

A mock sauna: For a soothing home sauna use two large towels and half to one cupful of blended herbs such as mint and camomile. Run the hottest water you can bear into the bottom of the bath. Pour in the herbs under the pressure of the tap water so as to disperse their fragrance. Don't get into the tub yourself but soak the towels in the scented water. Then, sitting on a sturdy stool next to the bath, swathe yourself, mummy-style, in the towels. When the towels begin to cool, unwind them.

Rough, scaly skin: You can improve rough, dry, scaly skin, which is usually very noticeable on legs, by soaking yourself in a warm bath, to which you have added a few drops of vegetable oil soap (available from chemists or health food stores). Make sure you rinse the soap off completely as soap residue can cause scaling. If you prefer you can use a bath additive instead of soap. Dry yourself very thoroughly using a friction movement. Then massage the affected parts with concentrated almond or turtle oil.

Quickie bath: If you need a bath in a hurry, run tepid water. Stretch out in the tub for five minutes, a wet face cloth over your eyes. Then scrub briskly and rinse yourself with the bath water. Next, turn on the shower as cold as you can take it. Rinse again. Towel dry to stimulate your circulation. That will really get you moving. Time taken – 10 minutes.

What a shower

Quick refresher: When speed is the criterion, there is nothing like a shower of whatever type, for waking you up in a brisk, invigorating manner.

Speedy body shampoo: For a three-minute shower spread a body shampoo all over your skin. Soak yourself thoroughly under the spray before lathering up, then rinse off. You can wash your hair at the same time as many body shampoos are gentle enough to be used as a shampoo for any hair type.

Good for hair: A shower is essential for an efficient hair shampoo. Wash your hair in the shower using a shampoo that conditions as it cleanses. Wet hair well first, then lather and rinse twice for good measure. The needle sharp spray ensures that you remove all traces of suds and grime.

For safety's sake: Equip your shower with a non-slip mat. Use soap that hangs on a rope around your neck or wrist or invest in a shower tray that hangs on the door and provides ready storage for soap, sponges, shampoo and such.

Sit down shower: It's wonderfully relaxing to shower while you are sitting down in the bath or in a shower recess on a sturdy stool that won't tip or slip. Scrub as usual with a sponge and plenty of soap. Then sit, legs crossed, and let the spray come down full force, especially on areas of tension such as the back of your neck and shoulders. You'll feel fatigue and strain literally wash away.

In a heatwave: Resist the temptation to take a cold shower when the weather is very hot. Set the temperature gauge to lukewarm or tepid. You will find that the cooling effect lasts longer because blood vessels all over your body will become dilated and release trapped heat. Shower for 10 minutes, if you can. Then, if you have time, allow your skin to dry naturally. Lie down and spray yourself all over with cologne. Then use lots of dusting powder.

Skin tones: A shower can liven up your skin tone. Make sure the spray reaches everywhere including the back of your ears, nape of your neck, under each foot, in between each toe. Temperature changes can help to freshen you up. Start with warm water, then switch to tepid mid-stream and finish with cool to rinse off.

Zipping it up: If you direct the jet to individual parts of your body, switching from hot to cold and back to hot again, you'll zip up the circulation in every area.

Backache relief: Soothe backache with a shower treatment. Sit on the floor of the bath, resting your head on your knees, and let warm to hot water pour down over your back, shoulders and the nape of your neck. Three minutes of this can relax muscle tension. (See Chapter 8 page 264.)

After the shower is over: After every shower apply dry skin oil or body lotion to your still-moist skin.

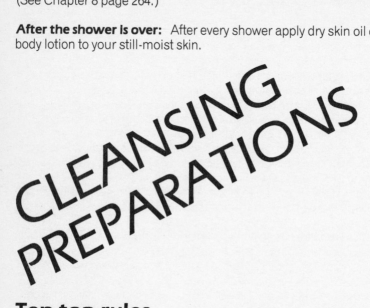

CLEANSING PREPARATIONS

Ten top rules

Don't be tempted: When you are tired, resist the temptation to fall into bed without removing your make-up. Stale make-up and the day's grime not only clog pores but will eventually coarsen your skin. Really deep daily cleansing is a most important part of all skin care. Use cleansing creams and lotions until the cotton wool or tissues come away clean.

Spotless: Always make sure that your hands are spotlessly clean when touching your face. Use just the tips of your fingers to apply make-up, moisturizer and cream working in light upward and outward movements.

Away with the cloth: Aim to do without a face cloth or flannel. No matter how careful you are, a flannel never dries out properly and there is always bacterial infection on it from the air, which is then transferred to your face. If you feel you cannot do without a face flannel, however, boil it after each use and jettison it instantly it has served its turn.

Clean basin: Make sure a wash basin is clean before filling it with water. If it is even slightly grubby, use running water rather than fill up the basin.

Morning cleanse: Never neglect to cleanse your face as soon as you get up. Even while you are sleeping, skin leads an active life. During the night hours, it still picks up bacteria and invisible dust particles from the atmosphere and, at the same time, breathes out body waste, excess oil and perspiration.

Value for money: Weigh up special offers as they are only good value for money if they are products that you would be buying anyway. Don't buy beauty products you don't want just to get the offer.

Cleansers are cleansers: As long as the consistency looks as if it's the sort you need (see pages 64–68), any cleanser can be a good buy. Look out for good sized cleansers in the sales and ask the assistant's advice.

An easy wipe off: On the subject of removers, it's important to realise that waterproof cosmetics are as easily wiped off as any other cosmetics. Make-up is generally resistant to soap and water and is best removed with a solvent, such as mineral oil or similar oils. Most cleansing creams, oils, lotions and eye make-up removers contain one or more of these solvents and will easily remove waterproof eye make-up.

With particular care: Eye make-up should be removed with particular care as the skin around your eyes is exceptionally thin and sensitive (see Chapter 3, page 94).

When chips are down: Nail polish removers can be drying. It's often wiser to touch up chips rather than remove all the varnish and start again from scratch. (See also Neat nails on page 106 for information on preventing chipping.)

For your face

Cleansing creams: These are designed to remove both oil soluble and water soluble grime and soil efficiently. They are quick to apply, easy to spread and easy to remove with a tissue and are ideal for dry; dry/sensitive combination skins as a night-time deep cleanser (see page 66).

Solid consistency: Some cleansing creams have a more solid consistency but become a liquid on contact with the skin. These are ideal for dry skin, especially at night-time, when you can leave the cream on until the last minute before you go to bed and benefit from its nourishing properties too.

Milk texture: Complexion milks are usually top-of-the milk texture rather than an actual pouring consistency. These are good for a quick cleanse for dry; dry/sensitive; normal and combination skins, because they spread easily and are speedily removed.

Wash-off creams: These are popular. They are first applied as a cream and then washed off with water. They are ideal for dry and normal skin (see page 66).

Clear liquid cleansing lotions: This type of cleanser is often recommended for the treatment of very greasy skins. It's also good for blemished skin as it cleans quickly and effectively and doesn't disturb the skin.

Good travellers: Cleansing tissues are ideal when you are travelling. They are usually packed in sachets and when opened up are about the size of a face flannel. The tissue is often a resin treated paper impregnated with a cleansing product. Another type consists of small circular flannel pads packed in a container with a tightly fitting lid. The pads are impregnated with the product.

Sloughing cleansers: These are a back-up to other forms of cleansing and help to remove dead cell debris. They only perform effectively after skin has been cleansed.

All-purpose creams: If you prefer, you can use an all-purpose cream, which doubles as a foundation cream and cleanser. For the latter purpose choose a creamy texture, which liquefies easily and is free from 'drag'.

Pore and cleansing grains: Preparations known as pore and cleansing grains contain little beads or granules and are intended for cleansing oily and blemished skins.

Soaps: Two ingredients, fat and lye, form the basis of most soaps but while cleansing they remove the natural oils from your skin, so after washing you should use moisturizer. Cake varieties of soap include transparent, super-fatted, triple or hand-milled (meaning soaps processed to a hard consistency to last longer). Some soaps are perfumed to match a whole range of bath preparations. Medicated soaps usually contain antiseptic or disinfectants.

Liquid soaps: These are a recent arrival and are gaining in popularity. They are rather like cleansing milks, except they do not lather. They are ideal for those who like the feel of a soap and water wash but whose skins need this milder form of detergent cleanser; like soap, they must be rinsed off thoroughly.

Astringent lotions: The second step in the cleansing operation is to apply an astringent lotion. This is recommended to close pores after the application and removal of cream or lotion and before the application of make-up. Astringents are also recommended for the correction of oily skin.

Enlarged pores: If you have enlarged pores or 'orange peel' skin, an astringent will help to close your pores and make them less noticeable. Pores are, in fact, the openings of hair follicles.

Skin tonics or skin fresheners: These are akin to astringents but less powerful. They are stimulating, cool and refreshing.

Face masks: You can choose a liquid or a paste face mask. After the mask has dried, or set, it will cleanse your skin and tighten it temporarily. Masks are pleasant to use and will leave your face feeling rejuvenated. Clay masks and earth masks will absorb grease and dirt from your skin. When removed, they will take skin debris and dislodged backheads with them. (See Chapter 6 for natural masks page 177.)

Wax-based masks: These are solid at room temperature and have to be melted and brushed on hot (usually a beauty salon mask treatment and not normally sold for home use). When the wax hardens you will experience a sensation of tightness as the wax film forms a moisture-proof barrier. This encourages profuse perspiration, which helps to flush dirt and impurities from your pores. They are used as part of a facial treatment, after a deep cleanse and massage.

Rubber-based masks: These dry out to form an elastic and water impermeable film on your face. This film causes heat to be retained by your skin with a resultant rise in your skin temperature and increased blood circulation. Rubber masks are easy to remove – you simply pull them off. After removal you will notice a slight 'plumping' of your skin. This effect is temporary and disappears after your skin respiration has returned to normal. They are ideal for dry skin as they help boost the natural moisture resources.

Gel-based masks: There are two types of gel-based masks. One which, after application, loses water and forms a flexible gel-film and another, a solid gel, which has to be melted before it is applied to your face. The sensation of tightness is produced by the eventual shrinking of the gel as it loses its moisture. They produce a toning effect in all skin types.

Earth-based masks: These include clay packs and mud packs, either ready-mixed or packed in sachets for mixing with water when required. The mask hardens and contracts as it dries on your face. They offer excellent cleansing, toning and stimulation effects.

For your hands

Heavy duty: Some hand cleansers are specifically designed to thoroughly cleanse hands after they have been in contact with potent, irritant and sensitizing substances. They reduce the risk of infection, irritation or contracting dermatitis. They will remove oils, tar and dye as well as grease and grime.

Look no water: Waterless hand cleansers were first introduced in the U.S.A. and bought by long-distance lorry drivers and private motorists, enabling them to clean their grease-covered hands when water was not available. Once applied to hands with a gentle, rubbing motion, the product liquefies and dissolves or emulsifies any ingrained dirt, which can then be removed with paper towels or tissues.

'Rolling' lotions: These help to remove coarse skin from hands, elbows and feet. These are in emulsion form and pressure-sensitive, so that when rubbed on skin, they form soft tacky rolls of wax, which pick up dead skin. They are only effective on skin which has been cleansed.

For your hair

Removing grease: The reason you wash your hair is to remove grease. Hair has a hard surface but, unlike wool and some other textiles, it does not pick up particles of dirt without the intervention of a grease layer. So when you remove the grease, you remove the dirt. The ideal shampoo washes the hair and scalp satisfactorily, while leaving them in good condition.

Built-in conditioner: Clear liquid shampoos often contain a built-in conditioner: a dual purpose product which shampoos and conditions at the same time, thereby saving time.

Special ingredients: Liquid cream shampoos are opaque. This category includes most of the shampoos containing eggs, milk, cream and other ingredients, which the manufacturers consider are beneficial for hair. They are specifically designed for certain scalp types and it is usually advantageous to pick one geared to your scalp condition.

Away with dandruff: Anti-dandruff and medicated shampoos are self-explanatory. They usually contain a suitable germicide and can be a clear liquid or an opaque lotion. If you suffer from dandruff wash and disinfect brush, comb and towels after each use (see Chapter 1 page 15 and Chapter 6 page 177).

Oil shampoos: This type of shampoo is ideal for a dry scalp and usually has to be left on the hair longer than most other shampoos (follow the manufacturer's instructions).

Dry shampoos: If you need to clean your hair without water, you can use a dry shampoo, which consists of an absorbent powder. This is sprinkled and left on the hair for about 10 minutes before being brushed out. Points against this type of shampoo are that it is difficult to get particles of powder to make contact with the grease. It is also difficult to brush the powder out of the hair. You can't hurry a dry shampoo. It is, however, suitable for emergencies, such as during a stay in hospital when you can't wash your hair or when you don't want to disturb a set.

For your mouth

Toothpastes: These are usually based on peppermint or spearmint flavours, but can be clover, wintergreen, eucalyptus, aniseed, rose or lavender. Menthol is sometimes included in order to back up the peppermint effect and to exert a cooling flavour. Toothpastes are popular because they contain a foaming agent, which both cleans and detaches food debris from your teeth.

Tooth powders: The forerunners of toothpaste and largely replaced by them, tooth powders are usually the cheapest form of dental cleanser. They are not as easy, or as pleasant to use as toothpaste.

Solid dentifrice: This is a product which in many ways is more akin to a soap than a tooth powder; it is usually coloured. It has been largely superseded by toothpaste but is often preferred by older people who grew up with this sort of product.

Mouth washes: Usually antiseptic, mouth washes have a refreshing taste and help to make your breath smell sweet. They won't disguise bad breath which has a physical cause. Some mouth washes aid gum disorders. They can be used as well as a tooth cleanser but never instead of.

Aerosol mouth fresheners: These are designed to freshen breath after eating, drinking or smoking and may contain a germicide. Spearmint and peppermint flavours are available. No specific claims are made about their ability to kill bacteria – treat them as an equivalent to chewing gum or as an alternative to a mouth wash.

For young skins

Topical treatments: Many topical treatments for teenagers are superficial peeling lotions which aim to produce a continuous, non-drying and sloughing effect on skin.

Skin hygiene: Products to encourage skin hygiene usually contain antiseptic agents. For men there are antiseptic soaps, medicated shaving sticks or shaving cream, medicated after-shave lotion and lightly coloured anti-acne face cream. For women there are antiseptic soaps, cleansing milks containing an antiseptic, medicated toning or astringent lotion and medicated tinted foundations.

Using a cleanser: To use a cleanser correctly take up as much cream as the two middle fingers of your hand can comfortably accommodate and begin to smooth it gently into your face and throat. Always use upward and outward movements, except over

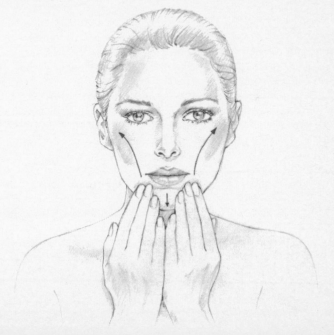

your chin, where you should bring the cream gently down over your throat. Tap the cream in lightly around your eyes where the skin is thin and has a tendency to stretch. Do this last when the cream is at its softest, warmed by the heat of your face.

Using a skin toner: To tone your skin take a small amount of cotton wool, then soak it in cold water, squeeze and shape into a spoon-shaped patter. Soak in the toning lotion and pat briskly all over your face and throat. Allow the lotion to dry before applying moisturizer, tinted moisturizer or foundation. Apply all these products with upward and outward motions.

Using a shampoo: To wash your hair correctly, first wet it, then lather it well with shampoo to remove the top layer of dust and oiliness. Rinse thoroughly and apply more shampoo. Each time you apply shampoo, massage your scalp gently with pads of your fingertips, never letting the fingernails touch the scalp. Finally, rinse out the shampoo completely, using four or five separate rinsings. For washing hair in a shower, see page 55.

High and dry: Dry your scalp well by putting a towel over your head, bending forwards and circling the palms of your hands gently, through the towel, from the nape of your neck to your forehead and from your ears up to the crown. Then, using another dry towel, massage your scalp again before you comb through your hair. It is essential to remove as much moisture as possible before you use a brush or comb on your hair. When hair is wet it is elastic and can be stretched and damaged.

Complete skin care plans

The following sections give a three-part skin care plan for different types of skins. The 'midday cleanse' could also read 'early evening cleanse' and is applicable for those who need to cleanse their make-up and completely re-do it at some point during the day.

For dry skin

Morning quick cleanse: Wash with a gentle lather of mild soap, spray on an aerosol skin tonic or decant some skin tonic into a spray. For a very dry skin – temporarily out of sorts – try a warm water rinse. Pat dry and apply moisture lotion and foundation lotion or cream.

Midday cleanse: Always cleanse your skin with cleansing milk before applying fresh make-up. Adding another layer of make-up simply aggravates a dry skin condition.

Night deep cleanse: Remove make-up with two light applications of cream or a creamy lotion specially formulated for dry skin. Remove cream with tissues and wash your face with

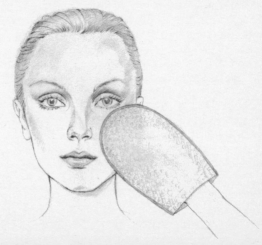

warm water and a bland, superfatted soap, using hands or the softest towelling mitt. Rinse with cool water and pat dry – never rub – with a soft towel. If your skin is very dry and isn't accustomed to soap and water, or if you are staying away from home in a district where the water is harsh, start by washing your face only once or twice a week. As your skin needs plenty of lubrication, use a super-rich cream to massage your face and neck for two minutes exactly. Then leave on the cream until the last minute before you go to bed. Once a week use a face pack for dry skins.

For combination skin

Morning quick cleanse: Wring out a pad of cotton wool in cold water, dot it with skin tonic and apply over your face and neck or splash your face with cold water and pat dry. Apply an astringent lotion in a small spray to your forehead, nose and chin. Apply foundation lotion.

Midday cleanse: Use complexion milk to cleanse your skin before you apply new make-up.

Night deep cleanse: Use cream or cleansing lotion to remove your make-up, then wash the oily parts of your face only. Work up the lather to a dryish consistency, apply it to the oily parts and pour over rinsing water from your cupped hands or a small plastic beaker. Rinse your whole face in hot water and pat your skin dry with a soft towel. Apply nourishing cream to the dry parts only. Once a week give yourself a face treatment with a pack suitable for an oily skin but apply a little nourishing cream over your cheeks before putting on the mask.

For normal skin

Morning quick cleanse: Wash your face with a mild complexion soap and tepid water. Massage well in with the tips of your fingers and follow with a tepid water splash. If your skin feels at all tight, use a moisturizer.

Midday cleanse: Cleanse at least once more during the day, using either a cream or a creamy lotion. Or, you can use cleansing cream pads – ideal for keeping in your office desk.

Night deep cleanse: Use a cream lotion to remove all traces of make-up, then wash your face with a mild complexion soap. Tone your skin after cleansing with a mild skin tonic. Once a week use a face pack specially for normal skin.

For dry sensitive skin

Morning quick cleanse: Cleanse your face with complexion milk followed by a splash with cold water. Apply a light powder base.

Midday cleanse: Cleanse with complexion milk and apply make-up as before.

Night deep cleanse: Cream cleanse your face and neck and wash with warm soft water and super-fatted soap as for dry skin. If your skin is unusually sensitive, wash only once a week and between washes clean your face with two cream cleansings, removed with tissues, and then with a pad of cotton wool wrung out in cold water. Finish by wetting your skin with a milk skin tonic.

For the blemished skin

Morning quick cleanse: Splash your face with cold water, dry and apply a foundation lotion or cleanse with special medicated cleanser and then apply foundation.

Midday cleanse: Cleanse with complexion milk or medicated cleanser and apply fresh make-up.

Night deep cleanse: If there are no spots which have come to a head, remove make-up with complexion milk and wash with very hot water and antiseptic soap, using your hands. Rinse with hot water, then cold water, and pat dry. Apply medicated cream or lotion. If there are open spots, clean with medicated lotion instead of soap and water, and dab each with antiseptic lotion.

For ageing skin

Morning quick cleanse: Smooth a few drops of cleansing cream lotion over face and neck. Start at the base of the neck and go straight up to the chin and over the face. Tissue off cleanser and freshen with a soothing, non-drying skin lotion. Apply a rich moisturizer. On the days when your skin positively laps it up, apply a second time.

Midday cleanse: Use cleansing cream followed by skin lotion and moisturizer.

Night deep cleanse: Cleanse with cream or lotion, going right from base of neck over chin and face. Soak a damp pad of cotton wool in skin lotion and pat this all over from your neck to your forehead to stimulate circulation. Apply a rich night time nourisher, using upward and outward movements and paying special heed to throat, chin, jowls and forehead.

On the move

Waste not: Don't decant preparations into smaller containers unless you're really short of space; decanting does mean you waste a certain amount. Ideally use a range of products which is uniform in shape and size and pack in well, side by side.

Less is more: Don't go off burdened with too many different products, especially if your skin is not used to them. Even in hotter climates all you are likely to need is a more liquid cleanser than you might normally use, and switch from clear moisturizing lotion to a tinted one for better day-long coverage. Top up with loose powder rather than applying the compressed compact variety, which might cake on your skin in a very hot climate. (See also pages 154–161 for hints on how to stay cool.)

Before landing: Just before landing after a long flight, cleanse and freshen your face. If possible use lotion cleanser, otherwise quick cleanse with skin freshener on cotton wool. Don't disturb your eye make-up. Cleanse round it. Apply moisturizer and foundation, a stick variety is ideal, and add pressed compact powder and a touch of blusher.

Good resolutions

The secret of success: Resolve to make the most of skin care preparations. Memorize instructions for use or paste them on your mirror. Remember that the secret of success is often in the small print. Treatment creams will only work with correct application and manipulation.

Never too busy: No matter how busy you are, don't neglect skin care. Choose a cleanser-tonic preparation, a moisturizer that does for face, body and hands. Choose a face mask that paints on in seconds and sets invisibly, so that you can move around.

Taking stock: The first free moment you have, take stock of your beauty paraphernalia. Give away products you aren't going to use, wash shabby labels off half-empty containers, and throw away dingy puffs and moulting make-up brushes. Replace the latter with natural fine-textured sponges, which are ideal for the application and even blending of foundation, blusher and shadow. Sponges can be washed regularly in warm, soapy water and always come up as good as new. (See also page 115, Chapter 3 for hints on make-up maintenance.)

Use a spatula: Don't dip your fingers into products that are expected to have a long life; instead use a clean spatula to scoop the cream on to the back of your hand and use this as a type of palette. When you have to use your hands, make sure they are newly washed and rinsed.

PERFUMES

There are seven types of perfume: single floral – the scent of one flower; floral bouquet – an intricate blend of many different flower notes; spicy – containing ingredients like cinnamon, clove, ginger, often combined with spicy flowers such as carnation; woody, mossy – known as 'green' scents – sandalwood, rosewood and other aromatic woods combined with oakmoss and fern; oriental blend – warm, intense notes of musk, ambergris and other exotic ingredients; fruity blend – with a clean, tingling scent of citrus fruit or a mellow suggestion of apricot and modern blend – the sparkling products of chemistry that sometimes resemble other natural fragrances and sometimes are totally individual.

Different strengths of fragrances

Perfume: Perfume is the most concentrated and longest lasting form of fragrance. If you try one, and like it, aim to buy that formula. If you prefer the eau de toilette, then that's what to look out for.

Eau de parfum: This is the next in line. It has a high concentration of essential oils and is stronger and more lasting than the parfum de toilette.

Parfum de toilette: This is a fragrance which is slightly diluted with distilled water.

Eau de toilette: This is lighter than parfum de toilette.

Eau de cologne: This is the lightest concentration of all.

A new concept: The fully fledged eau de toilette fragrances (i.e. they are specifically designed at this strength) are a relatively new concept created to meet the demand for a fresh, all-day fragrance. They're not derived from concentrated perfumes and, therefore, not on a scale of varying strengths, but exist in their own right.

Choosing perfume

An early start: When choosing perfume go shopping in the morning, when your sense of smell is at its best.

What should you try? Anything that takes your fancy. Don't be put off by a name. Similarly if you've tried, and disliked, one perfume from a house, don't let that put you off the others from the same house; one of them could be a winner.

Body chemistry: Your eventual choice of perfume depends on you and the reaction of your body chemistry to different perfumes. Scent only becomes 'visible' when it touches the warmth of your skin, so it is essential to try before you buy. Try one fragrance at a time and allow the application to dry before sniffing. Even if first impressions please you, don't buy immediately. If after half an hour it has disappeared, then no matter how much you thought you liked it, it is not the one for you. Ideally, one application should be with you for four or five hours.

Beware the bargain: It is easy to fall into the trap of thinking that the bigger the bottle the better the bargain. The larger container will only be a better bargain if that is the one that suits you best. To select the large size only because it is bigger is unwise.

Trial size: When buying an expensive perfume for yourself it is wise to take the handbag trial size first and then buy the larger bottle if you find you really like it.

Costly mistake: The most costly and common mistake you can make with perfume is to buy a particular brand because you like the smell on someone else. You might like it but it must like you.

When buying duty free: Bear in mind that even if you do test and try a perfume in the duty free shop, with the tensions of travelling, your skin will not be in its normal condition. You are most likely to be sweating slightly and the perfume's balance will be upset, so you will not necessarily make the right choice.

Rare ingredients: The cost of perfumes depends on the rarity of the ingredients. Staying power is not necessarily a gauge of high quality: some inexpensive scents linger longer than the most precious fragrances.

Using perfume

Correct use: To use perfume correctly bear three points in mind – that heat brings it out, that it rises, that after a time your own nose develops a resistance to it thus, people have been known to insist that the second bottle of perfume that they buy is not as strong as the first, though this is not the way it seems to other people!

A new perfume: Provided it suits you as well as the old one, a new perfume can be just as much a fillip to your spirits as a new dress and you won't suffer from the danger of a perfume blind spot when using it.

Don't dab: Don't just dab on perfume in a desultory manner. It is best to spray perfume on the places where the warmth of your body gently diffuses its fragrance, so that the scent seems to come from within. These areas are the inside of your wrists, your temples, the crooks of your elbows and knees, and the palms of your hands. Never dab perfume behind your ears or down the sides of your neck or you will damage your skin.

At all times: Perfume should be part of you. Use it at all times. Enjoy it in its subtle variations. Bathe with it, experiment with it.

Perfume clings: In a confined space perfume clings. By the time you get off a plane, for instance, you can be sick of the scent of something. Full-strength perfume is definitely something to avoid for this reason. Toilet water and cologne are a much better bet.

Evocation: Never forget the evocative powers of perfume. Think how the aroma of coffee can conjure up memories of drinking it hot and sweet in blazing sunshine at a Greek pavement café and you will realize how your perfume can create an image of your personality.

A signature: If you'd like one perfume to be your special signature, one you'll be remembered by and that will be associated with you and no one else, don't change your fragrance for at least a year. Sample all the forms it comes in – bath oil, dusting powder, soap too. Some popular scents are also available in hair spray, bubble bath and other forms.

Scented soap: Keep a cake of soap, suitably perfumed, in your lingerie drawer.

Making perfumes go further

Cream version: Switch to a cream version or a solid version which seems to linger longer on the skin.

Bath oil: Another trick is to buy an expensive, but highly concentrated, bath oil and use a touch of that.

False economy: Don't think you are economizing by using perfume sparingly. Kept too long a perfume will lose its delicacy, especially when exposed to light or temperature changes.

Large bottles: If you are to be given a present of an enormous bottle, remember that a 'musky' fragrance stays true much longer than a light, elusively fresh one.

Economical atomizers: Spray atomizers are good value, especially the totally enclosed type, which prevent evaporation. Although a spray tends to be used more frequently than other types of perfume, because it is so easy to press the button, it is, nevertheless, economical. The fine spray diffuses the perfume and one squirt goes a long way.

For special occasions: Tuck a little cotton wool saturated with perfume in your bra.

Scented halo: Give yourself a fragrant halo by adding a drop of perfume to the final rinse water when you shampoo your hair, or set it with cologne and water.

A fine mist: Be lavish with cologne and then follow it with several dabs of a fine mist of perfume for a finishing touch. You can spray cologne in wardrobes and drawers, inside your shoes, in the rinsing water for lingerie and sweaters as well as hair.

Keeping cool: Keep the bottle of perfume in the fridge during the summer. It will be a deliciously cool refresher for tired feet or for cooling the nape of your neck before you go to sleep.

Empty bottles: When you've used the last drop, scent your lingerie drawer with the empty bottle, and your hankies or scarves with the stopper.

Resealing: If you own a big bottle of perfume, funnel some of it into an atomizer for everyday use and reseal the bottle with a few drops of melted candle wax.

Matching up fabrics and fragrances

Perfume and clothes can either clash abominably or team superbly. It's nothing to do with the style of an outfit. The material is what counts.

Non-absorbent: Man-made fibres do not absorb, so they are best teamed with a fairly strong fragrance.

Natural fibres: Wool and other natural fibres take on fragrances more strongly and lastingly, so that even a light medium fragrance is transmitted over a longish period.

Pointers on the care of perfume

Dark place: Keep perfume in a dark place, in a brown bottle, if possible, to protect it from the light. Perfume oxidizes when exposed to heat and light.

Large into small: Transfer a small amount of perfume from its large container into a small one, just enough for a few applications. You do not waste your perfume, by evaporation or oxidization, when it is used this way.

Stubborn stoppers: To open stubborn stoppers, try holding the top briefly under running hot water.

Tape it up: Stick adhesive tape round the stopper of your perfume bottle if you are leaving the bottle behind for any length of time – before going away on holiday for instance.

MAXIMIZING ON MAKE-UP

FACTS ON FOUNDATION

Banishing blemishes (and slight imperfections)

Dealing with face faults: Very few of us have perfect features or an ideal face shape but we can make sure that our make-up minimizes any slight imperfections. The golden rule to remember is that foundation and powder which are much darker than your natural skin tone diminish the flaws, while make-up lighter than your skin tone serves to accentuate them.

Skin Improver: Another way to make up for the deficiencies of nature is with a good foundation. So for a smooth skin texture, always use one whether you are finishing off with a loose powder or a pressed powder. Use foundation **after** moisturizer to achieve the best effect.

Broken veins: You can disguise broken veins by using a green-tinted moisturizer under make-up or a green-tinted face powder. A cheaper alternative is a touch of green powder eyeshadow.

Blemish base: If you suffer from blemished skin or acne, then use a medicated liquid or a germicidal block foundation.

Covering slight imperfections: It can be very useful to have two different 'weights' of foundation in your beauty box because they can provide the same camouflage as a special 'concealer'. If you use a fairly light-textured foundation buy a heavier cream one, in the same basic skin tone, but two shades lighter, to cover spots, bumps or slight imperfections. Do be careful to blend the edges of the heavier foundation cream well into the lighter textured base. Any hard edges will defeat the purpose of this method of camouflage. Alternatively, you can use a purchased concealer stick or cream over the spots.

Does an oily skin need a moisturizer? Yes, just as much as a dry skin, but it must be the correct type. Ignore the creams and choose either an emulsion or a liquid. Use this under your foundation to give a really smooth base for the rest of your cosmetics.

Greasy skin base: If you have a greasy or a combination skin, such as an oily panel around the nose and cheek area, and have a tendency to shine a short time after applying your make-up, choose one of the special water-based foundations, which will keep you shine-free for several hours. For an oily skin apply this matt-finish liquid all over your face. If you have a combination-type skin, use it only on the oily centre patches and use an ordinary foundation in a matching shade on the rest of your face.

Enhancing young skin: Even the lightest foundation may be a little too heavy for young fresh skins, especially in summertime. An alternative is to brush a little corrective cream on to any areas of the skin which have a slight blemish or imperfection (a stray spot perhaps or a hint of shadow under the eyes) and then take a light translucent powder and whisk it over the entire face, using a clean piece of cotton wool.

Too many freckles: You can only disguise freckles to a certain extent with your foundation and powder. If you consider heavy freckles a nuisance, then the only way to lessen them effectively is to use a fading cream, which is designed specially for this purpose. Do bear in mind that many people find freckles attractive (See also Chapter 1, 'Freckles', page 32.)

Camouflage cover: Birth marks or scars can sometimes be covered with ordinary foundations. There are, however, special products which will provide a very good disguise. Look for them in the specialized cosmetic ranges.

Colour check

Take a closer look: The shade the foundation **seems** to be when you look at it in the jar or bottle is almost certainly **not** its real shade, so don't ever buy it on this basis. Always try a little on your face or neck. If there is harsh neon lighting at the cosmetic counter then go into the daylight and look at the dab on your face in your pocket mirror.

Blending beautifully: If you blend your own foundation – using two shades mixed to get the perfect match for your skin tone – it's a good idea to tip both bottles into one larger one. Shake the contents thoroughly, so that the two shades are really well blended. Only two lotions can be mixed successfully by this method. It won't work with creams.

Corrective colours: If you're not happy with your skin tone you can change it by using a tinted moisturizer under your make-up. If your cheeks are a little too red (or too pink) go for green; if you think you are just a little too pale for prettiness, or are perhaps suffering from a heavy cold, then try apricot to bring a great deal of extra warmth and a glow to your skin; if you have a tendency towards sallowness, mauve can work miracles by giving a much brighter look. The trick of course – whatever colour you choose – is to apply it with a gentle touch, so that the corrective colour is not obvious and you end up looking like a clown!

Complacent about colour? Avoid the trap of buying exactly the same shade of make-up base for years, assuming that, since it suited you when you first bought it, it will continue to do so. A face can change, as can skin, so try to update your foundation from time to time. Test it on your skin just to the side of a cheekbone to check whether the shade really is the ideal match for you. If not, then change it. If you're in a rut with a cream, or perhaps a stick, consider a liquid. You may find it more flattering.

Getting the shade to suit your skin tone: The following is a general guide. Most skin tones: mid beige or medium peach. High colouring: a flat beige or an olive base. Pale skins: a warm beige or a pinky tone. Medium skin: beige with a hint of rose or peach; in summer a darker beige. Dark tone: dark beige or light olive.

Individual mix: Blend together two different colours of foundation lotion to achieve a totally individual effect. Mid beige and tawny peach mixed together make a good basic shade and you can experiment with other colours. This, incidentally, is an excellent way of using up leftovers in jars, or colours which you've grown tired of, or which no longer suit your skin tone.

Getting a good match: When trying out various shades of foundation, don't test them on the inside of your wrist, or on the back of your hand, but dab a little of the liquid, or cream, on the cheekbone area of your face, on the part between the bone and the side of your face. Try to do this when you are not wearing make-up, so that the test can be done on your bare skin or wipe off a little of your make-up with a removing pad before applying the foundation from the tester.

Best for black skins: Preparations designed primarily for white skins are not likely to be ideal for black or very dark-coloured skins. Go for foundations from special ranges created for this particular skin type. Alternatively, just a touch of a bronze gel can give exactly the right look, but no powder on top!

Foundations and applications

Take it in steps: After applying moisturizer to your freshly cleansed face, wait for five minutes before applying your foundation. This will give the moisturizer a chance to get into the skin surface and give a smooth rather than a slightly tacky surface.

Smooth base: Use a moisturizer under make-up. It not only protects the skin in centrally heated surroundings but also provides a smooth base on which to apply your make-up. It prevents preparations changing colour after being on the skin for a few hours.

Start with a warm foundation: If you put your foundation on to the palm of your hand (rather than straight on to your face) and blend it lightly with a fingertip, you'll find it will go on to your skin more easily, as by warming it you make it slightly thinner. This is particularly important in winter when cosmetics can become cold and slightly clogged.

Use a sponge: It's worth investing in a proper cosmetic sponge to apply make-up correctly. An alternative is to buy a large sponge and cut off small pieces, which can be used for a limited time and replaced when necessary.

Applying foundation to best effect: Where you apply your foundation is very important. Always take it under your chin a little way, blending it away to nothing as you get down towards your neck to avoid a hard and unattractive 'edge' of colour. Never take your foundation too far into your hairline but fade it out as you get to this area. If you have any tiny lines (around the eyes is the usual place for these) then use foundation very sparingly otherwise it will simply go in between the lines and make them look twice as obvious. Never apply foundation under your brows and on your upper eyelids. It may look fine initially but will soon form a crêpey texture if you apply either powder or eye shadow over it.

Getting a good blend: Foundation must never be applied with a heavy hand or the result will be something akin to a clown's mask. What you want to aim for is an 'invisible' effect. Your skin should seem smooth and even in tone. So, the golden rule is, use sparingly, blend thoroughly into the skin with no edges showing around the chin or the sides of the face.

Watch that nose!: Your nose is the one part of your face which tends to get a shine most quickly but don't overdo the foundation and put a thick blob of it on the end of the nose. It will look wrong when you apply powder. The only thing to do is re-powder when the shine appears.

Dot ... dot ... dot: Put small dots of foundation over the central area of your face rather than blending it in straight from the bottle or tube. Put the dots on the bridge of your nose, on and below your cheekbones, on the central part of your brow, on your chin and on your upper lip. Then, with a small damp sponge or piece of cotton wool, join up the dots and blend thoroughly all over your face. Finish off by patting lightly with your fingertips.

Foundations for different skin types: If a foundation is to provide a really good smooth base for make-up and last for a reasonable length of time, it is important that it should be chosen for your own particular skin. Dry and mature skin: a cream or moisturized emulsion. Dry and sensitive: cream or oil based. A combination skin (usually dry on the cheeks and oily in the region of the nose, forehead and upper lip): liquid or an all-in-one base which has the powder contained in it and does not require topping with powder. Oily: one which is either astringent or water-based. Do not use a water-in-oil type of foundation. Blemished skin: something with a medicated base (cream or liquid according to your own preference). Extra sensitive skin: any foundation which is hypo-allergenic (which means that all substances which are likely sources of irritation have been removed). Dry skins: creams with a good rich texture come in jar or stick form – both are good. It's a matter of personal preference. Apply sparingly or you'll get a 'clogged' look.

Matching face and neck: Nothing looks worse than a beautifully made-up face which stops short under the chin (or at a harsh line on the chin) and leaves the neck and shoulders unmade-up and bare. When wearing something with a low neckline, take your foundation down well into the neck and shoulder area, spreading it more thinly than on your face. You could mix a little moisturizer in with it to make it go on easily and give a lighter texture. Blend it gently away to nothing towards the dress. A light dusting of translucent powder in the same shade as the one used on your face will add the finishing touch.

Black skins: The liquid or gel type of foundation is good for dark skins. Heavy creams are not recommended.

Cake or blocks: Apply cake or block foundation by rubbing a clean cosmetic sponge over the cake or block (dampened with a little water) and then smooth it over your skin. This is better than using your fingertips.

The liquids: If you are in doubt about which sort of foundation go for a liquid. These are by far the most popular today and suit most skins (in particular the under 35s).

Care with liquids: Thin liquids are easy to apply but what are known as semi-liquids and all-in-one foundations can be tricky. Be gentle when you apply them and take care not to drag your skin.

Non-tints: Although tinted foundations form by far the largest share of bottles and tubes on the cosmetic counters, you can buy a colourless, light textured cream. These are ideal for a young skin where all that's required is a natural look and a base to 'hold' a dusting of translucent powder.

Clean start: Use cotton wool – changing it every day – to apply your powder, in preference to a powder puff which tends to become clogged and dirty. Anything slightly dirty used on your skin can cause blemishes. (See also page 116 for advice on cleaning powder puffs.)

Not too wet: Don't soak the cotton wool or sponge you use to apply your make-up. It should be just damp.

Glitter and shine: A hint of shine is hidden in some modern foundations but do be careful about using these all over your face. They can be used to pretty good effect to highlight certain areas and then blended into your normal foundation.

Making application easier: Thick sticks of foundation are often used for shading the face but can cake easily soon after application. Instead, experiment with small amounts of liquid foundation in a dark and light shade. They may take slightly longer to apply but will give a lighter and longer lasting finish.

All-in-one mixtures: Foundation and powder in an all-in-one form can be quick and time-saving if you lead a very busy life. Treat them warily however. They do not suit dry skins. For an oily skin though, they can work well.

Make-up freshener routine: You can now buy mineral water in spray form. Carry some in your handbag and give your make-up a quick spray in your lunch break or before an important appointment. The mineral water treatment will not only give your skin a healthy glow, it will freshen up your morning face at midday!

Perfect finish: To 'set' your loose powder perfectly – and to keep your make-up intact throughout the day – dampen a small pad of cotton wool, squeeze it out, then press the pad gently all over your finished make-up.

Avoiding a mask-like look: Some liquid foundations are very easy to apply but they tend to give a mask-like quality to the face, so that your natural skin hardly shows through at all. The purpose of a good base is to enhance the natural skin, not cover it completely, so with this type of foundation, gently massage it over your face with your fingertips to bring out your own colouring.

Tips worth considering

Quick removal job: Sometimes you don't want to touch up your make-up during a working day. Before a special appointment or interview, you may prefer to go right back to bare skin and start afresh. If cloakroom facilities are limited, the easiest way to do this is with facial cleansing pads which will whip off your make-up without mess and freshen up your skin at the same time. They do have a slightly astringent effect, so use a moisturizer when you apply that new face.

Summer skin: Even if you are not actually sunbathing, but you have a pale, delicate skin, you may burn in the summer sunshine. In hot sunny weather pick a foundation which contains a sunscreener to filter out the harmful rays.

Bathing beauty: Don't apply your make-up straight away if you've just had a hot bath or shower, because your skin is likely to be flushed and pink and not its normal tone.

Doing double duty: If you have a very good skin which doesn't require extra coverage, you could economize by using only a tinted moisturizer rather than a moisturizer plus foundation.

Perfect powdering

Plenty of powder: Always be generous when applying powder. Take a piece of clean cotton wool and carefully 'fluff' off the excess. This will give a good lasting effect. Too little powder patted in can result in a shine fairly quickly.

Care with fine lines: Powder will also sink into, and emphasize, any small lines around your eyes, nose and mouth, so hold back and put on only a very, very light dusting.

Matching up: Remember that powder tends to go a little darker when it is applied to the skin, particularly if the skin is at all greasy. A delicate pink can look quite deep a few minutes after it has been applied. So if you have difficulty deciding which powder shade is best for your skin, go for a cool beige, or neutral.

Translucent or transparent? A translucent powder is an extremely light one but it does usually have some colour. If you want no colour at all but just something to 'set' the make-up and allow your make-up base to show through, then go for a transparent powder.

Order of application: Face powder should be put on **before** any other **powder** cosmetics, such as blusher, eye shadow and so on, but **after** any **liquids** or **creams.**

Compressed powder: Powder already blended with foundation and packaged in a compact is a popular type of make-up but do be careful to wash the powder pad which is supplied with it at least once every few days and dry it thoroughly. This is most important if you have a greasy skin as the pad will transfer the grease from your skin on to the surface of the compressed powder. It will then become sealed and difficult to use (see Greased up compact page 116).

Drying effect: Compressed powder is certainly very useful to carry around in your handbag for touching up purposes. Many people find it so convenient that they use it all the time instead of loose powder. However, these compressed powders have a drying effect on some skins, so choose one with its own moisturizer. An alternative is to counteract this effect by using a tinted moisturizer underneath your make-up.

Black skins: Face powders from ranges intended for white skins can give a rather greyish or yellowish look to black skins. It is best to use a powder from one of the ranges specially formulated for this type of skin.

Check for excess: When applying powder alway check that no particles have become lodged in your eyebrows or lashes. If so brush off immediately.

PRETTY LIPS

Shaping up

Mouth too small? Leave your lower lip alone but extend the lines of your upper lip at the corners.

Need a new shape? You can block out your natural shape using either a green-toned moisturizer or a foundation stick to match the surrounding skintone. Then, with your pencil, draw in the shape you want, going inside or outside the natural line as you feel necessary. Try to make your lips match in terms of width and length.

Livening up lips: A mouth which droops at the corners can have its shape changed slightly by careful use of make-up. Simply extend your pencil outline on the lower lip slightly upwards at the sides and on the top lip stop the colour short of the outside edge.

Lip gloss: Don't apply lip gloss right to the edges of the lips or it may well cause the colour to run over your lips.

Steady hand: When applying lipstick it's a good idea to rest your elbow on a dressing-table surface – particularly when doing the initial outline. This will keep your hand steady and prevent mistakes.

Lip pencils: Always use a sharp pencil to achieve a clear outline and have different coloured pencils to match or blend with the lipsticks you have in your beauty box. Use a brown-toned pencil with a beige or coral-toned lipstick for instance, never a deep red, and a deep pink pencil to outline fairly light pink. If you have run out of lip pencil you can use a light brown eye pencil, provided it's of the soft kind.

Creeping lipstick: If you're bothered by lipstick that works its way into the fine wrinkles around your mouth, here's the solution. After the first application of lipstick, pull your mouth wide, and blot; then powder over the lipstick with a dusting of translucent face powder, still keeping your mouth wide. Now relax your mouth to its normal shape and apply more colour, keeping just within your actual lipline.

A colourful smile

Buying new colours: Testing lipsticks in the shop on the back of your hand doesn't always give a true picture of their colour, which can change when you apply them to your lips where your skin is a deep pinky tone. Allow for a small colour change and to compensate as much as possible put the test lipstick on a pinky part of the palm of your hand, or on one of the pads on your fingers.

Mix 'n' match: If you're tired of the lip colours you have, or are looking for something to match a new outfit, try blending them. For instance, apply a first coat of a sludgy brown shade, blot and then use a pale coral tone on top. Mix a beige with a pink; use a matt red with a pink frosted or shimmer on top of it; use a darker shade on the outer part of lips and a toning light one in the centre area.

New colours from old: You can come up with some appealing new lip colours by mixing the stubs of old colours together to make **one** new colour. Dig out the last remnants of lipstick in the bottom of the cases and put them together in a small pan. Melt over a gentle heat, stirring the colours until they are well blended. While still warm, pour the new colour into a small container and apply the new shade with a lip brush. Don't be afraid to put all kinds of colours into the 'mixture' – reds, browns, pinks, shimmers, frosted, whatever you have and certainly add any lip colours you know you'll never use. You can't be absolutely sure of the colour you will create but watch the mixture as it develops, adding darker or lighter stubs to achieve the right shade.

Lips and nails: Nothing looks worse than lips and nails which are trying to compete with each other in terms of colour, so it's a good idea either to match lips and nails exactly or to use different tones of the same basic colour. You could use a gloss on your lips and matt on your nails or vice versa to get an interesting effect.

Echoing a silky look: If you are wearing something silky, such as a dress or blouse, try wearing a lipstick which also has a hint of a shimmer to pick up the light from the fabric.

Lip colours to match outfits: For an interesting effect find a lip colour which is an exact match for a special outfit. If you can only find a near match you could try blending the lip colour (see above New colours from old) for the right effect.

Lip lines: Shimmering lipsticks tend to accentuate lines on lips. It's better to use a plain one plus a gloss.

Lip lore

Keeping lips slick: No matter what lipstick you wear, it won't look good if your lips are chapped and cracked. Protect them from cold winter winds and keep them moist and in good condition with lip salve under your lipstick. Rub a little moisturizer or hand cream into your lips before you go to bed.

Double coated: Always apply two coats of lip colour. The first coat should be blotted with a tissue to absorb most of the colour. You can either apply a second coat or use a gloss which gives an excellent effect when you want colour on your mouth but not too much of it!

A touch of powder first: Before you apply any lipstick (or gloss if you are using this as your only lip cosmetic) press a tissue to your lips just to absorb any moisture and then press a piece of cotton wool dipped in powder all over your lips. This will prevent your lip colour 'bleeding' over the edges of your lips as some of the moist ones have a tendency to do.

Holiday lips: Sun, sand and wind can damage lips and no lip covering, whatever its colour, will look its best. If you feel like abandoning lipstick or gloss altogether, use an emollient stick containing a sunscreener.

For the more mature woman: Soft pinks, corals and soft red lip colours are a better choice than brighter shades. For something a little different, try a soft shade of plum. Avoid shimmers and frosteds and go for a matt type with a touch of gloss on top.

LIGHT AND BRIGHT HIGHLIGHTERS

Blend with care: There's no doubt that clever highlights on cheekbones, eye sockets and the underbrow area can add enormous interest to a face, but they must be blended in. Light patches standing out from the surface of the skin can look theatrical!

Keep it light for day: A transparent highlighter just under your browbone is best for daytime. So pick a cream, pink or beige for the best effect.

Emphasize the mouth: If you have a good mouth shape and want to draw attention to it, try a tiny dot of a white highlighter just above your upper lip (in the little hollow in the centre).

Making black more beautiful: A black skin has a beautiful natural glow and it's best to enhance this rather than to try to play it down by giving it a matt texture. Put a touch of a transparent pink highlighter over your cheekbones and pink shadow around your eyes. This looks super during the day as well as the evening.

Girls who wear glasses: You can afford to add extra light to your eyes if they are hidden behind a glass lens. Matt highlighters are too subtle. Pick an iridescent one (even for daytime) to add extra emphasis to eyes and make them look lively.

Matching eyeshadow: Pick up the colour of your eyeshadow by using a highlighter in the same tone in the centre of the eyelid.

Fine lashes: These can benefit greatly from a touch of highlight placed at the inner corner of the eye.

In the pink: If you're wearing any shade of pink – from rose to wine – try a touch of pink highlighter eye shadow on the eyelids for extra colour co-ordination.

Blushing beautifully

Different types: Cream products are much softer in effect for very dry or mature skins. They also last quite well throughout the day. Powder type blushers are easy to apply with a brush but they can lose their effect when you re-powder. Powder is applied on top of your face powder. Liquid, solid stick or gel should go on just after your foundation but gel, which is intended to create a very delicate almost transparent effect, should be worn on its own without powder on top.

Which blusher? There are so many colours of blushers to choose from that it can be difficult to know which one to buy. The following is an easy-to-remember guide. **Most skin tones**: a basic peach tone. **Pale or fair skins**: try to avoid the more striking blushers like purple and orange. **Slightly sallow skins**: coral or pink are best; avoid the browns and russets.

Run out of blusher?: If you find you haven't any blusher left in the pot or cake, then just use a lipstick stroked on to your cheekbones. Choose a dark shade if possible as some of the light pink lipsticks can, surprisingly, look a little un-natural on cheeks. Avoid frosted or shimmer lipsticks!

High colour? Anyone with a high colour should certainly avoid using blusher to excess; only a light touch is required.

Where to apply: If you have no special contour problems, place three dots of blusher on your cheekbone area – one roughly in a line with the iris of your eye and just on your cheekbone, the other slightly higher towards the side of your face and the third below your cheekbone roughly between the other two dots. Blend all the dots well with your fingertips not taking them too far in towards your nose. Powder should be dabbed on lightly with a brush. If you find the colour is too strong you can blend it out slightly by applying a dab of loose powder.

Coloured skin technique: If you have a black skin, you may want to steer clear of the more usual shades of blusher. Instead try the pretty cheek gels in a copper or bronze shade. Don't aim for a matt effect but try to keep your natural glowing look.

Working out your natural colour: To match a blusher with your own natural colour, pinch the skin on your cheeks (lightly). This will bring the colour to your face and that's the blusher colour you want for a really natural look.

Matching lipsticks and blushers: You can use your lipstick (the shade you are actually using on your lips) as a blusher on your cheeks too. This is one sure way to get perfect toning between lips and cheeks.

Blending in blusher: Blusher must be blended in carefully with the rest of your make-up or you may look clownish! It's always better to use too little rather than too much!

Is a blusher a shaper? People often think of a blusher as a means of shaping a face but it was not really intended for that purpose. The function of a blusher should be to give you a bit of a glow, to brighten up your entire face.

Best for oily skins: Powder blushers give a pretty, matt finish and if you are troubled by an oily or a combination skin, then this is probably the best kind to choose. They are ideal, too, if you want to add an extra touch of colour to your cheeks during daytime, because it can go on top of your powder. This is not possible with the cream variety which goes on under the powder.

Glowing points: A blusher can be quite a versatile cosmetic and give a glow to other parts of your face too. A dot on your chin, on your browbone, and even your earlobes is quite in order (careful about the ears in wintertime though because the cold tends to make them glow sufficiently anyway).

Time of day: The shade you put on your cheeks should always take account of the time of day. Nothing too strong or garish for daytime when you should aim for a soft and pretty effect. When the lights go on though, it's best to change your blusher as well as your outfit and select a strong, brighter shade.

A little at a time brings results: It's very tempting to apply a quantity of colour straight away and then rub it in as best you can. This is a bad technique, because when you rub off the excess colour, you bring the natural colour rushing into your skin. The result can be confusing if you adapt the artificial colour to suit and then a few minutes later find you look far too pale. Put a little on at a time, whether you're using powder or cream, and blend that in thoroughly before adding a little more.

Beautiful on blondes: If you have blonde hair, and either blue or green eyes, a coral blusher used with a matching lipstick can produce a particularly flattering effect. If your outfit demands something other than a straight coral, then choose a coral with a very strong hint of pink, once again matching the cheek and lip colour as precisely as you can.

Blusher at the bosom: If you're wearing a low necked dress in the summer, or a swimsuit with a dip in the front, then flatter your figure with a dab of blusher just at the cleavage.

Variety is the keynote to success: More than one colour is needed in your beauty box. You will want to vary the shade you use on your cheeks according to the lipstick you are wearing and also the clothes in your wardrobe. Bear these colours in mind when choosing your blusher.

Colour toning: When you wear wine or purple, use a deep pink blusher. A peach or tawny blusher goes well with orange and yellow outfits and a russet shade with beige and browns.

Only a blush: If you are lucky enough to have a really good skin, you can use blusher on its own to give a hint of colour (but if you dispense with foundation, then do use a **liquid** blusher). Just blend it under your cheekbones and carefully fade at the edges.

Blending beautifully: To apply either a cream or a liquid blusher to your skin expertly and unobtrusively, use a damp brush.

THE EYES HAVE IT

For the best effect

Eye make-up routine: To achieve maximum effect, apply make-up in the following sequence. **First**: shape and colour your eyebrows. **Second**: apply eyeshadow, highlighter and eyeliner and fix on false lashes if you wear them. **Third**: Apply mascara. This sequence provides the basic frame which is then filled in. You can vary the sequence for a special effect, but it's a good guideline for everyday make-up.

Getting a good line: If you are not very expert at lining your eyes it's a good idea to use a cake liner rather than a liquid one. With a fine brush, draw a line right at the base of your lashes, not a little distance from them. Then quickly, with another damp brush without any liner on it, go over the original line, just softening the edges of it a little as you go. Be careful not to smudge, just to soften. (See also page 95 for use of eye pencils.)

Applying eye make-up: It's very easy to smudge colour or mascara, so keep a few cotton buds handy, or one of those

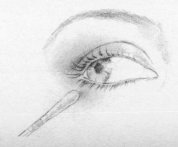

sponge-tipped sticks, so that the moment you make a smudge you can wipe it off. This is important because once on, liner and mascara can dry very quickly indeed. A bottle or tube of eye make-up removing cream will help remove stubborn smudges.

Switching emphasis: If you feel that your eyes are your best feature, draw attention to them by using a pale shade of lipstick on your lips. Dark or really bright lipstick tends to bring mouth and eyes into competition.

Bringing out the best: To bring out the best in eyes with the minimum of make-up, forget about liner, shadow and such and simply use a light-coloured highlight over the brow bone, a transparent cream or beige shade for preference. Don't use heavy shades or shine and glitter highlights during the day. A delicate but bright look is best for nine-to-five.

Best for a mature skin: While cream shadow is probably the easiest to apply, it is not always best if you have a mature skin, because this does tend to crease and leave dark streaks of the colour. Substitute a powder cream for a pretty, matt appearance which will remain soft.

Special spectacles: You can buy spectacles with lenses that can be hinged up individually to allow you to see yourself apply make-up to one eye at a time.

Whites a bit jaded?: Brighten the whites of your eyes by inviting the contrast with blue make-up. Try a mid-blue on your lids, a touch of white highlighter just under your brow, and a dark blue line drawn under the bottom line.

Keeping skin firm: When you are putting on eye make-up with a pencil or with fingertips, be careful not to drag the fine skin around the eyes (this applies when removing eye make-up too). The skin in this area is particularly delicate and once damaged can never quite regain its initial tautness. So – handle with care is the motto.

Removing eye make-up: When using eye make-up remover, always apply it to a closed eye. Gently rub it in with the fingers, leave for a few seconds, and then take a small piece of cotton wool and wipe off. Wipe **away** from your eye, going towards the tips of the lashes and from the inner to the outer corners of your eyes.

Bringing extra warmth: If you want to use a minimum of eyeshadow but still want to bring warmth to the skin surrounding your eyes, dab a little pink or peach-toned loose powder lightly over your eyelids, along your eyebrows and even under your eyelid. All you need then is a light touch of brownish shadow along the edge of your lashes and similarly on the lower lid (using a fine brush to get a really delicate effect).

The well-shaped eye

Mix and match for maximum effect: Although eye pencils do come in a considerable range of colours, you can achieve striking and individual effects by mixing two together. Try lining your lower lids in forest green and topping that with a touch of a brown pencil. Try deep blue with a soft white line blended in on top. For a dress of shot silk or taffeta in green with a glow of blue as the light catches it, mix a blue and a green line on your lower lids. Experimenting with the colours you have in your beauty box can be fun and produce some intriguing results.

Experiment with colour: Sometimes you buy a shadow which is almost the correct shade, but perhaps not quite; sometimes you can become bored with a shade you've used for years; and sometimes you just can't find exactly the shade you want. So why not blend your own? It is quite simple. Powder shadows can be 'mixed' on the back of your hand using a fingertip. Experiment, adding a little of this and a little of that. Two shades of the same basic colour can result in an even prettier variation and dark greys mixed with brown and then given a dash of something lighter can give an excellent 'smudgy' shade. Once you have created something which suits you apply the blended colour with a small brush.

In the purple? If you want to try purple shadow on your eyes, do be careful how you use it. Always use with a highlighter at the outer corner of the brows and **don't** match it up with a harsh mascara and eyeliner. What you want is a mascara in a matching purple and no liner.

Highbrows

An alternative to eye pencil: If you feel that emphasizing pale eyebrows with an eyebrow pencil creates a harsh effect, use a plain brown block of mascara with its own brush instead. Moisten the brush, rub on the block and then gently brush your brows into shape. The mascara will deepen the colour of the hair without giving a harsh, artificial effect. Use a waterproof mascara if possible to prevent eyebrows running in the rain!

Unruly eyebrows: To keep your eyebrows in a smooth shape, try this simple taming technique. First brush the eyebrows into shape with a dry brush. Then wet your finger and rub it lightly over a cake of soap. Rub the finger gently over your eyebrows with the soap solution pressing them into shape as you go and capturing any unruly hairs at the sides of the brows. Wait a few seconds and as the soap solidifies a little it will hold the eyebrows in shape. Not something to do too often because soap can have a drying effect on the skin, but useful in an emergency for taming eyebrows for a special occasion.

Eyes in the forties: Often at this age the eyebrow area begins to fill out a little and overhang the eye slightly. The result is that the eye itself looks rather deep set. To counteract this, use contrasting strengths of colour when applying shadow. Light shades on the area under the brow with a flick of white highlight in the centre and keep the colour mostly to the outer area. Then, with your darker shade, apply to the eyelid itself, from the centre to the outer edge, keeping it fairly close to the base of the lashes.

Extra attention trick: To attract extra attention to your eyes, use a little shadow in whichever colour matches your eyes, right at the end of your eyebrows.

Eyebrow shaping: Eyebrows can be shaped to give a different look to your facial contours. An angular shape can give a touch of elegance to a rounded face. A rounded shape can show large eyes or a wide forehead off to their best advantage and also give an appealing look to a young face. Eyebrows which sweep outwards and upwards add interest to a narrow face and can also help to balance an over-large mouth or nose. The sweeping shape also leaves a greater area for applying shadow, highlighter and other types of make-up.

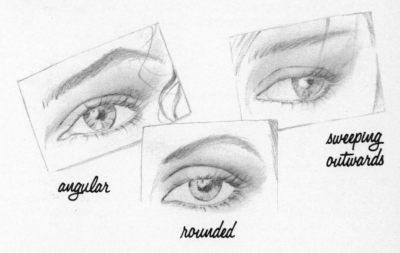

angular

sweeping outwards

rounded

Lashing out

Fine lashes – easily clogged: If your eyelashes are fine and more than one layer of mascara clogs them up making the lashes look sparse, avoid a mascara which is based on fibres. With a non-fibre one you can confidently use several layers to give lashes a good build up, making them substantial in appearance as well as glamorous.

Prone to smudging? Lower lashes do tend to smudge more than the top ones after mascara is applied, particularly if there is the slightest moisture on the skin. It's a good idea to powder the lower lashes before you apply mascara. The powder should take away any moisture on the surrounding skin.

Rules for redheads: With fine red hair and a light-coloured skin it's important to choose a suitable make-up colour. In the case of eye make-up for instance, anything harsh can over-dramatize delicate looks, so avoid black mascara and treat even brown with some respect. Best of all, choose rust, now available to tone in with those russet eyeshadows.

Eye make-up without tears: Should you find it tricky to apply mascara right at the corners of your eyes without getting some of it actually inside the eye, maybe you should change the shape of your applicator! The normal shaped wand or brush can be awkward, so change to a brand which has its own **curved** brush.

Tinted for glasses: Anyone wearing glasses may find that mascara can look a little heavy. If you have very long lashes and apply several layers of mascara to emphasize this, the tips of the lashes can sometimes touch the lens as you move your eyelids leaving little smears. An alternative is to have your eyelashes tinted.

Put a curl in your lashes: To get a really good upward sweep on your eyelashes, curl them. Use an application wand or for really straight lashes, a special small curling tool, which will shape them into a nice curve.

Curling procedures: Always curl eyelashes **before** applying mascara, never afterwards. When you do curl them, apply mascara from underneath the lashes only, sweeping upwards to maintain the curl. Curling from the upper side can straighten them again. Do be careful to use a lash curler properly and avoid trapping the lashes and pulling them out when you open it. Remember too, that lashes, like hair, when treated regularly with heated rollers or a curling instrument, can become dry and damaged. To avoid any adverse effects on lashes, don't curl them too enthusiastically or too often.

Applying mascara evenly: Put mascara on to upper lashes first, pressing your brush or wand downwards over the top of the lashes, then following with an application from underneath.

Thickening lashes: To make lashes look extra thick, simply dip a pad of cotton wool into a box of loose powder, shake off the excess and gently 'powder' over your lashes. Now brush on your mascara. The 'powder' treatment can be repeated before putting on a second coat of mascara to give a really luscious look.

Add a touch of gloss: Give eyelashes a gleaming look by carefully adding a small touch of petroleum jelly after applying mascara. Also apply a little jelly before going to bed (after all your eye make-up has been removed) which will help to keep lashes in good condition.

Separation technique: If your lashes have become dry, or if you have applied mascara clumsily and the lashes have stuck together, the easiest way to separate them is to use a small comb designed specially for this purpose. Keep it clean by dipping in hot soapy water at regular intervals or it will also become clogged.

Removing waterproof mascara: We all want a mascara which will stay on our lashes without running but those which are designed to do just that are difficult to remove. You can buy special creams and lotions to do the job (see page 57).

Lashes looking brittle? Some mascaras can set so hard that lashes look a little brittle. So try to choose one which contains a special conditioner. These tend to be a little more expensive but they are worth the extra.

False lashes: Fine lashes simply increase the thickness of one's own very slightly and give a rather natural effect. Heavier lashes can look artificial for daytime wear, so partial lashes are a good compromise. Place these at the outer corner of your own lashes and remember that you will, as a result, have half a line (the base of the lashes) so you must carefully complete that line along towards the inner part of your eye. Always use an orange stick to press lashes into position rather than your fingertips and hold the stick against the lashes for a few seconds for maximum adhesion. Lashes must be fixed really close to the base of your own lashes or

the gap between yours and the artificial ones will be only too obvious. If you want to put false lashes on the lower lids, then its best to restrict them to partial ones only used at the outer edges. If necessary cut them to fit.

False lashes lore: When applying false lashes, first of all draw a line very finely above your natural lashes and then stick the false ones on top of the line. Finish off by using a little liner at the outside corners of your eyes, or below lower lashes, to balance. If you don't use additional lining, false lashes can look rather top heavy.

Protecting the skin from smudges: It can be very tricky, especially for a beginner, to apply mascara underneath the bottom lashes without smudging it on the skin beneath. To avoid unsightly blobs take a tissue, fold it and slide it under your lower lashes. That way, any excess mascara will go on to the tissue and not your skin and if your hand slips the tissue will prevent disaster.

Contact lens wearers: If you wear contact lenses and find that even the hypo-allergenic mascaras still make your eyes run, then have your eyelashes tinted. Just a touch of petroleum jelly will add extra emphasis.

Slim for sparse lashes: Sparse lashes can become clogged with mascara and stand out in spikes. You can buy especially slim spiral applicator mascaras which are ideal for sparse lashes.

FACE SHAPING

Playing down a square jaw: The best plan is to emphasize your eyes, play down your mouth and make your eyebrows a smooth rounded shape rather than an angular one. You can add a little extra length to your face by using a light tone shader on your chin.

Broad forehead: If your forehead is broad make it look narrower with a darker make-up on your temples.

The high-cheekboned look: To achieve an elegant high-cheekboned look, use a dark shader just below your cheekbones towards the sides of your face and downwards in a long, slim triangular shape. Blend in with the main base you are using.

Widen the jawline: Light and dark shader, cleverly placed, can widen out your jawline if you want to create a broader-face effect. Apply a light shade all over the outer area of your cheeks and dab dark shadow on your chin blending it in to round out the point.

Long and narrow face: You can shorten both your forehead and your chin by using a shader which is actually darker than your own skin tone. Then use a dark foundation in these areas. On the sides of your face use a foundation about two shades lighter than your normal skin tone.

Lengthening a low forehead: You can 'lift' your forehead a little by using highlighter near your hairline.

Tiny, tiny ears: Very small ears can look attractive but if they bother you, place a line of light shader on each ear.

Too large ears: These should be darkened with a medium to dark base and just a touch of a brownish blusher.

Double chin: Dark base contrasting with light can work wonders here. Use a light coloured base on your chin area and then underneath your chin line and extending down part of your neck, use something about two shades darker. Blend this in carefully to avoid any suggestion of a harsh line where the two shades meet.

Shaping with blusher: If your cheeks have a slightly sunken appearance, use a light pink blusher right on the high point of your cheekbones. For a round face concentrate blusher more towards the centre of the face rather than towards the ears. Similarly with a narrow face, you can attempt to broaden it out a little by applying blusher more towards the sides of your face and sweeping it outwards.

Slimming the nose: If the lower part of your nose is broad or fleshy, apply a small dot of a much darker foundation than you are using for the rest of your face just above each nostril and blend it in to your main foundation shade, working it back slightly towards the sides of your nose. If you'd like to make the bridge of your nose look slightly narrower, then dot a little dark base right at the top of the nose, at either side and right up at the insides of your eyebrows. Again blend the edges of the darker shade into the rest, so that no tell-tale marks remain.

Nose a little uneven: Not everyone has a nice, neat nose. Sometimes it can be uneven and a little bumpy on one side only.

Apply a dark foundation just on the **bumpy** side of your nose. To make a nose look straighter, put a line of foundation all the way down the centre, fading at the tip.

Nose too narrow: One way to diguise a slender nose, is to pluck your eyebrows to take a little off the inside edge, thus making them seem to be set further apart. This is because close-set eyebrows can elongate an already long nose.

Nose too long: You can effectively shorten your nose by using a light shader on the lower half of it (from the middle of the bridge to the tip) and a dark foundation on the nostrils area at the front.

Slimming down thick nostrils: Dramatize your eyes to take attention away from the nose area! But you can help your nostrils a little by stroking dark shader on the sides of them.

Lengthening the nose: Draw in a full upper lip to reduce space between your mouth and your nose. Give your eyebrows a nice high arched shape to make your nose seem less short. If the tip is slightly too obvious compared with the rest of your nose, then darken this and use a twice-as-light shade on the main part.

Sculpting your own nose shape: It is quite possible to change the shape of your nose in a rather dramatic fashion by the clever use of light and dark foundations or shaders. Remember that the dark shades disguise and the light shades emphasize. Sit down at a good mirror and experiment until you get the shape you like.

To shorten the nose: Put dark foundation under the actual tip and not just on the end of the nose, if you wish to make it look shorter.

A question of balance: To balance a small nose, gather your hair up at the back, if it's long. Try a tousled urchin cut, if it's short.

Play it down: To detract from a large nose, avoid anything severe like a strict centre parting or very symmetrical lines for your hairdo or a flat fringe. A wavy hairdo with height at the crown and a fluffy fringe will be flattering. You could also try an asymmetrical geometric cut for a more sophisticated look.

To detract from a long nose: Use a lip brush to extend and widen the corners of your upper lip if you feel your nose is too long.

Narrow bridge: If your nose narrows at the bridge, wear a soft highlighter shadow in the inner corners of your eyelids to help widen the whole eye area.

A good disguise: To disguise nose to mouth lines, use a lighter foundation to fill in the groove.

Extra emphasis: A dot of brownish-pink blusher put **under** the nostril area of your nose can make it look a little broader.

Help for heavy jaws: Your jawline can be made to look less heavy if you dramatize your cheekbones with a dab of white or ivory highlighter on the outer edges and then apply a slightly darker shade of foundation on your cheeks.

Beware of blushers: If your face is either round or squarish, do keep your blusher well away from your ears and use it more towards the centre section of your cheekbones.

Light and shade: Highlighters plus light and dark shaders can help to restructure your face shape. Your upper cheekbones,

highlighter

browbones, your upper lip and even chin can all benefit from clever touches of highlighters. Experiment to see what suits you.

Shading takes time: It takes time and patience to achieve good results with face shaping. Streaks, blotches and what look like 'dirty' patches make things worse not better. So use only tiny amounts of light or dark shaders and blend them in to your main make-up base so that there is no 'join'. If you make a mistake it is best to cleanse your face and start again.

A full face: If you have a full-shaped face with a tendency to a double chin – avoid wearing white or any of the widely reflective colours which will highlight the heaviness and make your face look heavier as a result.

Seeing things in the right light

Daylight: To be a success, make-up must be both applied in a good light and designed for a specific type of light. For instance, if you intend to be outside in daylight, then apply your make-up as near as possible to a window. Make sure there are no shadows falling on any part of your face as this can produce deceptive effects. Try to get the light full on your face.

Summer light: When the sun is shining, pale colours can look stronger. You can, if you wish, use a sunscreener on its own without your foundation and go easy on eye make-up. If you prefer bare lips, it's still wise to use lip gloss to protect them from the heat. Something peach coloured is perfect for this time of year.

Candlelight: To look your best at a candlelit dinner, apply your make-up in the ordinary strength light in your bedroom or bathroom and follow these rules: steer clear of harsh shapes for either eyes or lips (avoid orange shades in particular). Be generous with your blusher, choosing a browny shade rather than a bright pink. Go for a smoky look about the eyes with soft greys, mauves and grape shades, picked out with a touch of ivory highlighter. Your lips should have a soft but strong colour too, perhaps one of the wines, blotted after the first application just to let the colour take, and then topped up with a gloss. After applying your make-up in ordinary light, check it out by sitting with a hand mirror in a lower wattage light or candlelight. If you feel that any part of your make-up is too harsh, dab with a tissue and smudge the edges of the colour slightly. On the other hand, if the result seems a bit wishy washy, add a little emphasis.

Neon lights: Offices, supermarkets and even cocktail bars often have neon lighting which tends to be harsh. If you are wearing anything pale on your lips and cheeks the result may be rather ghostlike. The trick is to opt for warm vibrant shades: peaches, coral, bronze, copper. Lips can take some shimmer to add an extra glow. Be careful of colours with even a hint of blue, which will be picked up and accentuated by this type of lighting. If pink is the colour you normally like for your lips, choose a shocking pink shade – one from the frosted range perhaps.

Disco lights: The dazzling, winking lights in a disco provide an opportunity to experiment with some really striking effects on your face. Colours you'd consider much too bright and glittering for day wear or for ordinary electric lights even, can be used. Aim for an exciting, exotic look rather than a garish one.

NEAT NAILS

See also pages 36–38, Chapter 1 for nail care.

Prevent chipping: To prevent polish from chipping, make a hairline across the top of each nail as you paint it, by drawing the thumb of the opposite hand across the top of each nail.

Extra protection: Seal with a top coat carried right over your nail, including the hairline, and under the tip of your nail for added protection.

A question of flattery: Darker colours flatter older hands which may have lost their creamy skin tone.

As near to natural: If you prefer a natural look on nails, simply buff them to a shine and drawn a line underneath the tip of the nail with one of those special white pencils.

Coat with care: A first coat of special base and then several thin coats of polish to follow is the way to make your nail colour last. One thick coat will peel very quickly.

Strengthening nails: Soft nails which are inclined to flake need a nail hardener (see also Chapter 1, Toughen them up, page 37).

Time to dry: It's important to allow each coat of nail polish time to dry thoroughly before applying the next one. Three thin coats are best for long lasting effect. Don't use your hands for at least half an hour after you have painted your nails.

No time to spare?: To dry newly painted nails in a hurry, you can buy a special aerosol spray which speeds drying and also prevents smudging.

Drying aid: You can use your hair drier to 'dry' your nails. Use it in the same way as you'd use it on your hair but don't put it too close to your nails or you'll begin to feel the heat. A gentle draught of warm air is best.

Get a good grip: Hold the nail polish brush firmly before applying colour, so that it does not slip out of your fingers (polish on clothes can be hard to get off!). Take the brush between your thumb and index finger and steady your hand with your little finger. If you do put polish on your clothes, blot as much as possible, then treat from the back of the fabric with non-oily nail polish remover. Follow this with an application of white spirit, and then methylated spirit, which will clear the colour. (Acetate fabrics can't be treated this way. They need to be dry cleaned.)

Cleaning off: When cleaning off old polish, don't dab away at random with a remover-soaked pad. Start with the smallest nail and work up to thumb nail. This way you won't smear colour all over your fingers.

Applying fake tan: A tan out of a bottle should always be applied carefully and evenly. Nothing looks worse than patchy orange streaks. It usually lasts only two days and you will have to re-apply it every other day until you acquire a tan from the sun. Try to keep the colour the same from one day to the next. Apply the tanning lotion, or cream, right under the chin and on to the neck as well as on the face.

Fake tans don't protect: Instant tanning lotions may make you brown but they provide no more protection than an ordinary make-up base. Always use a sunscreener on top of an instant tanning lotion for the necessary protection.

Not a sun worshipper? Not everyone likes the sun, although most of us want a healthy tanned look when we are on holiday. Use a light bronze gel if you are fair skinned, a darker bronze colour if you are a brunette, without powder and you will have a pretty sunkissed look. Unlike a real tan it will come off on clothes – so be careful not to brush a sleeve across your face. (Make-up can be removed from most fabrics with detergent and warm water; using a dry cleaning solvent on non-washable things.)

Go for maximum protection: Even if you do love soaking up hot sunshine, it's unwise to leave your face bare. Instead of your usual foundation, use a tinted sunscreen oil and do not powder on top. The same screener can be used over the rest of your body too. You'll find most sunscreeners are numbered and for maximum protection you must match this up to your own requirements. If pale skinned, go for one with a protection factor of 6 to 8 until you begin to acquire a natural tan. At that point you can change to a 3 to 4 and when you get a really good bronze colour, a product with a factor of 2 or 3.

Stick with the same brand: You may find that different brands of instant tan give different effects on your skin and one may be slightly darker than another. Try not to mix brands in the one application or you may find that, although evenly applied, the shade and depth of the tan varies from one part of your body to another. That may not matter so much on your arms, legs and body but it may produce a rather strange effect on your face.

First time tan: You may find that an instant tan in liquid form is easier to apply than a cream. This is because the liquid doesn't dry so quickly while it is being applied and will give a smoother, more even coverage. To be sure of the best results, design your own 'plan of action' and stick to it. Start with your forehead perhaps, do your left cheek and left side of your face, your nose and then your right side and finally the area under your nose and your chin. Always keep the instant tan well away from your eyelids and lips. If you can use both hands and do both cheeks at once, you will produce a good, even result.

Getting skin ready for the sun: Searching summer sunshine can easily emphasize dull and dreary skin and pinpoint every tiny blemish. So, to feel and look your best during these first few holiday days on the beach, prepare your skin before you go. Cleanse it thoroughly – with a professional treatment in a salon if you can afford it – or with a home treatment which involves steaming your face, cleansing with cream or liquid and then toning with a mask. If your skin has a tendency to dryness then do use plenty of moisturizer in the weeks before your holiday, not only in the daytime but at bedtime too after taking off your make-up. And take the moisturizer with you on holiday too!

Dealing with a streaky look: If you end up with streaks and blotches, it is not quite such a disaster on your arms or legs but it's certainly not acceptable on the face! You can try to even out the effect by using a dark foundation on the lighter patches, blending this into the edges of the tanned patches as unobtrusively as possible. If the worst comes to the worst, the artificial tan does only last **two** days.

That panda look: If you've been sunbathing with your sunglasses **on** and have rings of pale skin around your eyes, you can fill in the pale patches with make-up by applying a bronze gel or a dark tinted foundation. Remember to take off your glasses next time!

Lovely legs: It is best to buy a product which is designed specifically for legs, rather than double up with a face gel, which may not look right and will certainly prove expensive. The body suntan is a smooth cream which goes on easily and quickly and gives a stunning silky look in a natural bronze colour. It won't streak and it lasts quite a long time.

In the summer time

Keeping a tan: A tan, however rich, will fade if you are not continually exposed to the sun. To retain the lovely glow for as long as possible, keep your skin well lubricated. If your skin becomes dry and starts to flake off then light skin will begin to show through. So apply lots of moisturizer both during the day and after you take your make-up off at bedtime.

Sunscreen base: When you are in a hot summer sun, your make-up will not always provide adequate protection from burning. In this case it is a good idea to substitute a foundation which contains a sunscreener.

Summer time faces: Gel foundations are ideal for summer when your skin probably has a light tan and a natural glow anyway. Try to choose a waterproof formula in a shade which is either the same as your own skin tone or one which is about one shade darker – anything too dark can look rather theatrical. No need to use powder on top of a gel, just dust a little translucent powder on the tip of your nose and centre of your forehead where there may be a shine.

MAKE-UP MONEYSAVERS

Tackling tubes: It is difficult to squeeze out all the liquid when a foundation is packaged in a tube. However, if you carefully cut open such tubes with a pair of scissors you will be surprised how much useful liquid is still lurking around inside.

The last precious drop: Many liquid foundations and moisturizers are packed in narrow bottles which trap some of the product on their base and sides. To reach this, you can either dip in a make-up brush with a long narrow handle and apply the liquid to your face straight from the brush or you can, if you have time, stand the bottle upside down for twenty-four hours to allow the trapped liquid to drain into the cap.

Nail polish thick and lumpy?:   If you leave nail polish in a drawer for a long time or forget to put its cap back on, it will become thick and difficult to apply. To make it smooth and free flowing again, add a little nail polish remover (liquid not gel) and shake thoroughly to blend.

Repairing a lipstick: You can mend a broken lipstick by heating the entire surfaces of both pieces over a low candle flame for a few seconds and then pressing the two ends firmly together. Make sure the candle is held securely in a holder or on a flat dish. Allow the lipstick to cool and set properly before using.

Lashes last longer: Make your false lashes last longer by dipping them regularly in warm water to clean. After this, roll them around a pencil and secure overnight by gently wrapping in a tissue so that the 'curl' shape will remain.

A little water makes the product last longer: Always use damp cotton wool to apply any kind of liquid cosmetic to your skin. It will give more coverage this way.

Emergency face powder: If you find you have run out of loose powder (or mislaid your compact) a little talcum powder dusted over your nose, chin and forehead will take away the worst of the shine. But take care or a floury effect could result.

No lip gloss?   A touch of petroleum jelly on your lips makes an excellent substitute for your usual lip gloss. Apply with your fingertips or with a fine brush.

Brushes on a budget: There's no doubt that it's better to apply make-up with specially designed brushes but they are expensive. Ordinary water colour paintbrushes make a good substitute. The advantages are that they are cheap, come in quite a variety of thicknesses and can be trimmed easily with a pair of scissors to the exact shape you want.

The beauty box

Beauty kit for beginners: If you are a teenager still at school, make-up is likely to be worn mostly after school hours and the cost of cosmetics is important when pocket money rather than a wage packet is involved. The following items would make a good basic beauty kit:

- A **cleanser** (perhaps one of the soapless soaps)

- A **toner**

- A **moisturizer**
  (These three items should be chosen according to your skin type, whether it is oily, dry or normal. All are available at budget prices in ranges for the young skin by various cosmetic houses)

- **Translucent powder** in a neutral shade, such as beige

- **Powder blusher** in a basic browny pink

- **Two lipsticks** from the special cheaper teenage ranges – one pink, perhaps, the other a caramel colour with a touch of gleam

- **Lip gloss**

- **Eyebrow pencil** (a soft type which will double for eye liner)

- **Runproof mascara**

- A budget-range compact of **powder eyeshadows**

Adult beauty box: Most people have too many items in their basic beauty box. It makes a beauty routine a lot easier if you stick to several simple items which you use regularly and which you are confident will work well for you. Get rid of any you do not use and plan as follows:

- A **cleanser** (a liquid type is a good all rounder which works for most people, but you can experiment with one of those cleansers you apply and then wash off with water – and if you have oily skin and like the feel of that type of cleanser, then stick to it)

- An **astringent** or **toning lotion** of some kind (according to your skin type). If you like natural cosmetics, buy some rosewater or witchhazel from your chemist. These make good toners – witchhazel is the stronger (see also page 198, Chapter 5.)

- A **moisturizer**

- **Blusher** – one powder, one cream if you can afford it (the powder is handy for giving an extra glow on top of cream)

- A **white pencil** for highlighting under brows

- **Eye pencils** – a basic in black, grey or brown, according to your colouring and perhaps a double-ended one in shades to suit your eyes

- **Mascara**

- A palette of **eye shadows**

- **Lipsticks** – one pink-toned, one coral, one caramel and one red makes a selection to cover most occasions

- **Lip gloss**

- **Foundation** – one dark and one light-coloured in the same texture (that is cream, liquid or whatever)

- **Translucent powder** in a neutral shade

- **Mineral water** in a spray to set your completed make-up

- Lots of **cotton wool** for cleaning off make-up and for applying powder

- **Nail polish** and **remover**

- **Lip pencil** to draw an outline before applying lip colour (Although these are available in a whole range of shades, a brownish one will work well for most lip colours)

- As many **brushes** as you can afford, but at least one for applying lipstick, another for powder blusher, another for eyeliner

Portable cosmetic bag: Pack a few items into a small plastic bag to take with you in your handbag, so that you can freshen up your face during the day. For the basic minimum:

- **Pressed powder** in a compact

- **Powder blusher**

- **Lipstick**

- **Eye pencil** and **colour**

- **Face cleansing pads**

Make-up maintenance

Taking stock: Every so often it's a good idea to go through your entire collection of make-up. Throw out anything which has become hard or dried up, such as nail polishes and foundations. If a cap isn't secure then transfer the cosmetic to a container which is secure.

Clean containers: All make-up containers must be kept clean. If it's a plastic bag, empty it out every month. Turn the bag inside out and sponge with warm soap and water, dry, then replace the contents. Do check that the bag itself is in good shape. If the plastic is torn or the zip broken, buy a new one – most chemists and chain store beauty counters sell inexpensive ones.

Wash and brush: Mascara brushes, sponge-tipped applicators and lipstick brushes, indeed any kind of brushes, must be kept clean and unclogged if they are to work well. So, once a week check through brushes you use regularly and clean them all thoroughly. All you need is a bowl of warm soapy water; dip in each brush head and, using your fingers, rub and squeeze gently to get rid of any excess make-up. Rinse the brush thoroughly under the tap and then dry with a tissue.

Powder puffs: It's most important to wash powder puffs regularly. Hot soapy water should do the trick. Rinse with clear warm water and leave the puff to dry in a warm place. The thin foam pads, which come with some make-up, can be washed by dipping them in hot soapy water. Squeeze out with your fingertips, rinse and then leave to dry naturally.

Pencil sharpeners: These come in a small size for eyebrow and liner pencils and in a jumbo size for those lip and eye colour pencils. Both can become clogged up, especially if you tend to break the fresh point, because you use too much pressure when sharpening. They should be cleaned regularly. The best way to do this is to dislodge, with the sharp point of a needle or something similar, any pieces of coloured 'lead' or wood which have become stuck inside the sharpener. Then give it the soapy water treatment using a stiff brush to get rid of all trace of pencil. An old toothbrush is just the thing for this. Dry thoroughly.

Lipstick care: Sometimes lipstick escapes from its container on to your fingers. If you see any traces of colour on the metal or plastic base of the container, always wipe off immediately with a tissue. Then roll up a tissue to form a sausage shape and put it inside the top part of the lipstick container and twist it around. This will remove any lipstick that has escaped.

Greased-up compact: All too often a compressed powder compact develops a greasy film across the top, which makes it very hard to use. The only remedy is to scrape the surface gently with something sharp such as an old (but clean) kitchen knife. To prevent a film forming, use a clean piece of cotton wool as a powder puff.

Keeping the cap on: The tips of cosmetic pencils can be damaged if they are left lying around carelessly on a dressing table or in a handbag. Always keep the little metal or plastic caps on.

DRESS SENSE

THE RIGHT FOUNDATIONS

Gone are the days of hard and fast fashion rules and regulations. Today's fashion sees no social barriers nor does it recognize rigid age limits on styles of dress. It reflects individual tastes and priorities rather than designer dictates. No one colour, length or style rules. So dress to please yourself **first** and protect your personality. Never allow friends or relatives to influence your own personal instinct. Feeling good in your clothes means creating an air of confidence. Always dress to suit **your** lifestyle. Only ever buy clothes based on **your** needs, your budget and your priorities. Fashion is more a matter of getting the proportions right than slavishly following every latest fad and fancy. Finally, take care to look well-groomed from top to toe no matter how insignificant the day's duties might appear – chances are, if you don't, it will be the one time you'll regret throwing on the nearest clothes to hand.

The basics to build upon

What is a well edited wardrobe?: A successful wardrobe is one where colour, textures and shapes have been planned to coordinate and where old and new items blend harmoniously. Learn how to detect your fashion mistakes by questioning the amount of times your clothes have been worn. Did they feel 'right'? Did they receive compliments?

Simplicity is the key: The best fashion perennials are the classics with minimum structure in good quality fabrics. These are the most favoured long-term investments.

Fashion mileage: Separates provide more scope for ringing the fashion changes and are therefore the most economic buys. One dramatic dress offers fewer options than permutations around a separate theme, which gives endless wardrobe workouts. Always aim for maximum mileage from the minimum amount of clothes.

Clever calculation: Be prepared to rethink your clothes when you make new purchases to find multiple ways of wearing them. Do this by using colour as a linkline. Time spent rethinking and planning your wardrobe is energy well invested, as it may well produce several new combinations from one new item.

Inventiveness: Fashion inventiveness doesn't begin and end with the designer. Consider uncharacteristic ways of wearing things; perhaps turn a V-necked sweater back to front for a different effect; pick a man's parka jacket if you yearn for a really chunky oversized effect; a man's singlet vest looks super on a woman as an economical summer top.

Fashion know how: Having style doesn't necessarily mean buying lots of new clothes, it is often a matter of thoughtful teaming. There's nothing to prevent you from wearing a vintage favourite jacket with this season's latest skirt. Invent your own ways of wearing different clothes together.

Easy dressing: It is always better to dress under rather than over, if the degree of formality is not known. Aim to create an impression of effortless ease, not a laboured effect.

Details and colours that count

Quality rather than quantity: A sound principle to remember is that buying 'cheap' in terms of tatty manufacture is a false economy. Better to have one **good** pair of well-cut flannel trousers than two pairs in a cheap coloured synthetic fabric that seat and lose their shape, after the first few wearings.

Colour as a link line: Colour is the foundation to any successful wardrobe. Choose your most flattering neutral shade as a base for big buys like coats and jackets. Decide upon a colour theme to form a link between old clothes and new buys.

White for all seasons: Neutral classics like beige, grey and white are firm fashion favourites whatever the weather. White, generally accepted as a summer colour, looks even more sensational in wool flannel for winter jackets and coats.

Colours to suit: Strict rules on wearing certain colours next to the skin obviously vary so much according to personal taste. Some tried and tested colour tips: **red heads** and freckly faces always look their most dramatic in earthy tones of beige and green to reflect their natural gold highlights: **dark brunettes** with olive skins look dynamic in bright electric colours and deep red tones: **blondes with English rose complexions** can all too often fade away under pale pastel shades and beiges. Go for grey and colours in the blue spectrum which flatter and look most attractive: **mousy, mid brown hair** is flattered by burgundy colours or those in the blue colour spectrum, especially when mixed with white to give clarity to a sallow skin and mousy hair colouring.

Palette pick me ups: White is the purest pick me up and the best neutral for adding a healthy glow to the palest of skin tones and hair colouring. See the difference a crisp white collar makes to a plain navy dress.

Doom and gloom: Black, though particularly stunning with a sun tan, is the hardest colour to wear. It needs immaculate grooming to make it effective in a fashion context. Never wear black if you're feeling anything but radiant. Black is guaranteed to age the wearer, though it does have a slimming effect.

Safe bets colourwise: Though difficult to wear, black is the safest bet if in doubt about the formality of an occasion – hence the well-worn remark about 'little black cocktail frocks'.

One colour wonders: A total look in one colour – say all navy – is extremely smart and elegant but needs careful working out and good grooming to go with it. Better, perhaps, to go for one colour **in tones**. For example, team a beige tweed jacket with a cream silk shirt and darker tawny beige trousers with corresponding beige/cream shoes. This is a much easier way to wear all one colour in a stylish manner.

Looks in harmony

Mixed interpretations: Don't be afraid to mix and match colours, textures and patterns in clothes. Some of the cleverest, and most successful, designers have made their name around intricate texture mixing. For example, mix a tweed herringbone jacket with a similarly coloured Fair Isle patterned sweater and toning coloured checked wool skirt. Stamp your own creativity around the different ways you blend and harmonize your separates.

No singular sensations: Base print mixing around the more traditional designs like paisley, checks and stripes, rather than on high fashion prints of the moment, which need their own pride of place as singular sensations.

Hard and soft: There's no reason why a hard masculine fabric like leather shouldn't be teamed with a soft feminine fabric like silk. Opposites attract in the fashion world as well and make for the most imaginative fashion themes.

Wardrobe care

Sifting and sorting: If you cannot face a daily crisis of sifting and sorting through racks and shelves of clothes, keep a well-edited wardrobe. This means making sure that everything is immediately on view and easy to locate. Racks and shelves with everyday clothes should be at eye level.

Storage savers: With space continually at a premium, aim to make the most of every available inch of wardrobe area. Invest in space-saving storage devices such as: **shoe racks** to locate shoes readily. Always store shoes in tiptop condition. Keep a shoe cleaning box and shoehorn to hand; **tier racks on backs of wardrobe doors** which provide hooks for hanging handbags and mirrors; **storage trays** on a pivot which allow for instant access.

Footnotes: Wellies and boots can be stored upside down on wooden boot racks to dry out and prevent dust settling. Tights and stockings should be stored individually and tangle-free in large pocketed bags.

Instant hideaways: Precious jewellery can be hidden from burglars in one of the new miniature safe hideaways disguised as a double electric power point. The drawer is unlocked with a key, which should be hidden from prying children's eyes lest they try to copy on real electric sockets.

Ventilation: Always keep your wardrobe well ventilated. Hang sweet smelling fragrant sachets inside wardrobe doors and in drawers and cupboards.

Classify: See your wardrobe as a workshop full of ideas to test and try for endless permutations. That means approaching it as a filing system. A well-planned wardrobe needs classifying in colour groups, so that everything you have already tested together can be found at a glance.

Wear and tear: Clothes are costly outlays that deserve the necessary care and attention in storage. Always put clothes away in **perfect condition**. Check for missing buttons and flaws and mend immediately if necessary. Check for cleaning and laundry straight away. Never wear any single item more than one day at a time, to allow the fabric time to recover.

Headlines: Use baskets to store wide hats. If brims are squashed, steam them gently back into shape over steam from a boiling kettle.

Discipline: Adopt the attitude that your wardrobe has no doors and is on full view to a total stranger – that way you'll discipline yourself to keep it neat and tidy at all times.

Keeping in good shape: Wire coat hangers distort the shape of clothes. It makes sense to invest in top quality coat hangers. Use trouserpress hangers for skirts and trousers and shaped padded hangers for bulky items like jackets and coats. Place tissue over hangers for fragile items like silk shirts to prevent any extra creasing.

Knit knacks: Never hang or peg out knitwear. Always fold generously and pack in drawers preferably with a layer of tissue in between each item for extra care.

Hang free: Use double hanging rods in smaller wardrobes for better working efficiency. This way shirts can hang at the top and their relevant matching skirts or trousers below them.

Crease free clothes: Keep an ironing board, iron, a squeezy water spray and spray-on starch within easy access. Instant ironing effects can be achieved with the steam from your bath. Hang clothes ready to hand in the bathroom.

Standing alone: Do your clothes coordinate with other items in your wardrobe or stand out as singular failures?

Remove and recycle: Though fashion moves in circles, your original versions of today's look might not look quite right now. Your yesteryear mistake might turn out to be tomorrow's fashion favourite for someone else. In either case investigate secondhand clothes shops to help soften the financial blow of making a fashion mistake.

Habit: Forget old habits about dividing your wardrobe into distinctive seasonal groups. Autumn and spring clothes often have an all-year-round life. For example, a plain white T-shirt can be worn in summer with shorts and in winter under Shetland sweaters with jeans.

Right clothes for the right shape

Remember, no shape is the **wrong** shape. It's a matter of finding the clothes that are most flattering for you. For instance, you can make an asset of being boyish or petite, rather than think of either as a hindrance. Few women are totally happy with their figure type and nobody's absolutely perfect!

Perfect posture: Carriage and posture are vital. No matter how beautiful your body, bad posture ruins the effect of good clothes. Hunched shoulders, slumping and slouching adds years to your looks. However, the right choice of clothes can help camouflage any bad posture points. Avoid tight-fitted styling or ribby knits which emphasize protrusions. Concentrate instead on loose, easy fitting styles and square shoulders. Work at improving your posture with a well planned exercise routine (see page 247).

Proportion pointers: Analyse your own proportions and figure faults to help find the best styles to suit you. Though your natural proportions can never be changed you can, if you are aware of your assets and defects, camouflage or show them off accordingly. Always dress to flatter your size. This means choosing the right fashion shapes, lengths and colours.

Too petite: Small women should concentrate on simple fluid lines, nothing too frilly, flouncy or fussy. Fashions with waist definition help. Balance your clothes to suit your small frame. Avoid overwhelming prints or jazzy colour contrasts. Opt instead for single colour blends all the way through to toning tights which help to add length. If you are tiny, you don't have to wear high heels all the time. Provided there is enough depth between your skirt length and heel height, flat shoes can look just as effective.

Too tall: Theoretically there is no such thing as being too tall. Most of the world's famous fashion models are shoulders higher than most mortals and look at their success! Again, it's all a matter of having the right proportions. If you are tall, you can get away with more flamboyant styling, capes, oversized big coats, wide voluminous layers, bolder prints and wilder colour blending. You may find that trouser legs are often too short but these can be tucked into boots and leg warmers to help bridge the gap. If you are very tall, you will know that your biggest problem areas are skirt lengths. When in doubt it's best to keep your tights colour matched to your skirt to help alleviate the gap.

Pear shaped: The classic British figure type of small bust and large hips is best dressed with separates that emphasize the shoulderline, like easy raglan sleeves, tailored styles with padded shoulders, double-breasted fastenings. If this is your shape, avoid ribby knit dresses and tight trousers. Eyecatching necklines and ruffles help take the eye upwards. Steer clear of tops that cut across the broadest beam. Pick wide swirly tent dresses that skim easily over hips and can be belted to flatter your waist.

Top heavy: Big busts often suggest slim, small-boned hips with good, shapely legs. If you want to camouflage a well-endowed figure, balance it by wearing wide full skirts, perhaps pleated over your hips. Help minimize a big bosom by concentrating on soft loosely-shaped tops with small lapels and a minimum of stitch and pocket detail. Obviously, clingy, fitted lines will accentuate and exaggerate. Only use these if you want to make the most of a generous bosom!

pear shaped

small

tall

top heavy

Figure failings and slimming tricks

Thick waists: Those with straight up and down tomboy shapes with no waists should make the most of hips as their best body asset. Long generous overshirts with hip slung wide belts are always flattering. Drop-waisted dresses, sashed or belted on the hips, help take the eye away from the waist. Beware of drawstring waists and opt for soft waist pleats instead of full gathers.

Low full bustlines: Start by choosing the right bra for a low, full bust, a style that will provide the best support. It should be underwired with well-set non-stretchy straps. Avoid body hugging sweaters and tight waistline emphasis. Opt instead for overblouses and low drop waist styling.

Short necks: Low bustlines often go hand in hand with short necks. Try to suggest length with V-necklines, low rever collars, necklaces and low slung scarves. Always avoid round, tight necklines or bateau necks that cut straight across.

Long necks: Necks that are too long need an attractive cover. Play up your top half with cowl necklines, high ruffled collars, scarves and mufflers, even chunky choker type necklaces.

Big bodies: Big bodies can be beautiful. Big bones do not necessarily mean fat. Beware of clingy knits and jersey fabrics. Avoid wild prints, bold stripes and loud colours. Simple tailored looks in clear neutral colours are best. Soft, generously cut shirtdresses with stylish accessories and toning coloured tights provide a slimming effect. Steer away from cropped top half shapes, opt instead for longline figure skimming jackets, tunic tops or threequarter length cardigans.

Legs eleven: We are all leg conscious but few of us have perfect legs. However, the new wealth of wonderfully wearable textured tights (even in support styles) help camouflage problem areas such as varicose veins, scars or blemishes. Try shoe and boot styles until you hit upon the most flattering length and heel height. The right heel height depends on your skirt length or trouser style and not on your own individual height. In principle, mid calf length skirts compliment most legs, with the exception of very thick ankles. If this is your problem, take your skirt lengths to just below your knee to show the full curve of your upper calf. Whatever your legs are like, pick trousers and shorts sensibly. Heavy-set thighs look better in a divided culotte skirt rather than Bermuda shorts. Trousers with lots of top pleat detail draw attention to heavy thighs, so concentrate instead on easy, track-style shapes or full baggy boilersuit styles, with a belt to show off a curvy waist.

BEST FOOT FORWARD

A shade on the dark side: Dark colours have a slimming effect – this applies to all clothes including stockings and shoes. Heavy set legs should never wear white tights, which will only make them look larger and giant-sized feet should steer away from white shoes. Opt instead for white as a trim, used in moderation, or beige which is a much easier shade to match with legwear.

Running through the ladder: Consider the texture and denier (the hosiery term for density) before you buy. Generally speaking, the lower the denier figure, the finer the tights or stockings. The sheerest, ten and even seven denier, are usually the most expensive luxury items and much more elegant that the average twenty and thirty deniers. Micromesh tights are cheaper but tend to be heavier than fine knit tights or stockings.

See through: Choose extra fine tights, or stockings. with a sheer sandal heel and toe to wear with sling back or peep-toe shoes in the summer.

Tights tip: Expensive hose deserves the appropriate care and attention. Wash tights separately by hand in a mild detergent. Dressing with chapped hands and badly clipped nails is often the cause of snags and ladders in hosiery. An instant remedy to avoid a ladder spreading is to apply a transparent nail varnish at the top of the run to seal the surface. When you want to look your best, an emergency fail-safe bet is to keep a spare pair of tights to hand.

Tights talk: Tights, socks and stockings are basic wardrobe accessories. Manipulate the colour and density of your tights to your advantage when creating a co-ordinated look. By altering the density of your tights, you can switch moods, for example mixing a full tweedy skirt with thick ribbed tights and flat shoes creates a country feel – whilst mixing the same skirt and shoes with fine lace tights gives it a much more feminine touch.

Wide ankles: It's best to avoid ankle-straps and fancy lattice work detail if you have wide ankles. Concentrate instead on shoe designs cut low at the front.

Large feet: Too-pointed shapes make feet look longer. Soft almond toes and higher front coverage are more flattering for large feet.

Wide calves: Beware the fitted boot if you have wide calves. This type of boot will sag and usually wrinkle at the ankle. Go for wider cow-boy shapes that offer roomy space and make heavy set legs seem daintier by comparison.

Flat feet: Shoes with a slight heel are best for flat feet. Do not wear completely flat pumps and really high stilettoes which strike an ungainly balance.

Boot bonus: Create the effect of wearing boots by teaming ribby tights with simple, same-coloured brogues.

Spacious wellies: Always buy Wellington boots just that little bit larger than your normal shoes, so that you can wear thick woolly tights or socks inside them.

Two are not always a pair: Always try on **both** shoes for a perfect fit when buying shoes. It's quite common for one foot to be slightly larger than the other.

Cool approach: Avoid trying on shoes when your feet are hot and therefore slightly swollen.

Keeping in shape: Use a shoe horn when putting on shoes to keep them in shape.

Doubling up: Avoid buying shoes that can only be worn with one special outfit. If you need a strappy evening shoe, go for something that can double up as a summer sandal too. Traditional satin dancing pumps or velvet carpet slippers make economical instant evening shoes for that sudden special occasion. Likewise, some low-heeled loafer styles and moccasins make unusual slippers to wear at home.

Shoe shiners: Massage saddle soap into new leather shoes or boots to help protect the skin. Apply soap with a small sponge, allow to dry, polish up and shine ordinarily.

Soft on suede: Use a protective spray on new suede shoes to help prevent rain spotting. Brush regularly to keep pile soft and dust free with a special suede bristle brush. Store suede shoes with tissue in between for added protection.

Boot care: Stuff wet boots (and shoes) with newspaper in the toes and dry away from direct heat (or upside down on a shoe rack). Always store boots with special boot shapers.

A stitch in time: Always have boots and shoes repaired before they are too worn-down.

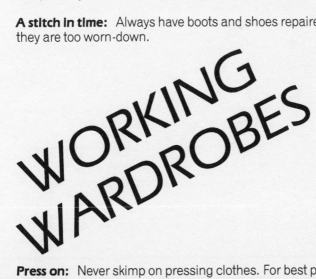

WORKING WARDROBES

Press on: Never skimp on pressing clothes. For best polished end results, some fabrics like linen need a quick press every time you wear them. A general guide to iron temperatures –

- cool 110°C

- warm 150°C

- medium 180°C

- hot 200°C

- very hot above 200°C

and to fabrics –

- synthetics like nylon require a cool iron

- silk/wool requires a warm iron

- viscose fabrics require a medium iron

- cotton requires a hot iron

- linen requires a very hot press

Dab when damp: The success of pressing depends on the perfect balance of pressure applied with moisture, therefore never press clothes that are over-dry. Iron with sharp dabbing motions. When pressing with a cloth rather than using steam, do not slide the cloth around – it may make extra creases. The best sort of pressing cloth is muslin, which retains the moisture well and can be folded when necessary to reduce the heat and shine.

Test out: Too much pressure when pressing can flatten the pile of ridged fabrics like corduroy – too little will have no effect at all, so always test fabric first in a corner of the garment to achieve the right balance.

Zip up: Close zips and buttons, so that clothes can hang perfectly in the wardrobe.

No bones: Never put wired or boned bras in the washing machine. It distorts their shape and could cause damage to the machine if wires go astray.

SHOPPING STRATEGY

First come – first served: Avoid the mistake of leaving your purchasing of major items right up until the last minute. Shops have a nasty habit of running right out of swimwear in May when you are off on holiday in August. Try to plan ahead and pick from the best possible choice early on in the season.

Window shop: At the beginning of each major season, window shop to see who's stocking what and how to put the new fashion looks together. There may be one style of skirt you really like in three different shops all at different prices. Retailers' mark-ups on fashion merchandise, and particularly on jewellery, often vary. Check likely sources to get the best buys.

Where to shop: Never allow yourself to be talked into buying things by a friend against your better intuition or by a shop assistant who may well be out for a quick sale. Seek out the shops and chain stores where assistants really offer a service, where they give constructive advice and honest appraisal and where goods, if not completely satisfactory, can easily be exchanged.

Best of both worlds: A good working wardrobe is usually made up with clothes bought from both chain stores and small, more exclusive shops.

When to shop: Do you buy in one spree or as and when you need to? Always take the latter option unless of course you live too far from any major shopping area. Better to spend time working your initial purchase in with your existing clothes before you plan the next stage.

Just looking: Clothes you need to buy urgently when you have little time to spare are always the hardest to find. Best buys are often made when you are 'just looking'. Trust your intuition, impulse buys can be successful.

Shopping logic: Good fashion shoppers have good memories to match. Attempt to hold a colour in your mind when you shop for best colour matching. If you find this difficult, take the belt or the item you wish to find a partner for out with you. Always check colours in daylight if possible.

Before saying yes: Check for cut, fit and detail before you make any fashion purchase.

Trying on tactics: When trying clothes on **always** do the following:

■ check back and side views

■ investigate for imperfections, perfect zips, missing buttons and loose threads

■ wear simple, no fussy underwear to get the best impression

■ keep jewellery to a minimum to avoid snagging clothes, especially knits

■ wear the sort of shoes you might expect to wear with your new purchase

Small budget – big challenge: You can look good on a big or small budget. Style is more a matter of having the personality to carry a look off. A small budget forces you to be disciplined and think in a more creative way. Turn it into an advantage rather than a disadvantage, adapt, improvise, sew, mix old clothes with new.

The cost of upkeep: Never make the mistake of buying expensive clothes if you can't afford their upkeep. It is no use sending an expensive taffeta dress to the instant launderette! Special clothes need specialist cleaning.

Good buys: What suggests itself as a basic necessity in one woman's wardrobe, may seem an extravagance to another. Therefore, tailor your purchasing around your own individual, clearly defined needs. If you're at home all day with the children, there is no sense spending most of your money on a dress for one special occasion. If you are shopping with some important event in mind, try instead to cut costs by splitting the buy into three easy pieces, say a jacket, a silky shirt and trousers that can also be adapted to suit daywear as well.

Invest in extras: It's not always true that you have to spend more on a dress than you do on shoes. You can often pick up a good chain store dress but it is much harder to find cheaper stylish shoes. It is always well worth spending more on those telling fashion extras.

Buy bigger: If circumstances force you to buy the cheapest – then buy bigger. Cheap clothes are usually skimpily cut. For example, inexpensive plain T-shirts are best bought two sizes too big to allow for shrinkage plus wear and tear.

Know how: The simplest fashion shapes are the hardest to find in cheaper high street stores for these are the clothes that rely on good cut and fine fabric. Track down designer theme basics in some of the most unlikely places. For example, if a designer theme is sailor style, check the real nautical shops; cow girl looks can be found in western stores; peasantry ideas at ethnic Indian shops and don't forget that men's fashion adapts to women's clothing and is often cheaper. A flat tweed cap looks alluring on a pretty face; a fisherman's tote bag makes a practical hold-all for students or schoolgirls.

Sales sense: Remember that a real bargain is something you have worn a lot and always felt good in. When buying in a sale always question why the item is in the sale? Because the shop bought too many? Because it simply did not fit anyone or hang right? Because it's out of fashion? Because it's an awful colour? Because it's badly shop soiled?

Seconds out:　Only buy seconds if you know what the fault is and know you can live with it. Never buy anything just because it's marked down or if it's out of character with your usual style of dress.

Designer labels:　Good sales buys can be those designer labels you covet but cannot afford. In sales these tend to be the more extreme styles, so be sure they are something you are going to be able to wear before you commit yourself.

Best sales buys:　Genuine bargains and really sensible buys are the quality goods that you know you'll always need, like leather handbags and luggage, quality knitwear, nightdresses, a classic raincoat. Stock up on basic buys like tights and underwear.

Sales shopping strategy:　Sales shopping should be planned strategically for best results. Basic pointers to follow are:

- check papers for details of sales that might interest you

- check beforehand in the shops to see what you would like to buy marked down and make a bee line for it

- avoid shopping during the busy lunch hour panic

- wear something cool and comfortable, as temperatures soar, so tempers will fray

- keep other purchases packed in one bag to avoid loss or theft

- if in doubt about sizes, take two of the same style into the fitting room to avoid disappointment as someone else makes off with your bargain

Fashion antiquities:　Never let your own standards drop when buying antique or secondhand clothing that you intend to wear, no matter how cheap. It is pointless to buy anything that is too frayed, stained or requires totally reshaping.

Something unique:　The main reason for buying something old is to acquire clothing that is totally individual because the work and handicraft lavished on it would be impossible to recreate for a similar cost today. The best fashion bargains in old clothes are found in country markets, jumble sales and antique shops that mix bric-à-brac with clothing, rather than shops that specialize in nostalgic clothes.

Granny hand-me-downs to pick you up:

- old watches (but make sure they still work) have become classic antiques

- lace – getting harder to find as its popularity grows. Use it for collars and scarves

- evening bags – far more original than modern day versions

- shawls – particularly the richly embroidered kind. Use as an evening wrap

- knits with lovely old-fashioned buttons

- nightdresses for purists – can be worn as blouses too

- jewellery – collector's items from any period. It is often worth having precious gems re-set to suit modern taste

- fans – a long-forgotten fashion treasure that provides a final flourish to an evening outfit

PACKING TO PERFECTION

Plan ahead: Wherever the destination – whether a weekend in the country or a week in the tropics – the golden rule is to do your home work before you set off. Know what temperatures to expect, whether the beach is near the hotel, what rules (if there are any) about dining attire, what kind of transport is on offer. There is no use arriving at the station expecting a limousine and having to take the local bus if you are loaded with luggage.

Bags and baggage: Expensive luggage is a waste. Modern travel, though fast and efficient, often means that your precious suitcase will be pummelled into chutes, chalked on and thrown about on airport buses.

State your case: Always have each item of luggage clearly labelled with your name, address and destination and airline carrier plus flight number.

Airline custom: Keep hand baggage on planes to a minimum. Airline rules allow one piece of hand baggage plus duty free bag and handbag and these are often strictly applied.

Near to hand: Choose a nylon or other lightweight fabric grip that can be stowed easily under your airline seat with anything you need for the journey immediately to hand at the top. Keep toothbrush and cosmetic bag with comb at the ready on long distance flights.

In Transit: Comfort is the most important priority whether you are on a car journey or long distance flight. Choose favourite well-worn clothes – never new shoes – and never tight skirts or restricting jeans. Avoid very high heels, especially on long flights when feet swell. Go for fabrics that are flexible, like jersey, velour or corduroy. They may 'seat' slightly during long distance travelling but this is preferable to long hours of discomfort in tight clothes.

Packing without panics: Packing is mostly a matter of common sense but here are some basic rules:

- roll clothes when packing in a squashy holdall, to pad out the sides and avoid jumbled chaos

- place shoes, individually wrapped in tissue to prevent scuffing, in the bottom of your suitcase, filling in all around with minor items like underwear

- pack tissue in between each layer of clothes for best non-crease results

- knits, T-shirts and non-crushable fabrics should be packed first

- roll, rather than fold, pleated clothes, so they spring back into shape

- put jewellery into a jewellery roll to ensure padded protection

- pack sewing kit and first aid basics

- take a travelling iron, but check voltage requirements first

- decant beauty basics into miniature plastic containers for lightweight travel or take sachets and cleansing pads rather than large bottles

- take extra polythene bags for wet swimsuits, dirty laundry or to wrap up precious new purchases

- take a miniature container with laundry detergent, some cotton wool and tissues. These items can cost twice as much abroad

- remember your address book for post cards

- place nightwear on top of your suitcase in case you arrive late and don't want to unpack

- and remember to leave room in the suitcase for those holiday buys

What to take: Whatever type of holiday you choose, select comfortable clothes you know and trust with maximum versatility from the minimum number of items.

Start with a list: Make a comprehensive list beforehand noting all the situations you are likely to need to dress for on your itinerary; such as sightseeing, swimming, the theatre.

Swimwear: Wear your skimpiest swimwear for initial tanning (and don't forget the sun tan lotion) to allow for maximum exposure without ugly sun strap marks. Take a khanga (see page 144) rather than cumbersome towelling robes but do pack a beach towel as hotels don't like their towels taken to the beach.

Jewellery: It's better to take fun or costume jewellery. If you take valuable jewellery with you, it will have to be left in the hotel safe.

Head start: Keep cool with a packable Panama hat, which can be rolled into your suitcase and will spring back into shape when needed. Or take scarves to be worn as hats (see page 148).

Sun specs: Don't forget to take your sun specs and visors which are effective over real specs.

Accessories: Think through accessories and shoes carefully, so that they match up with the maximum number of your outfits.

Easy care: Take plenty of cool T-shirts to hot climates where you may have to change several times a day. Plan your holiday wardrobe around easy care fabrics that can be washed simply every evening.

Scarves: Take lots of scarves not just as sun shields but also to provide instant accessories to change the look of an outfit.

In the cool of the evening: Take an extra warm knit or giant shawl even in a hot climate – it often gets very cool in the evenings.

Beach mat: Consider buying a roll-up mat that folds into a beach bag; essential on some holdiays where beaches are all shingle.

FIGURE FITTING FACTS

First step: What to wear under your clothes should be given just as much care and attention as what goes on top, to make the most of your good points or diminish your bad ones and to create a streamlined overall impression.

Moment of truth: Badly fitting underwear can cause minor medical problems, so make sure you know your true measurements.

Correct figure faults: Admit your figure faults and disguise them with the right foundation underwear. Nowadays this does not necessarily mean rigid constricting fabrics but new lightweights that stretch and feel flexible next to your skin.

Sensible colours: Buy basic day-to-day underwear in sensible colours such as beige and cream tones.

The right bra: To confirm that a bra really fits, check that the underbust band sits comfortably, and lean forwards so that you can slip gently into the cups. If you bulge out over the top, the cup is too small; if the bra wrinkles, the cup is too big. It is important to try on a bra before you buy it, unless you are so familiar with a particular brand that you know your right size or you're sure you can exchange it.

Sizing up: Generally speaking a wide back denotes a small cup size and a narrow back, a large cup. The cup size and bust measurements are two different things. Cup sizes start at AA (the smallest) up to DD (the biggest). The principal of measuring across the fullest part of the bust is grossly inaccurate because a 90 cm/36 inch bust could be all back and no bosom.

Measuring up: To discover your exact measurements, first measure all round your rib cage directly under your bust. Then measure across the fullest part of your bosom noting the difference between the two measurements which should fall approximately within the gauge of 10–22.5 cm/4–9 inches. The cup fitting code is as follows:

AA cup equals 10 cm/4 inches in difference
A cup equals 12.5 cm/5 inches
B cup equals 15 cm/6 inches
C cup equals 17.5 cm/7 inches
D cup equals 20 cm/8 inches
DD cup equals 22.5 cm/9 inches

Size assessment: To assess your size, add 12.5 cm/5 inches to the underbust measurement. For example, an underbust measurement of 72.5 cm/29 inches (plus 12.5 cm/5 inches) equals an 85 cm/34 inch bust. If the actual bust measurement is 87.5 cm/ 35 inches, the 15 cm/6 inches difference indicate the cup as 34B.

Bra spectrum: Large, low busts should be fitted with bras designed with non-stretch straps for complete support. Never shorten bra straps too much as this will distort the shape and push your bosom forward in an uncomfortable manner. Maximum comfort can be best achieved for smaller to average size busts from the wealth of sheer moulded bras, which offer more lightweight control plus flexibility.

Foundation wear to suit the outfit:

Under clingy rib dresses: Conceal severe midriff bulges with a body shaping all-in-one, for clean smooth polished lines. For more perfect figures, wear sheer tights with built in panty reinforcements.

Under tight jeans, trousers and skirts: Never wear pants that have a visible line showing through. Go for smooth pantigirdle shapes that provide a wrinkle-free finish.

Under low plunging necklines: Wear a deep plunge bra with front fastenings, if you do not want your underwear to be seen, or a pretty lace edged vest. Choose one of the many thermal designs for extra warmth, if the style is casual.

Under see-through tops: Go for a flesh-coloured bra with minimum stricture. Choose moulded bras that are completely wrinkle free. Never wear a see-through blouse if you haven't a bust that deserves 'showing off'.

Under strapless tops: It's best not to wear a bra if the outfit has no straps but if you need one, select a bandeau bra like a bikini top or, for sex appeal, a waspie which gives midriff support too.

Under backless dresses: There is such a limited range of backless bras on the market, that if you really need support, only buy a dress that provides built-in help by means of clever seaming under the bust.

Beating the bulges

Bikini versus one piece? It depends entirely on personal taste and figure limitations, and to a certain degree on social etiquette, as to what type of swim costume you choose. It is best to go for a racy one piece suit in public swimming baths at home, if you are seriously swimming for exercise. Restrict your bikini to holidays and sunning.

Going topless: Though topless bathing is becoming more commonplace on beaches abroad, do check before you derobe, for some countries have strong rules regarding exposure.

Shape rather than age: Your style of swimsuit should depend on your figure rather than your age. A one-piece swimsuit is usually the most flattering for less than perfect figures.

Suit yourself: swim slimming tricks

- **Short legs:**
  Suits that are cut high at the sides create an illusion of length on short legs. Vertical stripes help too. Avoid suits or bikini briefs cut straight across the tops of the thighs.

- **Heavy hips and thighs:**
  Go for simply cut one-piece suits with high cut legs preferably in a dark single colour. These give a flattering leggy feel taking the eye upwards and away from the problem zone. Particularly effective are long V-neckline suits with high cut legs. Avoid bold patterns or skirted styles, which add on extra bulk around the problem areas.

- **Top heavy:**
  Bikini or one-piece suits need to have good underbust
  support, either by seams or light boning, not necessarily
  through cups which tend to give the impression of an even
  larger bust. Find a suit with wide-set supportive straps,
  preferably cut high under the bust. Avoid styles with fussy
  bra top details like ruffles, lacing and fancy clasps. Opt for
  simple, clean cut lines perhaps with patterning around the
  hip line zone to draw the eye down and provide a more
  balanced proportion.

- **Small busts:**
  Re-adjust your proportions by opting for a suit or bikini top
  with pretty top detail like ruffles, shirring or a bandeau style,
  rather than a suit with built-in bra cups. A light bra top and
  dark bikini bottom brief effect will also help even out irregular
  proportions.

- **Skinny all over:**
  Terry towelling shirred fabrics that most women find difficult
  to wear often make the most stunning swim-cum-playsuits.
  Skinny shapes can wear suits that provide fullness in their
  fabrics or by means of novelty singular prints, horizontal
  stripes or maillot-style racing suits on old-fashioned bathing
  belle lines. Avoid bikini briefs that are cut too low and show
  scraggy hip bones.

- **Wear and tear:**
  Always wash your swimwear in cold water after each wear for more lasting results. Never hang damp swimwear on wire hangers, it can cause rust marks.

- **Khanga cover up:**
  Make an instant khanga coverup to protect you from the sun with a giant square of fabric measuring at least 1.2 metres (4 feet) by 1.5 metres (5 feet). A khanga can be tied in a multitude of different ways provided it is large enough.

Three ways with a khanga

A sundress: Wrap the khanga around your body lengthways, bringing the sides together to one side and knot the ends together. Twist the knotted end several centimetres/inches away from your body to form an armhole. Slip one arm through and adjust the knot on to your shoulder to form a single shoulder strap.

Sari style: The regular way of tying a khanga is sari style, wrapped around your body and folded into large pleats which are rolled under (this can also be done at waist level).

South Seas style: Alternatively, it can be wrapped around your waist lengthways and tied firmly between your waist and hip at a slant South Sea island style.

COLOURWISE
Looking on the Bright Side

A new shade: If you fancy a new hair colour, consider the colour of your eyes and think about a hair shade that will enhance them. Brown eyes and mid-brown hair fade into each other, but red-brown or golden hair make eyes seem much more vividly brown. Smoky eyes, the irises of which seem to be made up of different colours, can be startlingly green beneath auburn hair; fair hair can accentuate them too, reflecting eyes as truly blue. Hazel eyes team stunningly with dark brown hair.

Skin tone: Take your skin tone into account when you are trying to decide on a hair shade. The ideal colour for a pale complexion is copper or dark brown, both of which lift the skin. Darker shades of red give warmth to sallow skin. The most flattering hair colours for a pinky skin tone are all the shades between mouse to dark brown and black. When your hair turns grey you will find that nature balances the tones in your skin so that this, too, is lighter. Therefore, it is sensible to copy nature and if you want to cover your grey, choose a slightly lighter shade than your natural colour used to be.

Lighting-up time: Daytime colours can fade away after dark and look pale and washed out, so a stronger make-up is needed. Use two shades of blusher on your cheeks, darker in the hollows and a lighter tone elsewhere. Light up your eyes and your lips with lots of gloss and highlighter, using strong colours as your basis, and line them to give a clear emphasis. Take a black, or very dark grey pencil or liner round your eyes and draw a sharp line round your lips. This is the time to try a touch of iridescent highlight. Put it on your browbone, on your cheekbones and just the merest dot on your lips (in the centre of your lower lip). Experiment with a highlighter and discover where it suits you best.

Shading cheeks: If you feel you want only a little extra warmth on your cheeks and that even the most delicate of blushers is too bright, then you can use two different shades of powder for a pretty effect. Use a powder about two shades darker than your normal one on the area under your cheekbones (a warm dark beige with a hint of peach) and carefully blend it at the edges into the lighter powder, so that no harsh line of definition of any kind is obvious.

If you are long-sighted: Your lenses might have the effect of making your eyes more prominent if you are long-sighted, in which case you might want to play them down with neutral colours. Use taupe or grey eyeshadow, apply it over your eyelids and in the creases. Draw a thin line of eyeliner close to your upper lashes; thicken it slightly towards the outer corner. Keep your brows fairly full with a low arch.

If you are short-sighted: Your lenses will make your eyes look smaller if you are short-sighted. Use a light pastel or white eyeshadow just up to the crease to play up your eyes. Taupe shadow on the bony prominences under your eyebrows will play down this area and accent your eyes.

Soft shades for glasses: Colour used around your eyes can very often be magnified by lenses – depending on what your particular sight problem is and what lenses you wear – so avoid garish eye make-up. Go for pretty soft shades but be sparing with eyeliner which can easily look harsh! If you want some definition, it's best to use a brown or grey pencil and dot on the colour (rather than drawing a firm line) then smudge it slightly with your fingertip.

Eyes Right for Colour

Drawing the line: Eyeliner can be used very effectively to emphasize and dramatize the eyes but remember that a little goes a long way! A line drawn on the eyelids should always be light and soft to give emphasis without the line itself being apparent. A tapered brush gives the best results and the line should always be drawn as close to the roots as is possible and smudged a little to make it more subtle. To achieve additional colour brilliance, draw a line in brown, grey or black and then apply a line of bright colour very carefully alongside it. If you are lining upper lashes, then do the same along the lower lashes or you may produce a top heavy effect.

Splitting shades: Get an interesting two-tone effect on your eyes by using two shades of the same shadow on different halves of your upper eyelids. Use a dark forest green on the outside corner of your lids and a light green on the inside corner, blending carefully in the middle. The same trick works with dark blue on the outer and light blue on the inner part of the lid. You can carry the colours in this 'half and half' fashion right up to the base of your eyebrows, again blending carefully wherever the shades meet.

Eye make-up for a coloured skin: Go for something striking: sludgy, muddy shades are not for black or brown skins. Frosted shadows, even those with a touch of iridescence, are ideal. Reject blues and greens as a general rule and discard dark navies altogether. Choose russets, bronzes and apricots and, for something a little different, a gentle pink. Don't skimp on eyeliner but use it on the lower lid rather than the top and possibly choose one which matches the colour of your eyes. Bronze is a good general purpose alternative. If you want to use a highlight, go for ivory rather than white.

Get a smoky-eyed look: You can use a soft pink shadow and smoky grey to give an unusually pretty effect to eyes. Use the pink shadow on the browbone area and bring it right down on to the inner half of your lids only. Then add dark grey shadow on the outer part of your lids. Finish with a line drawn in a dark grey close to your lashes.

To add extra lightness and interest, place a small spot of white highlight in the centre of each upper eyelid. If you feel that the result is a little dramatic, soften it by taking a brush dipped in powder blusher and gently smudge it over the grey and pink at the outer corners of your brows only.

Autumnal tones: For a stunning effect with velvet and coral materials in lovely autumnal colours, use emerald mascara, a pale green shadow just above your lashes and then blend it gently into a soft russet. Add a tiny touch of a soft gold at the outer corners of your eyes.

Blues for blondes: If you are blonde and have the sort of lashes and eyebrows which are practically invisible, try this trick to enhance them. Instead of putting eyeshadow over the entire lid, use either blue or green shadow just above your upper lashes and a touch just below the lower. Use whichever colour matches your eyes. Then, with a pencil in a matching colour, draw a fine line round your eyes and finish off with a mascara which closely matches the shadow and lines.

Dramatic effect: If you want to get a really dramatic effect, use a coloured mascara and match that up to eyeshadow and then to finish off draw a line of matching colour with an eye pencil right along the base of your lashes. Complete the effect with a spot of ivory highlighter in the centre of your upper eyelids and just under your eye brows (at the outer edge).

Emphasize oriental eyes: Should you be lucky enough to have lovely slanted sloe eyes, then make the most of this feature by using make-up to draw attention to them. Use plenty of liner on your lower lids, swinging it up slightly at the sides. On your upper lids, use a pale shadow on the inner side and a dark shade at the outer edge, sweeping this outwards. If you feel that your upper lids lack emphasis, then apply a very fine line with a dark grey pencil and go over it gently with your fingertip, smudging very slightly to avoid any suggestion of a harsh outline.

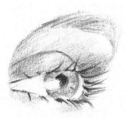

Accentuating small eyes: Don't use a dark eyeliner to outline your eyes if they are rather smaller than you'd like them to be, because this will make them look even smaller. Instead draw a fine line at the outer edge of your upper lids only, winging it just slightly up at the sides. Use a soft pencil for this rather than a brush and liquid liner, and touch the line lightly with your finger to smudge it a little. Then on your lower lids, apply some white highlighter as close as possible to the base of the lashes. For eyeshadow, choose a light shade which looks well with your eye colour and use a darker shade of the same colour under your eyebrows, swinging it out and well away from the nose area. Finish off with a touch of white highlighter at the outer edges of your upper eyelids. For a more adventurous colour combination, use one of the pale purple shades of shadow, with the white highlighter in the same position as before.

Eyes too close?: If your eyes are close-set, they may look smaller than they are. Make-up can help here and the careful use of colouring can give the impression that your eyes are more widely spaced. Apply lots of white highlighter to the skin area at the sides of your nose and then carry this up to the inner edges of your eyelids. Eye shadow should be smudged on the outer areas of your lids only and not all over. The shape of your eyebrows can help space out your eyes too, so try to wing them out and upwards at the outer edges. Keep your eyebrows light and use pencil on them very sparingly, as heavy brows will emphasize small, close-set eyes.

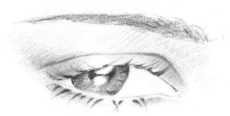

Eyes too narrow?: Instead of putting eyeshadow over the entire surface of your eyelids, use a touch of highlighter in the centre of each lid. This tends to make narrow eyes look more rounded and a little larger too. You can use this technique with any colour of eyeshadow.

The Well-Shaped Eye

If eyes are deep set: Don't use a dark shadow around your eyes as this will accentuate the problem. Use a very light colour. Start off by dusting loose powder over your lids and eyebrows, pressing it in and then flicking off the excess with a tissue. Use a powder which is paler than your own natural skin tone. Then, on top of that, smudge ivory and white highlighter for a pretty soft effect, using this on both lids and under the brow area. On the browbone itself, brush a hint of dark shadow. This should complement your eye colour. If you have hazel eyes, choose dark brown blended with a little forest green – blue eyes will be flattered by dark grey with a hint of navy blue, or navy with a hint of lighter green blended into it. Be very sparing with mascara and add a little petroleum jelly to your lashes for extra shine. **Don't** use liner or pencil to define the eyes. Eyebrows should not be too heavy.

Prominent eyelids can be disguised: Apply a fairly sombre but still rich shade of shadow to your upper lids to make them a little less obvious. Next, lighten the area under your browbones to detract attention from your lids by using a light shadow and a touch of white or ivory highlight. Colour combinations which work well are plum on the upper lid and a medium pink on the browbone area, a green/bronze shade on the lid and a very pale creamy green on the brow skin.

Light and bright: To make eyes look brighter, you can lighten the area under your brows using highlighter in an ivory tone. Reflect the highlight effectively by using it on your cheekbones just above the cheek shading.

Lips too full?: If you have a 'generous' mouth, try this trick to make it less obvious. Use a darker lipstick in the centre section of your lips and a lighter shade (but from the same basic tone) on the outside. Don't take the colour right to the edges of your lips, instead draw an outline with your pencil just inside the natural line.

Lips too thin?: You may have exactly the opposite problem from above, in which case use a pencil in a medium lip colour to draw your outline just slightly outside the natural line of your lips. Then fill in the shape completely. If your top lip appears thin by comparison with the lower one treat them separately when applying colour. Use a good colour and lots of gloss on the narrow lip to accentuate it; use a paler shade of the same colour on the fuller lip and avoid gloss.

Pencilling an outline: Cultivate the art of applying lipstick in order to achieve a professional and attractive result. For a really clean outline on your lips, always use a lip pencil to draw round the outside edge (correcting the shape slightly as you go, if necessary). Then fill inside the line with either the lipstick straight from the case or, better still, with a brush.

Uneven lips?: If your particular problem is that your upper lip is too thin in comparison with the lower, achieve a balanced effect by using a slightly lighter lipstick colour on the upper lip. Reverse the procedure for a thin lower lip.

Pretty and pale: If your hands are not your best feature, avoid the bright shades of nail polish which draw attention to them. The most flattering are the paler, more natural-looking nail polishes.

Lengthening nails: Short and stubby nails will look longer if you apply polish down the centre section of the nails only leaving the sides plain.

Half moons: If you have fairly slim nails you can, for a change and a very pretty effect, leave your half moons plain.

Colour and shape: If your nails are round or square, don't use deep red or wine shades. Choose one of the soft, muted beiges, browns or pinks. Fan-shaped nails look best with frosted or pearlized polishes.

Perfect application: Always apply polish with bold, positive strokes rather than little dabs and work from the base of the nail upwards towards the tip. If you are not covering the half moons, put the first touch of the polish from one side of the moon right across the top edge of it to the other side. Fill in the rest of the nail with normal upward strokes.

The collectables: Concentrate on building up a backbone of good basic items like a perfectly fitting navy blue blazer and plain white T-shirt tops. Ideally, your wardrobe should include: well-cut flannel or gabardine trousers; easy-fitting shirt dresses; a plain and simple black skirt; creamy coloured shirts with various necklines for maximum options; good quality knitwear ranging from simple, homely Fair Isles to (if budget allows) the ultimate luxury of cashmere which never dates.

Think through: Spend time thinking through the right shoe for the right outfit. All too many women make the mistake of wearing the newest fashion look with well-worn shoes. When the budget cannot stretch to new shoes for a new outfit, base your major investments around shoe styles that will team with more than one of your outfits and that will happily stand the test of time. Styles that are **always** in fashion whatever current trends dictate are:

- a classic court shoe with almond toe and medium heel

- a real leather brogue

- a traditional loafer or deck shoe

- an evening mule

- a correspondent (two-colour) slip-on

- a canvas sneaker or espadrilles

- a classic riding boot

- a green country Wellington boot

Stepping out: If you wish to call attention to attractive legs, or use hosiery as a vital fashion accessory, play up your legwear. Innovations on the hosiery scene provide for endless scope: lacy tights, novelty motif designs, seamed tights or stockings, ribbed and bouclé patterns, glittery blends for evening glamour plus a whole array of leg warmers and fun socks.

Versatility and Variety

One item – many ways: Never underestimate the endless possibilities of wearing a simple fashion item like a basic V-neck sweater in many different guises, such as:

- over a white T-shirt and with classic twill trousers
- with a pretty blouse and leather belt over a full swirly skirt
- with a check scarf to fill the neckline and workmanlike jeans
- casually strewn over the shoulder of a shirt dress for fashion impact and colour co-ordination

Swap accessories: You can transform one set of clothes into a totally different mood by swapping accessories. For example, add a piece of black jet jewellery, some sexy court shoes and black tights to a grey sweater dress to switch it from a daytime image to a ritzy evening feel. It can then take you from the office to a cocktail party with little extra effort.

Getting knotted: Scarves are fashion's most versatile accessory – learn how to ring fast changes with them. Depending on the size and texture, one scarf can be worn in at least twelve different ways:

tied peasant-style, low over your eyes and knotted at the back ▼

with a large-brimmed hat worn over the top, Carmen Miranda style ▼

Sloane Ranger style tied under your chin ▼

as a bandeau with perhaps another scarf plaited over to provide interest ▼

▲ on your head and wrapped several times around your neck and tied at the back for a resort feeling

▲ bandana style around your neck, knotted at the back

A scarf can also be worn as a turban; as a cravat; slung and knotted as a muffler; as a large floppy bow, fixed at the neck; as a soft snood gathering in all the hair at the back; as a giant shawl thrown over your shoulders.

Colour partners: Here are some suggested lip colours to team with different outfits.

Blue: almost any shade of pink or true red lip covering but not one with blue in it. For a more adventurous choice, try a peach or coral, especially to team with soft blues.

Pink: a matching lipstick or one in a softer or darker shade than the outfit.

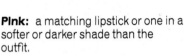

Red: try to match your choice of lip colour exactly with your outfit. If you want a paler muted look, apply the lip colour, then blot off the excess with a tissue and apply a touch of gloss. Another alternative is one of the russets.

Green: any of the corals, peaches, pinks or russets look great.

Yellow and orange: these can be awkward to match with make-up. Play safe and choose peachy or russet lip shades with a shimmer or a lick of gloss on top.

Colour mix: Real fashion pundits know how to mix their colours to great effect in the same hue, even, without letting the colour take accessories over. For example, a khaki safari dress can be matched with a khaki dishcloth-type of scarf, bronze jersey, canvas/leather rope belt, tan sandals and a giant brown leather satchel for a really co-ordinated, stylish look.

Colour psychology: Critical colour blending of accessories can emphasize your best features. If you want cheering up, a bright red fashion extra such as a cotton kerchief tied round your hair makes a strong fashion statement with a denim jacket; or bright pink ankle socks give your jeans more impetus. Brights quite naturally add razzamatazz. Neutrals add dimension in terms of texture.

Looks in Harmony

Patterns and plains: Forget old theories about only wearing patterns with plains. Mix patterns together, provided they are of the same basic colour hue. Take blue denim for instance: mix a plain denim jacket with an indigo blue printed T-shirt and team it with a blue floral printed skirt. Then pick up on accessories, perhaps a woven blue check kerchief and ethnic robe belt. The result will be a stylish do-it-yourself designer mix.

In the mix: Mixing patterns and textures together in one outfit requires a good sense of colour. Follow the principle of mixing the print, so that it matches in **colour** and in **style** – for example a classic paisley design in blue with a classic tweed based on blue. Never mix prints from a completely different family group, such as paisley with gingham, which will create a disorganized jumble. Mix your patterns in different weights of fabrics for the best results. Stick with small prints, such as floral sprigs and paisley designs, if you're mixing in major doses. Large, wild abstract prints need their own pride of place and are more difficult to blend.

Printed matter: Best results are achieved when the dominant print is used for the most dominant part of the outfit – for example, a large check skirt with a small check blouse and shawl pulling the look together.

QUICK INSTANT UPDATES

Accessories to ring the changes: Accessories should complement, not compete with your clothes. New accessories breathe new life into old favourites. Always buy the best you can afford. Budget for accessories as you would main buys. Though obviously not the foundation of a wardrobe, they provide extra fashion impact and can update far more efficiently than any new single separates item. For example, the latest looking low-heeled pumps give an old fashioned smock new fashion appeal.

Accessories to update: Your everyday accessories, such as shoes and bags, should be bought with care, so that they fit in with as many items as possible for an economical outlay. Your special accessory updates can smack of whatever is brand new in fashion. As fashion swings towards hats, you can buy the latest beret to give this season's look to last season's coat.

Belt it up: You can lift last year's look into this year's style by the right choice of belt. Be inventive and improvize. Belts can be made from scarves or from strips of contrasting fabrics like hessian to complement a Japanese-style kimono dress or with rope to go with T-shirt dresses.

Focal points: Belts help create the right proportions with regard to the length of your clothes. Belts worn on the waist project a completely different feeling from, say, belts worn low on the hips. Both are always 'in fashion' and are relevant within the context of the shape you wear them with. For example a loose linen shift dress can be hitched to mini length and teamed with a wide leather belt on the hips – or it can be elegantly belted on the waist with a narrow leather belt.

Clever combinations: Unexpected combinations can work, such as an inexpensive cotton T-shirt dress with an exclusive designer belt. Mix and match according to your budget. It is often worth spending more on little stylish things.

Bags of mistakes: Bags are often the letdown of an otherwise well thought out outfit. Consider the size of the bag in relation to what you are wearing and what you actually need to carry with you. Don't carry unnecessary extras.

Handbag essentials for evening: Cloak room and gratuity loose change, lipstick, powder pack and comb plus a tiny mirror and a pretty hankie should be all you actually need.

For daytime: Pack your bag according to your day's needs and clear out superfluous things immediately. Never let things stockpile. When you change your bag remember to switch all contents.

Double purpose bags: Pick bags that are double purpose, such as a neat medium-sized shoulder strap style that can be worn with suits and coats as well as dresses or one with adaptable straps. Avoid clutch bags for daily use, they are cumbersome to carry.

The right bag: It is not essential that a bag should match your outfit or shoes, in exact colour replica, but it should be in the same mood. Base your mainstay bags on neutral colours, such as tan, or brown, and sport one light beige or khaki bag to match summer lightweights.

Budget limitations: If your budget cannot stretch to leather, consider jazzy alternatives, such as a canvas or a parachute nylon type bag with sporty summer T-shirt styles. Designers have become most original with their choice of materials.

No knuckle dusters: There is nothing that spells out your vintage years more than the wrong jewellery. Sixties-favourite knuckle duster rings worn on every finger are out of context with today's streamlined fashion looks. Even if you have favourites, wear them in moderation and matched to your outfit.

Simplify jewellery: Wear jewellery in moderation. If you are already wearing a large spangled belt buckle, then there is no need to wear an ornate dangled necklace as well.

Link ups: Use jewellery to link together certain features of your outfit. A pretty pearl choker for example is the essential link for a decolletage; a tiny set of gold stud earrings will soften a severe suit and short boyish hair-style; rows of ivory and ebony bangles will transform a plain sweater into a fashionable one.

Fakes add fashion impetus: Real jewellery can be mixed with fake. It is difficult to tell the difference when it comes to the more traditional gems, such as turquoise and amber. Consider ethnic combinations, which are inexpensive and often incongruous, such as wood, glass or seashells.

Self styling: Develop your own style with accessories. For example, the endless permutations of wearing a classic check cotton shirt can provide for some varying fashion statements.

- wear it over jeans or skirts with a wide low slung belt

- wear it tucked in, with a contrasting check scarf at the waist

- wear it buttoned at the neck decorated with a dickie bow

- wear it unbuttoned with a T-shirt peeping through

- wear it with a cravat and brooch tucked into the neck

- wear it with masculine style braces and sleeves rolled up

- wear it with a watch or multitudes of bangles over the cuff

- wear it with cuffs buttoned and armbands

- wear it loosely unbuttoned as a jacket over another shirt

Add drama: Use the relevant accessories to play up a key point in your outfit. A pretty Peter Pan collar, for example, could be made to look feminine with the introduction of a lace jabot (a cascading frill) at the neck. A strict, tailored suit jacket could be emphasized by wearing a dickie bow.

Day or evening: Never categorize accessories too rigidly into day and evening moulds. Many suit both. Pearls can, for instance, look right in the daytime with a plain cashmere sweater and in the evening with a grand style taffetta blouse.

Unusual sources: Remember the natural attributes of ethnic sources. Traditional holiday buys can give a plain outfit a stunning designer touch. A brightly coloured shawl spices up a simple sweater dress. Rows upon rows of silvery bangles give a plain blouse extra impact.

Scarves become hats: Scarves are the most useful fashion accessory and can be switched to make an attractive hat as well. To turn a scarf into a turban:

How is it tied? Whenever a scarf is worn, how is it tied? These are the telling fashion extras that make the difference between this year and last. Note how magazine fashion models wear their accessories, watch shop windows as a barometer of style.

Scarf trims: Scarves can also be trimmed in many different ways to provide a fashionable fillip to accompany your outfit. Ten ways to trim a scarf:

- machine ricrac braid to a plain kerchief for a rustic feel

- scatter fine sequins into a chiffon scarf to make your evening snood

- make rouleaus (tiny twists of contrasting scarf) to go around your scarf when it is tied peasant style

- mix two or three long woven check scarves together to tie bandeau style for impact

- wear your scarf as a headscarf swathed around the neck with a large visor worn over, resort style

- attach tassles to the ends of a scarf which can be tied gypsy style

- attach artificial flowers to the knot at the nape of your neck when a scarf is tied peasant style

- pin a brooch to a turban scarf

- fray the ends of a cotton scarf for a rustic feel

- fold a scarf into a bandeau, leaving the ends loose and trim with beads, twenties style

Scarves become belts: Scarves can also be swathed to form a belt. For instance:

- wear two or three plaited together to form a belt, tucking the ends under

- wear a scarf slung sideways around your hips, gypsy style

- wear a scarf wrapped around your waist to form a giant cummerbund. Wear a fine leather belt over for impact

- wear a tiny cotton square tucked into a wide leather belt to add a splash of colour

- wear a giant shawl over your shoulders tucked in at the belt for practicality plus style

Nice and easy: Wool, cotton and lace scarves are easy to control. Silk, though a beautiful fabric, is too slippery to wear in many of the ways described and linen, though often suitable, is inclined to crease more easily.

Hat trends: These are the basic hat shapes that are adapted and improvised according to fashion trends each season. They are always ostensibly in fashion:

- the bowler
- the straw boater
- the breton
- the trilby
- the cloche
- the beret
- the helmet
- the stetson

- the cap
- the turban
- the pillbox
- the picture hat
- the sombrero
- the fur hat
- the visor
- the toque

cloche

boater

cap

picture

Hats and hair: Hats can go with hair worn in a variety of different cuts. It is not always necessary to wear your hair scraped back. It depends upon the cut of your hair and the shape of your hat.

Hats and glasses: Earrings and glasses can also be worn with hats. Take extra care to choose the right shapes to suit.

Hats and face shapes: Consider your face shape and the way you wear your hair to find the right shape of hat to suit. Always try on a hat and view from all sides before you buy.

Oval faces: An oval-shaped face looks particularly good in a hat in most styles but not shapes that are too high at the top and add extra inches.

Round faces: Medium or small brims are best for round faces – nothing too extreme, nothing too head hugging.

Long faces: Sharp styles really suit long faces, especially angular shapes, such as a classic trilby.

Square faces: Large picture hats suit square faces but they should have soft lines, such as a straw hat elegantly trimmed. Avoid anything too tiny and petite which will look out of proportion.

Wide faces: Hats worn off the face suit a wide face best of all, especially medium brims, worn at the back of the head.

Heart-shaped faces: Petite hats look their best with heart-shaped faces, such as one-sided pillboxes and cloche hats.

round

long

wide

square

heart shaped

A good hair cut: Never wear a hat if you feel that when you take it off it ruins the effect of your hair. However, a good hair cut will fall back into shape as soon as you shake your hair. Wear your hat with panache, always pulling it down on your head to avoid the old-fashioned look of a hat perched over a hair style.

DAILY DIFFICULTIES

HOW TO REMAIN COOL

Keeping cool

Think cool: Your own mental attitude counts for a lot. Tell yourself you love the heat and enjoy every minute of it. Try to stay indoors during the really hot hours.

Take your time: Get up earlier than usual in hot weather so that you can start the day in a leisurely, unhurried fashion.

Avoid starch: Meals that contain starch and sugar will make you feel over-heated. Conserve coolness and energy with crisp salads, cold fish, meat and poultry and a minimum of bread and pastry.

Summer bathing

A good beginning: If you've an action-packed day ahead, try a refreshing and relaxing bath to which you've added a milky bath powder or seaweed-based bath additive. Soak, exercise if you like, wash, scrub and finish with a lukewarm splash followed by a quick cold one.

Massaging in: The action of 'massaging in' creams and lotions can make you feel hot and sticky. In a heat-wave, use nourishing and moisturizing body preparations which are an integral part of your bath or shower routine and don't require handling.

A summer soak: Moisturizing is soaking yourself in water, so fill the bath right up. Summer bath water should not be too hot and as too-long baths actually lead to dehydration, limit yourself to 10 minutes in hot weather, especially if you've been sunning yourself during the day.

Bath after swim: Bath as soon as you can after a swim in a pool or the sea to replace lost moisture when it's most needed. Salt water dehydrates and dries your skin.

After a bath: Pat yourself dry with a soft towel. Be gentle as vigorous rubbing will only make you warm.

Be generous: Choose a light flower fragrance for soap and talcum powder and be generous with talcum on your feet.

On with the eau de cologne: Invest in a large bottle of eau de cologne or eau de toilette. Use it on the back of your neck, your chest, the back of your knees and your arms. (See Chapter 2 Different strengths of fragrances, page 70.)

Daytime refreshers

Cool places: You'll feel refreshed if you apply cooling toilet waters, a cologne stick, or ice cubes to the areas where your veins are near the surface of your skin, such as the backs of hands, insides of wrists, and elbows, under arms, behind knees, inside shoulders and on ankles. Your veins act as cooling rooms for the blood as it courses through your body.

A pat on the neck: Cure that sticky feeling during the day by patting the nape of your neck with a piece of cotton wool soaked in cooling cologne.

Renew make-up: If possible, clean off all your make-up and renew it once during the day.

Cool to the touch: The cooler products are to the touch, the more you will enjoy using them in hot weather. Make space in the fridge for face packs, skin tonics and colognes.

Aerosols are best: Spray-on preparations are extra cool because as soon as the gas propelling the contents hits the air, it liquefies.

Clean and confident

Perspiration is a vital process, as continuous as your heartbeat, which maintains your normal body temperature. What's more it's a wonderful beautifier – all that natural body moisture keeps skin soft and pliable, which is, after all, the universal aim of costly creams and rejuvenators. It is worth knowing about the products available for checking perspiration. These include aerosols, creams and roll-ons in both emulsion and clear liquid varieties. It's very much a matter of personal choice.

Deodorants and anti-perspirants: These are not cleansers as such but their aim is to keep us clean smelling. A deodorant counteracts the odour of perspiration; an anti-perspirant checks wetness as well.

Is an anti-perspirant safe?: Don't worry about 'sealing' your skin. A 100% reduction of sweat is just not possible. Anti-perspirants reduce sweating by 40–50%, which is usually enough for comfort and to prevent your clothes becoming marked.

Perspiration: This is regarded as the most persistent nagging beauty problem but, dealt with firmly and quickly every day, it proves far less bothersome and obvious than the occasional spot or broken fingernail.

Regular applications: Apply your deodorant regularly, every 24 hours on average, and let the application set before you dress. Sprays dry instantly but creams take longer, up to 2¼ minutes.

Don't waste time: While waiting for an application to dry practise exercise for strengthening the pectoral muscles, which support your bosom by drawing circles in the air with your elbows.

A word of warning: Most anti-perspirants and deodorants, except the long life variety, are not water-fast and should be re-applied after a bath or swim.

Lack of confidence: When you don't feel confident that your deodorant is working properly, check after washing, and before applying the product, that every speck of soap is rinsed off. Any residue can interfere with the remedial action of a deodorant.

When to apply: The time to apply a deodorant is when you are relaxed, such as immediately before going to bed or immediately you get up. Don't apply when your whole system is in top gear because by that time your glands are very active.

Cover well: Check in a mirror that you are covering the entire radius of your arm pit. Unless you cover the whole area, some sweat glands may be missed, with obvious results.

Action packed: If you lead an action-packed life, are always on the go and full of nervous energy, then consider a miniature product as one of your handbag essentials. Your original application may well falter half-way through the day and you'll feel distinctly damp. Try to renew the application during a calm spell.

Try not to panic: Panic, emotion, anything that disturbs you, accelerates the rate at which you perspire.

A good alternative: If your underarms are wet only and there's no unpleasant smell, pat dry with a tissue and re-apply anti-perspirant deodorant. If the bacteria have got to work and you can't have a proper wash, a good alternative is to use a cleansing tissue – an unperfumed one – to cleanse the area and then re-apply anti-perspirant deodorant.

Underarm hair: This should be removed regularly as it can inhibit the effectiveness of an anti-perspirant deodorant, (see page 45, chapter 1) but what about the advisability of applying protection afterwards? Most product instructions suggest waiting at least a few hours. However, you can use anti-perspirant deodorant before shaving, but the action of the soap and razor is likely to remove the protective qualities, to some extent. Stick deodorants can usually be applied immediately after shaving although there can be stinging momentarily if a blunt razor has been used. Another post-shaving remedy is to use a finely milled deodorant talc.

You are what you eat: Food has an effect on body odours – garlic, for example. Our kidneys can't deal with some of the things we eat and drink and odours will be dispersed by our skin. Avoid too many strong foods, such as onions and salamis and rich cheeses and limit your intake of alcohol which in excess will overload your kidneys. (For cooling foods, see page 154.)

In times of stress: Recent research has proved that body odour can occur when you are under emotional stress. Sweating from heat alone doesn't cause the same sort of smell or the same sort of problem. (See Chapter 7 page 203 for further information on how to relieve stress.)

Hair in the heat

Sweet hair: Long hair tends to mop up scalp perspiration and doesn't smell so sweet. Rub the hair roots with a cologne-soaked swab of cotton wool between shampoos.

Quick pick me up: Push some cotton wool, which has been soaked in eau de cologne, into the bristles of a hair brush and brush your hair lightly before setting on to rollers. Allow to dry and brush out as usual. The cologne will take up any grease, making your hair bouncier as a result.

Between shampoos: If you have greasy hair, massage it with a spirit type tonic (i.e. a clear liquid with an alcohol base) and then pin it up. Wring out a towel in very hot water; place it round your head and remove when cool. Brush your hair and leave to dry. It will look glossy and shiny.

Braid your hair: A cool way to wear hair in summer is to braid it either straight after a shower, fresh from the pool or when your hair is already dry. Bend over, gather your hair at the crown and plait into a single plump plait. Where it narrows at the end you can wrap it with ribbon, string or beads.

Try a chignon: Do this on wet hair or apply a setting lotion. Comb your hair back smoothly, twisting each side into a coil, reinforcing the coil with pins where needed. Secure at the back with a covered elastic band and hairpins. Then roll up the extra hair at the back of the neck and secure with pins as well. Decorate the chignon with a flower or a bow.

Curly and natural: Relax and enjoy your natural curls with a good cut kept fairly short. Arrange your hair using a wide comb, or finger dry, fluffing it up with your fingers.

Long, straight hair: If your hair is long and heavy, gather a large section of it loosely at the crown. Twist it into a small, casual curl and pin it down off-centre. Then just let the rest fall smoothly down your back.

The pony tail: Update this style by pulling the tail out to one side. Curl it into a loose twist at the base and camouflage the covered

elastic band with tendrils of hair. Another idea is to have a tail on each side of your head or even two on one side.

The extremities (see also pages 60–61 for more hints on hands)

Hot sticky hands: If your hands are hot, you can feel hot and sticky all over. Hold your wrists under a cold, running tap. Alternatively, you could cup a little skin tonic or eau de cologne in the palms of your hands.

Anti-perspirant on hands: If your hands perspire a lot, a light touch of anti-perspirant won't harm your skin.

To conceal: Nail polish can conceal the rims of your fingernails, which may become dirty quickly in hot weather.

Bare beauty: Summer is the time for bare legs and sandals, so make sure that your feet and legs are as pretty as the rest of you. Legs should be clear of blemishes and silky smooth (see Chapter 1, For a smooth finish, page 44). Toe nails should be cleaned like fingernails with cotton wool soaked in cuticle cream wrapped around an orange stick.

Remember the soles: In summertime when you may go barefoot, the soles of your feet will show. Scrub off any roughness with soap and a pumice stone and smooth in a little hand cream.

Cool for feet: Solid cologne stroked over the soles of your feet will keep them cool and comfortable.

A summer face

Problem make-up: To keep make-up fresh on hot days, use an astringent or skin tonic first. Not only is it cooling and refreshing but it also closes the pores and provides a better surface, so that make-up lasts longer.

Sensitive complexions: Only you know how your skin reacts to sun, but there are at least three skin types which don't tan happily: the true redhead; the fair English rose with a fine, sensitive skin;

anyone with a skin both fine and liberally freckled.

Make it minimal: Keep make-up to a minimum. You'll feel cooler that way.

Gels for coolness: Gels are dry, transparent and matt. They are cool to the touch and ideal for hot weather make-up. (See Chapter 3 Summertime faces page 111.)

Colour adjustment: As your tan develops, remember to adjust your make-up and clothes to suit your new skin colour. (See Chapter 3 Getting the shade to suit your tone, page 78.)

In the day: For daytime make-up, choose face-bronzer or foundation to flatter your tan, set with translucent powder. Emphasize areas of natural sheen with a high-lighter (see Chapter 3 Highlighters page 88 and Seeing things in right light page 105).

In the evening: Apply gold highlighter as well as blusher on cheeks, hairline, temples and, if you like, along your collarbone and top of your shoulders. Cheek hollows can be subtly highlighted with glowing bronze-toned blusher (see also Chapter 3 Candlelight, page 105).

Keep dry with make-up

Waterproof make-up: This can be a joy as it resists heat as much as it does wet and your waterproof make-up will stay put for hours.

Soft and natural: Gel sticks of transparent face or cheek colour in medium, dark and bronze skin tones, slide on to your skin and dry to a soft natural look.

Creamy consistency eyeshadows: These repel water and are marvellous for holidays as they stay dry and intact even when subjected to underwater swimming.

Smudgeproof and waterproof mascara: This is a good buy all year round; it is equally effective whether you are swimming or caught in a sudden downpour.

HOW TO KEEP WARM

Facing up to winter

Don't wash: Never wash your face immediately you come in from the cold or just before you go out as it will increase the tautness of the skin. If you want to cleanse, use cream or lotion to help keep the skin pliable.

Dry face: If your skin is dry, take off your make-up at night with a swab of cotton wool soaked in baby oil. Put on a second application, then gently wash your face in luke-warm water. Rinse and rinse again, then pat your face dry and, while it is still warm, lightly smooth a third application of oil into the skin.

Against the cold: Just as skin needs to be protected from too much sun in summer, it needs protection against winter cold with a moisturizer and a film of make-up.

Central heating: Powerful central heating and roaring fires will dry your skin. The best defence is an invisible layer of moisturizer at all times.

Chapped lips: Even if you don't use lipstick it's a good idea to wear lip gloss during the winter, to protect your lips from the harsh weather.

Colour balance: Don't try to make up to your natural colour in winter. Use colours which counteract the effect the temperature may have on your skin.

Blue with cold: If you go blue in cold weather, choose make-up with a warm beige tone rather than anything pinkish and put aside lipsticks with a hint of blue. Use lipsticks with warm tones and glowing brown and violet eyeshadow colours.

White with cold: If you go white in cold weather, choose a warm foundation with a yellow tinge. Avoid anything with too much white in it.

Pale-skinned girls: If you have a pale skin and very blue eyes but want to wear blue, use make-up with warm tones.

Red nose: If your nose reddens in extremes of heat and cold, wear a green-tinted camouflage moisturizer under foundation or, alternatively, blot out the danger area with a cover-up cream before applying foundation.

Glowing good looks

Keep warm and pretty: Winter beauty requires good circulation. Improve your circulation by exercising (see Chapter 8, Warm up, page 276).

Morning rub: A morning bath or rub down will warm you up. Use a rough towel and rub vigorously.

Take a mitt: A quick rub over with a soft friction mitt soaked in cologne will do wonders for a sluggish circulation. A towelling mitt filled with kitchen salt and rubbed over your limbs after a hot bath will also tone up your circulation.

Head up, shoulders back: Walk briskly to the station or the shops. The more you huddle, the colder you will look and feel, so throw your head up, keep your shoulders back and step out. Tensing your body will make your ribs ache and teeth chatter, so relax and welcome the crisp cold air for its champagne-like effects – sparkling eyes and a glowing complexion.

Circulation 'chasers': A brisk walk after lunch and again before going indoors for the evening works wonders. Dancing – even if you're alone – is splendid for your circulation and figure.

Plenty of fresh air: In winter you may not get your optimum supply of fresh air, so stand in front of an open window with your head up and shoulders back and breathe slowly and deeply. Try to do this for five or ten minutes twice a day.

A show of hands

Extra care: Your hands will need extra care in winter. Cream them regularly working towards the wrists, kneading the skin between your finger and thumb.

Chilblains: Changes of temperature encourage chilblains, so try to keep your hands and feet warm all the time. Never warm up too rapidly and never wear damp gloves or wet socks.

Two better than one: Layered dressing is warmer. Two pairs of thin, loosely fitting gloves are warmer than one thick tightly fitting pair.

For rough jobs: If you are gardening or doing any outdoor jobs, slip thin gloves under large rubber ones, to give the necessary insulation.

Hands up: If, when coming into a warm room from the cold air, you find your hands are red and puffy and feel hot and numb, hold them up above your head for a minute or two to help the blood supply.

The chilly type: Keeping your wrists and ankles warm will keep your hands and feet warm too. Knit bands of ribbing to slip over as cuffs.

Chapped hands: Cracked finger tips and chapped hands are caused by dry skin. Avoid using strong soap and detergents and putting your hands in water too often. When they do get wet, always dry them well. Make sure your diet contains vitamins A and B complex which are found in meat, fish, eggs, green vegetables, carrots, milk, liver, wheatgerm, tomatoes and peas.

Use a barrier cream: Always apply a good lanolin barrier cream to your hands before putting them in water.

Winter hair care

Light perm: Your hair might need a light perm to keep it crisp and resistant in blustery weather. Spray it with lacquer before going out on damp days to avoid the problem of wispy ends.

Hot oil treatment: An occasional hot oil treatment will do wonders for your hair in winter. It will revive dull hair and the massaging which the treatment involves will also help stimulate the circulation. See Chapter 6, Oil treatment, page 185.

Dressing for winter

Keep it loose: Never wear tight shoes or tight gloves which can impede free-flowing circulation in your hands and feet.

Light is best: Fine, light woollen or thermal underwear, which should cover your thighs and abdomen as well as your chest and shoulder blades, is the best way to keep warm. It will also allow you to keep a slim shape.

Be consistent: Don't coddle yourself in warm underwear one day, and leave it off the next. This is a sure formula for developing winter ailments.

Care for feet and legs

Foot bath: Your feet should be as warm and relaxed as possible (see Chilblains above). A foot bath is comforting and relaxing after a cold hard day. Dissolve two handfuls of Epsom salts in a bowl of warm water filled to ankle depth. Soak your feet in this for not less than 15 minutes and then half-dry them and rub pumice stone gently back and forth across any calluses. Finally, pat your feet with cologne or skin tonic.

Chapped legs: If you expose your legs to the cold and/or roast them in front of a fire, they can become chapped. Wear warm stockings and boots; avoid extremes of temperature where possible and rub in generous amounts of hand or body lotion daily.

SHORT CUTS

Make-up aids

Day for night: If you are making up in daylight for an evening affair, as can so often happen in spring and autumn, draw the curtains and turn on the electric light while you do your make-up.

Evening blues: Artificial light takes the blue pigment out of colours, so when choosing shades of lipstick and blusher, select those which are already plentifully loaded with blue pigmentation – the true reds, the blue-pinks, the fuchsias, rather than the oranges or yellow tinted ones.

Hostess in a hurry: If you want to make-up well before your guests arrive, gel make-up is just the right consistency for not spoiling – no matter how early in the afternoon it is applied.

Instant face lift with colour

In disguise: When you're tired and your face gives the show away, choose a warm-toned foundation in the beige/peach/amber spectrum and top that with translucent powder.

Take to camouflage: Blot out any tell-tale shadows under the eyes with a beige-tinted concealer cream. See also page 8.

Hair that sticks up: If you find you have slept awkwardly on your hair and it is sticking up, pin it up in rollers or hold a section at a time round a cylindrical brush and spray each section with setting lotion, then blow dry or spray with hair spray and leave to dry naturally.

Pillow creases: Remove those early morning creases by splashing your face with hot water or massaging gently with cleanser or moisturizer.

Red nose from having a cold: Camouflage this with light, beige-toned, stick make-up; but if you are constantly having to blow your nose, you are probably better to focus attention elsewhere – for example, by putting a faint feathering of powder blusher high on cheekbones.

Puffy eyes: To soothe puffy eyes, relax for 10 minutes with folded tissues soaked in mild astringent lotion over your closed eyes. Splash with cold water and apply foundation or beige camouflage make-up. Avoid pearly eye colours which will only emphasize the problem. See also page 8.

Preparing for a long day

Clean and efficient: A mask is the most efficient skin cleanser available and, when you know you've got a long day ahead, it's a good idea to apply one early in the morning, ideally while you're bathing. Make-up that goes on to a scrupulously cleansed, cool-to-the touch skin lasts longer.

Take it with you: Soak a little pad of cotton wool in toner and take it to work in a waterproof bag. Or decant some toner into a natural spray – or top up with water even. Then, whenever you start to feel hot and bothered during the day, or before you go out for the evening, pat or spray your face without disturbing your make-up. This trick helps to keep the skin tone and temperature nicely balanced.

Just in case: Some portable items to take to the office to help your make-up stay put include the following: a camouflage stick for quick touch ups to the under eye area or any 'problem' spot; pressed powder; blusher – remember you need more colour if you're going out to spend the evening in artificial light; lipstick and perfume. It's also worth considering eye drops to refresh eyes that have been hard at work all day.

Dual purpose hair brush: As well as keeping your hairstyle in order, a brush can give you a quick pick-me-up before an appointment. Just before you go out, bend from the waist to send a rush of blood to the scalp and brush through your hair – the best reviving treatment there is.

Coping with hair in emergencies

Take a pipe cleaner: Even without your usual bag of tricks, you can still produce a hairstyle with movement and fullness: just use pipe cleaners. Divide your hair into six big sections; twist each one from root to end and wrap round at the root, into a coil, secured with a pipe cleaner. For a really curly effect you can sleep in the pipe cleaners but just popping them into dry or damp hair for half an hour in the morning gives a good degree of fullness.

A swift solution: For speed, partly dry your hair before putting it in rollers, to avoid any tell-tale ridge marks along the roots. This can be a problem when hair is dry or exceptionally soft and fine.

Titivate in minutes: Heated rollers can give a quick lift to your hair. The secret is to leave them in until they've cooled right down, then remove and quickly brush through.

Hair on the move: If you normally wash your hair every day or two and can't because you are travelling, dry shampoo is the answer. This is especially useful if you have fine hair and your head is rubbing against a seat back. That sort of friction will make your oil glands active and your hair greasy, See also page 62.

Dewy effect: Apply make-up before you bathe and you will achieve a cooling dewy effect and long-lasting results.

Well spread: A foundation will spread and blend more quickly and smoothly over your skin if it is slightly damp with skin tonic.

Use sparingly: The secret of success with foundation is to use it sparingly. Leave it on for five minutes before you finish your make-up; if you have used too much it will shine. Gently blot off excess with a tissue.

Quick mix: If you have difficulty spreading your foundation quickly, mix it with a little moisturizer.

Eyeshadow base: Use your foundation as a base for eyeshadow. It will give your skin a pearly undertone and enhance your eyes.

Pearly sheen: If you use the combined cream and powder type of make-up, press over it lightly with cotton wool wrung out in cold water. This will give your skin a pearly sheen.

Speedy eyebrow make-up: Use what's left on the mascara brush, or wand, after you've applied the colour to your lashes, to sweep lightly along the length of your eyebrows.

Use eyelash curlers: In seconds they produce a lovely curl which lasts all day and is as effective as three coats of mascara.

Dyed eyelashes: One half-hour salon session once a month saves minutes every time you make up.

Cotton-tipped sticks: These are excellent for applying make-up. Just throw them away when they're dirty. You will save time washing and drying an assortment of cosmetic brushes.

Pile on the shades: If applying two or more shades of eye make-up use a cotton-tipped stick rolled backwards and forwards over the shadowed area, to avoid hard edges of colour.

Fan the lashes: When using mascara, brush across your lashes to fan them out and keep the colour thickest on the outer lashes.

Sable brush: Treat yourself to a huge sable brush from an artshop. With this you can apply blusher in seconds; you can fluff over your whole face, lighting and lifting a tired make-up. You can buy the cheaper brands of blusher without an applicator.

Caught on the hop

Transformation: Transform your usual powdered eyeshadow into another shade by wetting it or use a palette and mix together two shadows.

Spot into beauty spot: Mask a spot with concealer cream and touch it up with brown or black eye pencil.

Double blusher: A blusher can double-up as a highlighter for your eyes. Smudge it on in a curve from nose to each eyebrow.

Different effects: One eyeliner pencil can provide many effects. Use it blunt or pointed and even hot or cold. If you run the pencil tip under hot water, or put a match to it for a second, you will achieve a marvellous intensity of shade.

Avoid a build-up: When touching up make-up avoid a build-up of matt colour, especially around your eyes; apply gloss shadow for a light translucent effect.

Wayward wisps: If short wisps around your hair line won't go the way you want them to, moisten them with setting lotion, comb them into place and let them dry.

Top to toe treatment in under an hour

0.01: Run a bath. If you haven't a bath additive to hand, try baby oil or even a cup of milk; the latter is very soothing and it foams well too.

0.03: Put in rollers to revive a tired hairdo.

0.06: Refresh tired eyes while you are soaking in bath. Use a wet flannel as an eye pad or even cucumber slices or cold, used tea bags.

0.12: Scrub around rough skin patches and goose-pimply areas.

0.15: Finish off with a cold shower to get the circulation going.

0.17: Rub in hand and body lotion all over your body. Don't forget your feet.

0.20: Whisk the white of an egg to make a marvellous tightening and toning face pack. Use it on your neck too.

0.25: While the face pack is working its wonders, soak your hands in slightly warmed olive oil. This will help to soften rough edges and cuticles.

0.30: Push back cuticles with a hand towel which is less finicky than an orange stick when time is at a premium. Then polish a little talc into each nail for a really good shine.

0.35: Apply foundation and a touch of beige concealer or eyeshadow to hide any circles under eyes.

0.37: Set finished make-up with a damp sponge; press it all over your face with a rolling movement.

0.40: Apply eye make-up, ideally a shadow with bits of iridescence in it, which will draw attention to your eyes in artificial light. Mix lipstick with a little castor oil or olive oil for a real glow.

0.50: Remove rollers and gently comb your hair. Apply perfume (see pages 69–74).

Fast keep-fit routines

Improvization: If you don't have enough time for an exercise routine, improvize by taking a few deep breaths. Sit cross-legged on the floor and hang your head down, nestling as close to your chest as possible. Breathe in deeply through your nose, filling right down to the bottom of your lungs. Now exhale slowly. Repeat for five minutes.

Poor sleep: If you're sleeping badly or feeling jittery as a result of being tense and over wrought, relax over a cup of peppermint or camomile tea instead of yet another cup of strong black coffee or tea. Another drink which will relax you is a tablespoonful of honey taken in hot water, with or without the juice of half a lemon. (See also Chapter 7, Sleep and relaxation, page 210.)

10 minute flop: When you haven't time for a proper rest, flop for 10 minutes in the beauty angle. Lie on the floor or a bed with your feet, legs and thighs supported, so that they slope gently upwards and your feet are 30 cm (12 inches) above your head. This will send blood to your head to feed and re-oxygenate your hair, eyes and skin.

Last minute face savers

Take a deep breath: When you've run out of time and need to pull yourself together quickly, take a deep breath through your nose. When you can't inhale any longer, exhale pushing out as much air as you can until you feel empty.

Uplifted brows: Slice some perfume across your eyebrows to smooth them and add a touch of fragrance.

Pretty mouth: Lip gloss is not renowned for its staying power but when there's no time for anything else, dab some on for a pretty glowing mouth.

Relieve tension: Reach round to the back of your neck with a dab of moisturizer or hand cream and massage for a few seconds on the trouble spot.

Cool hands: Wash and half dry your hands in cool water and then hold them to your face, cupping a cheek in each palm; you'll feel better and look better.

NATURAL
ALTERNATIVES

FRUIT

Almond

A good stimulant: If you have slightly dry skin, avoid face packs which have a drying effect, even though they may tone the skin well. Here's a recipe which uses fuller's earth as the toning, astringent ingredient but also contains an oil to guard against overdrying. Take a tablespoon of fuller's earth, put it into a container, add about half a teaspoon of rosewater (this has a very mild toning effect only but gives a good stimulus to skin) and then add as much almond oil as you need to make up into a smooth paste (you're looking for something of roughly the consistency of clear honey). Apply this to your face, massaging it into your skin slightly before leaving it on. Wait for five minutes, no more, then rinse off with lots of warm water and pat dry with a tissue.

Nutty nourisher: Pure almond oil from the nut tree takes a lot of beating when it comes to nourishing and softening dry skin. Keep some handy in a bottle and after you've been out in the sun or the wind, rub a little on to your face after you have cleansed it and repeat before you go to bed.

Apple

Banish dark circles: To fade the circles under your eyes, cut two slices from a juicy apple. Lie back, close your eyes and place a slice of apple over each eye, then relax for a while.

Apple cider nourisher: Apple cider vinegar mixed with other natural ingredients can be made up into a super smooth lotion to nourish dry skin. Take four tablespoons of apple cider vinegar, two egg yolks, one quarter cup sesame seed oil, one teaspoon comfrey and a few drops of peppermint oil. Add the oils to the egg yolk very slowly, as you would when making mayonnaise. Then add the comfrey and the vinegar. Mix together thoroughly and store in a bottle or jar in a cool place or refrigerator. It will keep for 8 to 10 days. Use it to rub into your skin before going to bed.

Avocado

Skin improver: Scoop two tablespoons of flesh from half an avocado. Place in a bowl with a few drops of lemon juice and mash together quickly with a fork to prevent the avocado turning brown. Add one teaspoon of honey and mix to a smooth paste. Apply this mixture to your face and leave it on for at least twenty minutes. Rinse off with lots of warm water and follow with a splash of rosewater on the skin. Then towel dry.

This treatment is excellent for softening the skin and, as it is non-drying, it can be used for most skin types. If you have a dry skin, however, leave the mixture on your face for 10 to 15 minutes only while soaking in a hot bath.

Hair conditioner: Hair which is lack-lustre can be helped considerably by giving it a conditioning treatment with avocado. Mash the flesh of half an avocado or put it in a liquidizer for an even smoother mixture. Rub the mixture into your hair, massaging it into the whole length. Leave on for 15 minutes to allow the beneficial oils to do their work and then rinse off with warm water.

Avocado abrasive: If you have rough, dry skin on elbows, legs or feet, indeed anywhere, a good way to get rid of the flakiness and restore your skin to its original softness is to rub with avocado skin. (When you have eaten an avocado keep the skin.) Repeat as often as you can.

Skin conditioner: This recipe will pep up jaded skin in no time at all. Take half an avocado and scoop out the flesh. Place it in a bowl with the juice of half a lemon, a pinch of sea salt, two tablespoons fine oatmeal and one teaspoon of comfrey powder. Blend everything together very thoroughly with a fork or a whisk, or put it in an electric blender, and then apply it to your face with your fingertips. Rinse off with lots of cold water. You can use this on your neck and shoulders too. If there is any leftover, the preparation will keep for up to a week, provided it is stored in an airtight container in a cool place.

Blackberry

From the hedgerows: Blackberrying is a common pastime and the berries can be used for other things besides jams and jellies! Put a level tablespoon of whole blackberries into a pan containing 600 ml (1 pint) of water. Add about 6 leaves from the bush. Bring to the boil, then remove from the heat immediately and allow to cool. Strain off the liquid into a bottle. Add a few drops to your bathwater for an invigorating effect. It has a super smell. If you have a freezer you can easily freeze some berries, so that they will be available out of season for your bath tonic!

Elderberry

Bath tonic: Elderberries are plentiful in the countryside and great favourites with home winemakers. The elder can provide beauty aid for bathtime, too. Infuse some berries and leaves in the following way. Add 1 level tablespoon of berries and a cupful of leaves to 900 ml (1½ pints) of water in a pan and bring to the boil. Simmer for 2 minutes, then remove from the heat and allow to cool. Strain off the liquid into a bottle. This makes an excellent addition to the bathwater, when you feel in need of some extra special soothing treatment: use one or two tablespoonsful.

Lemon

Stained fingernails: If your fingernails have become stained or discoloured, they should be soaked in a bowl containing 600 ml (1 pint) of warm water to which a tablespoon of lemon juice has been added. This should restore the nails to their original condition.

Lemon and lime mask: To make a mask for oily skins, take two teaspoons lemon juice, one teaspoon of lime juice, one teaspoon of orange juice and mix in a bowl with half a standard carton of plain unsweetened yogurt. Spread gently over the skin and leave for ten minutes. Rinse off with warm water.

Softening elbow skin: Dry skin on elbows, which is common in wintertime when arms are covered by thick sleeves, can be softened and cleaned with a fruit cup! Next time you are squeezing lemons for a cookery session, don't throw away the squeezed out halves of the fruit. Instead, sit at the kitchen table with your elbows actually resting inside the empty lemon cups. Just sit there for five or ten minutes then remove lemon halves, rinse your elbows with warm water and dry. You can massage a little oil on the point of your elbows, wiping off any excess with a tissue.

Lemon bath: Not only does lemon have a lovely fresh smell but its juice has a toning and whitening effect on skin. So put a few slices of lemon in with your bath water and use any empty lemon halves you may have in the kitchen after squeezing the juice for drinks, to rub lightly over all your body just before you step into your bath. This is really refreshing!

Lots of lovely shine: Lemon makes an excellent tonic for hair and gives extra shine at the same time. Put two teaspoons of fresh lemon juice into a bowl of really cold water (best to try in the summertime only!) and use this to give your hair a final rinse after your normal shampoo and rinsing with warm water treatment. The reason for the shine is that lemon causes the surface of the hair to lie in a certain way, so that it will reflect the maximum amount of light.

Get rid of dandruff: Lemon juice, if used regularly as a rinse (see hint above), helps to prevent dandruff.

Raspberry

Raspberry mask: Mash two tablespoons of raspberries in a bowl with a fork and then add two teaspoons of plain unsweetened yogurt and one teaspoon of fine oatmeal. Mix all three ingredients together thoroughly to form a paste. Apply this to your skin, leave for ten minutes before rinsing off with warm water. This is particularly good for dry and normal skin.

Soft fruit

Make your own masks: You can buy many fruit-based masks but it's quite simple, and usually cheaper, to make your own, particularly during the summer months, when soft fruits are plentiful, or perhaps available from your own garden. Different fruits have different properties, so which one you will use depends on what type of skin you have and what effect you want to achieve by using the mix. Raspberry and strawberry, for instance, have an acid effect, and so they should be combined with a cream to offset this to some extent (see below). You can vary the proportions of fruit and cream to vary the degree of acidity in the mask.

DAIRY PRODUCTS

Buttermilk

Facing up to freckles: Although freckles can be extremely attractive, some girls do try to get rid of them! This is not an easy task and proprietary products are not available to help. If freckles are your problem, you can try spraying buttermilk on to your skin regularly, or pat it on to your skin with your fingertips. It won't work miracles but it may help to diminish a freckle problem.

Milk and vegetable fader: Another old-fashioned and natural treatment for freckles is buttermilk mixed with horseradish. This is applied on pads of muslin to those areas of your skin which have freckles. Take two tablespoons of buttermilk and two teaspoons of freshly grated horseradish. Put the grated vegetable in the milk and leave in fridge overnight. Next day, strain off the horseradish, soak some pads of muslin in the liquid and apply these to the freckled areas and leave on for five minutes. Finally, dip your fingers into the liquid and rub in into your freckles. Rinse well with water to remove all traces of the liquid.

Cream

Rich facial: Here's a facial that will really help to nourish and enrich skin which is a little out of condition and rather tired looking – and it feels lovely on the skin, too. Mix two tablespoons of ground almonds (you can buy these loose or in pre-packed quantities in any supermarket) with two tablespoons of double cream. Stir together thoroughly in a bowl until the mixture forms a smooth paste. Don't spread this over your skin as you would a face mask but gently massage it into the skin with your fingertips for a few minutes first. Then leave the paste on for 10 minutes, filling in any areas where the massaging has left the paste a little too thinly spread. After 10 minutes wipe off the paste with cotton wool and lots of warm water.

Milk

Milky mix: An old fashioned skin toner and tightener which contains milk and starch is excellent for oily skins – but should not be used by anyone with a dry skin. Just mix one tablespoon of top of the milk – warmed, if possible – with two tablespoons of plain powdered household starch. Mix until they form a smooth paste and apply to your face. After ten minutes rinse off with warm water.

Puffy eyelids: Eyelids which are puffy respond very well to a simple, low-cost routine. Soak two pieces of cotton wool in some icy cold milk from the fridge. Flatten the cotton wool into pads to fit the shape of your eyes. Place the milk-soaked pads on your closed eyes and lie down for 10 minutes.

Emergency cleanser: If you run out of your regular cleanser, then raid the fridge for a pinta. A piece of cotton wool soaked in milk will remove make-up efficiently.

Yogurt toner: For this you need either a standard carton of plain unsweetened yogurt (bought or home-made) or sour cream (again bought or made by adding lemon juice to cream or top of the milk). Just dip your fingers into the yogurt or sour cream and spread it quite thickly over your face. Relax for at least 15 minutes before removing with plenty of warm water. Be careful to get rid of all the stickiness and finish off by splashing your face and neck with cold water. Dry with a towel or tissues. This is suitable for most skin types as it is not too astringent.

Mask for dry skin: Put one egg yolk into a bowl and add a teaspoonful of honey. Mix together thoroughly to make a thick paste. Spread this paste very thinly over your face with your fingertips and leave for 15 minutes. To remove the mask, take a pad of cotton wool and lots of warm water and rinse off, carefully removing all traces of stickiness. Pat your skin dry with a towel or tissues. This is excellent for improving the skin texture.

Egg mask for oily skin: Take one egg white, beat it in a bowl, then add a few drops of freshly-squeezed lemon juice and beat again until the mixture becomes frothy and slightly thick in texture. Apply to your face, but avoid delicate skin around your eyes. Leave on your face for about ten minutes during which time it will tighten and stimulate your skin. Rinse off with lots of warm water, then finish by splashing cold water over your face before patting dry with a towel.

Hair conditioner: One of the simplest but most effective hair conditioners, is a fresh egg yolk. It is excellent for brightening up dull, lank locks. Just separate the yolk from the white of the egg, put it into a bowl and beat thoroughly before applying to your hair after your normal shampoo and rinse session. As this can be a little messy to apply, the most efficient way is to use a tiny sponge (the kind you use for applying home perm lotion), then comb the yolk mixture through your hair, making sure that every section of it gets its share of the egg yolk. Leave the egg on your hair for 20 minutes before rinsing off with warm water. Rinsing must be done thoroughly because egg can stick stubbornly to hair and you must get rid of every particle of the yolk. Use fairly hot water for rinsing.

Egg wrinkle treatment: There is no way of avoiding wrinkles altogether but a little regular care can delay them. Take the yolk of one egg, put it into a bowl and beat lightly. Add sufficient bran (the natural bran from health food shops, not the sort which comes already made up into a breakfast cereal) to make a smooth paste. Apply the paste to the areas of skin well to the side of the eyes and to nose to mouth lines, which are most prone to wrinkling (do not apply immediately around the eyes). Apply it before taking a bath, then remove it afterwards extremely carefully, so as not to pull or drag the delicate skin. If you wear pads over your eyes at bedtime you can leave the paste on overnight.

Egg and gel conditioner: Egg is good for your hair. Add a few other items to it and you can make it into a conditioner, which is full of protein and will give fine hair extra body and bounce. Take one egg, one tablespoon powdered gelatine and two tablespoons of any shampoo you normally use. Mix these together and rub well into your hair after you have shampooed it and rinsed it. Leave on for a few minutes, then rinse off with warm water as for any conditioning treatment.

Incidentally, gelatine on its own – a tablespoon of the powder dissolved in a cup of boiling water, then allowed to cool just a little – can be poured into your rinsing water. This will help to give you a good set.

Skin mix: An enriching mix for your skin can be made with one egg yolk put into a container and beaten thoroughly, then mixed with enough 100% wheatgerm to make a fairly thick but smooth paste. With your fingertips, massage the paste all over your face. After massaging put a thin layer of the mix on your skin, leave for just a few minutes, then rinse off with warm water and pat dry with a tissue.

VEGETABLES

Carrot

Stop that spot: A carrot facial is good if your skin gets the occasional outbreak of spots. It is not very drying and is simple to mix. Take two new carrots and a little rosewater. Grate the carrots, using the finest section of your grater, into a bowl, add a few drops of rosewater to bind together and then apply the mixture to your skin. Leave on for 15 minutes before rinsing off with warm water. If your skin happens to be especially greasy and you really want to tighten up the texture, then mix the grated carrot with a little egg white instead of the rosewater and apply as above.

Cucumber

A slice is nice: If you have a glut of cucumbers in your garden – or just some slices left over from a salad – don't waste any of their goodness. Gently pat the slices of cucumber over your freshly cleaned skin for a few minutes. This is a super and effective skin freshener at little or no cost.

Cucumber face pack one: Take two tablespoons of cucumber, scooped out from the flesh of the vegetable and without any skin and mix this very thoroughly with an egg white. Spread the mixture over your face. Leave on for about 15 minutes before rinsing off with warm water and then patting your skin dry. This, incidentally, is particularly good for improving skin which suffers from small blemishes from time to time.

Cucumber face pack two: This will stimulate and improve the texture of your skin. You need some slices of cucumber crushed into a pulp with the back of a spoon. Add a teaspoonful of double cream and a few drops of rosewater. When mixed together this will produce a fairly soft consistency, which should be applied to your face and left on for 15 minutes before rinsing off.

If you have an oily skin, for extra toning properties you can add a whisked egg white to the basic cucumber mixture. In fact, the quantities of the cream, egg white and cucumber can be changed according to personal experience as to which particular mix gives the desired effect on your skin type. So it's well worth experimenting until you get a recipe which is absolutely correct for you. Do remember to make a note of the proportions used for a future occasion!

Leek

Bruises and swellings: If you don't happen to have medication handy, then try this treatment for bruises and swellings. Rub a cut leek against the spot to reduce the swelling and also the pain.

Olive oil

Luxury hand treatment: Put some olive oil into a bowl (enough just to cover your hands). Gently warm some of the oil (not too hot and **don't** boil it) and rub it into your hands, then dip them into the bowl and keep them there for ten minutes. Wipe off all the excess oil quite thoroughly with a tissue. This softens the skin and improves its condition by adding nourishment.

Insect bites: A simple ointment which will take the sting out of insect bites: mix two tablespoons of olive oil with the white of an egg, put in a bottle and shake well before using. It's an easy-to-make remedy when you are away on holiday and will keep for a couple of weeks in a cool place.

Onion

Itchy feet: Sometimes, if your feet sweat after a long walk you get an itch between your toes. Onion juice rubbed into the skin is a tried and tested old-fashioned remedy for this. The best way to apply it is to cut a slice from an onion and then rub the slice between your toes to let the juice come out on to your skin.

Potato

A pep up: If your eyes are tired and strained, lie down and relax for five minutes but before you do so, cut two slices from a fairly large potato and place them over your closed eyes. Leave on for five minutes and you'll find that your eyes feel refreshed.

Tomato

A tonic: Rub a slice of raw tomato over your arms two or three times a day, then massage the juice well into your skin with the palms of your hands. Let the juice dry on your skin, then wash off with some clear warm water in which a little borax has been dissolved. Follow with an application of glycerine and rosewater mixed together, then blot off any excess with a tissue. This tomato treatment helps to whiten and soften the skin on arms.

Vegetable oil

Oil treatment: For hair that is dull and out of condition, through too much sun or perhaps too much use of heated rollers or hair curlers, there are expensive oil treatments available professionally. However, you can give yourself a similar treatment at home at very little cost. Any vegetable oil is suitable. Just heat the oil until slightly warm. Rub a little into your scalp and then comb it through every part of your hair, massaging as you go to let it penetrate your hair properly. Cover your hair with a plastic shower cap or swimming cap and leave for two hours – or more if you can. Shampoo your hair in the usual way and rinse thoroughly.

Walnut

Natural brown tone: Walnut shells can be used to make a natural brown dye for light brown hair, giving the colour extra depth. Boil the shells in water and leave to simmer for two hours. Strain off the liquid and store in an airtight container. After you've washed your hair, apply the liquid thoroughly with a pad of cotton wool. Leave for two minutes, then rinse off with clear water.

PLANTS AND HERBS

Angelica

Ban spots: You are no doubt familiar with angelica as a green cake decoration. This is the fruit of a plant, which can be grown in the garden. An infusion of the leaves will produce a liquid, which has slightly antiseptic properties. Put a handful of angelica leaves in a pan, bring to the boil, then simmer for half an hour and strain off the liquid. Use to dab on any spots on your face before applying your make-up in the usual way. If you have a slight puffiness under your eyes, the application of angelica liquid will help to reduce it.

Basil

Where the bee lurks: Ease the pain of a bee sting by rubbing the spot with basil or savory leaves. If, however, you are allergic to stings, or the sting remains painful, see a doctor.

Henna

Henna hints: Although henna is a natural dye and is guaranteed not to cause any skin or scalp problems, there are one or two points to bear in mind when using it.

1. Don't use it if your hair has already been coloured, tinted or dyed with a chemical substance of any kind (and that means the proprietary colourants you buy in the shops as well as the tints you'll get in a hairdressing salon). This is because there is no way you can gauge the kind of colour you'll end up with.

2. Henna will produce a different effect on various shades of hair, so it's always best to test a small strand first. Be sure to keep a note of the exact time you left the dye on, so that when you do your whole head, you will get the right colour. It is possible to use henna on grey hair but only if the percentage of grey is very small (something less than five percent). Even then it can sometimes produce an unpleasant orange effect, depending on which country the plant was grown in. So, again, test a small strand of grey hair before venturing on to the whole head.

3. Remember that the quality and the property of henna varies according to the source of the raw material (the white flowered oriental shrub) so once you find a shade that suits you, it's a good idea to try to stick to the same brand.

4. Henna can be used just as a rinse to give extra shine to hair because it is rich in conditioner.

Bright for hair: If you want to brighten or colour your hair without running the risk of any allergic reaction to the chemicals which are often used in over-the-counter products, then henna provides an excellent alternative. Although better known as a dye to achieve a red effect, you can buy henna products which will add lustre and colour to all shades of hair. Available from chemists and health food shops.

Coffee bean colour: If you have dark hair and want to achieve an extra rich colour, instead of using plain water to make up the henna paste, use a strong brew of coffee from freshly ground beans.

Lavender and other herbs

Herbal toner: An infusion of herbs can make a good toner for the skin – it costs little and can be kept in the fridge for up to five days in an airtight container. Boil half a cupful of herbs in 600 ml (1 pint) water, then leave the liquid to stand overnight. Strain off the liquid and put into a screw-top container. Use whichever herbs you happen to have in your garden, or what is available in your local store, but bear in mind that different herbs do have different properties.

For dry skin – parsley and fennel. For oily skin – lavender, sage, thyme or peppermint. For a normal skin – balm and spearmint.

Lavender and peppermint oil: You can make your own fragrant oil from natural ingredients. It can be used to pat on to your face before going to bed or indeed at any time you think your skin needs a little soothing. To make up the oil, use fresh herbs rather than dried ones. Many of us have lavender in our garden and that would do very well, with perhaps some thyme, sage and mint. Crush up the leaves slightly to help release the oils and then put them into a jar with four teaspoons of cider vinegar and leave for five minutes. Top up with avocado oil, give the jar a good shake and leave for 24 hours before straining off the oil. Use as and when required.

Bath bouquet garni: Just as you can make up a bouquet garni of herbs to add flavour to your cookery, you can do much the same to give soothing and skin-softening properties to your bath. Use dried herbs and put a selection of them into a little muslin bag, then drape it around the water tap, so that the water runs over the bag and through its contents as it fills the bath. You can vary the contents of the muslin sachet according to what herbs you have available and what perfumes and properties you like. Camomile, lavender, thyme, mint can all be used and to add a real perfume, use a few rose petals or freesia flowers to the mixture. Experiment and you'll be able to produce your own special recipes. Dried lavender flowers, for instance, are an excellent bath basic combined with a few sprigs of rosemary and basil.

Sweet smelling steamer: Give your face a deep clean steam treatment. After cleansing off all your make-up, put a few dried, sweet-smelling herbs into a bowl of newly boiled water and steam your face by making a towel tent over the bowl. Let the steam penetrate your skin and open the pores. Stay under the tent for as long as you can stand the heat. Finish by splashing your skin with really cold water before patting dry.

Foot freshener: An infusion of lavender leaves can freshen up your feet. Make the infusion by putting either fresh or dried lavender leaves in boiling water and leaving them to soak. Allow the water to cool and then soak your feet.

Marigold

Go red with marigold: The marigold flower is a lovely orange/ tawny shade, so it is not surprising that if you infuse the leaves of the plant (which simply means boiling them in a pan of water and then straining off the liquid when cold), you can use this to give reddish tones to light-toned hair. If your hair is bleached and rather harsh in tone this is one way to give it a softer look without using any more chemicals.

Nettle

Nettle lotion: Nettles of any age can be used to make an effective liquid which, if rubbed on your scalp, will help to keep it free from minor disorders. Just boil two cupfuls of nettle leaves in a pan of water, leave to simmer for half an hour, cool, strain, bottle and use to rub into your scalp every time before you wash your hair. The liquid will keep for several weeks.

Oatmeal

Porridge and egg: Two tablespoons of porridge oats mixed with the white of one egg and then applied to the face makes an excellent face pack if you don't have any oatmeal in your kitchen cupboard.

Refining face mask: Oatmeal is excellent for oily and normal skins, but should not be used for dry skins. It both cleanses and improves the texture of the skin and is very cheap. For most beauty purposes a fine oatmeal is best. Coarse oatmeal can be ground until it is fine in your coffee grinder. Mix half a cupful of oatmeal to a fine paste with water, or lemon juice if you prefer the mask to have a more astringent effect. Apply it to all areas of your face except round your eyes, and leave for 10 minutes. This particular mask requires extra care in removal because oatmeal tends to cling to the skin, so rinse thoroughly with lots of warm water.

Oatmeal in the bath: Mix your oatmeal breakfast cereal with herbs to create an excellent skin refiner for bathtime. Get a pair of old tights, cut off the foot of one to form a bag. Into this bag, put a selection of herbs (whatever you have available but rosemary, lavender and thyme are particularly good since they are so fragrant). To the herbs add two tablespoons of medium ground porridge oatmeal. Tie the bag at the top with a long piece of cord and then hang it round the tap in the bath letting it just dip in the water. The oatmeal will produce a slightly milky liquid which is extra fragrant and soothing because of the herbs. This bath bag costs very little to make, is most economical because it can be taken out of the bath and left to dry and then used again. You'll be able to tell when it's time to renew it by the fact that the oatmeal is no longer producing that milky tinge to the bath water.

Oatmeal and hazel: Finely ground oatmeal and witchhazel make the basis of a mask for those with oily skin. Add sufficient fine oatmeal to a beaten egg white to make a paste but instead of applying to your face with your fingertips, moisten a pad of cotton wool with witchhazel and then use this to apply the paste to your face. When the mask dries, rinse it off with warm water and finish off by patting your skin with a little witchhazel.

Cleansing grains: A really good way to cleanse your skin and tone it up at the same time is to take a tablespoon of fine oatmeal and mix it with some warm water into a smooth paste. Massage this paste into your skin with your fingertips and continue to massage for a few minutes. Rinse off with lots of warm water and dry your skin with a tissue. This is good for rough elbows.

Oatmeal and carrot tone up: This is suitable for all skin types and for oily or combination skins, subject to acne, it is particularly effective. Take a tablespoon of fine oatmeal and put it into a bowl. Grate a small carrot finely and make sure you get all the juice off the grater and into the bowl. Add enough water to make the oatmeal and carrot into a fairly smooth paste, then leave in the bowl for ten minutes to allow the ingredients to thoroughly absorb the moisture. Add a little top-of-the-milk and apply the mixture to your face with your fingertips or with a spatula. Leave on for five or ten minutes according to the time you have available. If your skin tends towards dryness, then five minutes is sufficient. Wash off with warm water. Pat a little rosewater into your skin.

Oatmeal and orange cocktail: An alternative type of pack using oatmeal as a basis is to substitute orange juice for the more commonly used astringent egg white or witchhazel. Put two tablespoons of oatmeal into a bowl, add some warmed pure orange juice, mix up into a paste and spread on to your face. Leave to set for five minutes then rinse off with warm water.

Orange flower

Natural cleanser: An orange flower is excellent for removing make-up and lasts well, so is cost-effective. All the ingredients are natural, so it cannot harm even the most delicate and sensitive skin. Into a double boiler or a bowl over a pan of boiling water, place 15 g (½ oz) beeswax, 15 g (½ oz) spermaceti, 100 g (4 oz) petroleum jelly, and heat until melted, then add 90 ml (3½ fl oz) orange flower water, and 25 ml (1 fl oz) witchhazel a little at a time, stirring continually. Remove from the heat and keep stirring until the mixture begins to cool. Pour into a container (such as an empty cosmetic jar with a fairly wide top which has been well washed out first, of course). Use as you would any other cleanser. It has a fairly oily consistency, so apply a little at a time; allow to soak in to your skin and then wipe off with cotton wool or tissues.

Orris

Dry shampoo with the natural touch: Orris, which is another name for a species of iris, is used in the making of perfumes. Its root, which is dried and powdered, can be bought for home use quite cheaply and it makes an excellent dry shampoo. Use it when you either don't have time to wash your hair or, for health reasons, simply don't feel you can summon the energy to do it. All you do is apply the powder to your hair (taking it section by section as you would when doing a home perm or setting your hair). Leave the powder on for a few minutes only, then brush out thoroughly. It's always a good idea to clean the brush after the first brush through and then brush through the hair again to remove as much of the powder as possible.

Peppermint and plant oil

A creamy massage: Peppermint and plant oil combine to make a creamy massage for the face. If you can persuade a friend in to do the facial massage, then so much the better. Combine 4 tablespoons almond oil, 4 tablespoons olive oil and half a teaspoon peppermint extract. Place the bowl containing the ingredients over a pan of hot water and warm gently. Massage the warm oil mixture over your face using smooth flowing finger movements, with a very gentle touch around your eyes. Lightly tap your cheeks with your fingertips and use a circling movement. Don't forget your neck. Massage for five minutes. Don't use water to remove the oil, simply wipe off any excess with a clean tissue.

Pine needles

Forest fresh: Pine is one of the most common fragrances used in proprietary bath beauty products and you can get your own fresh-from-the-forest fragrance at no cost at all if you live near pine trees. All you do is put a handful of pine needles into 1.2 litres (2 pints) boiling water and leave them to soak in a basin overnight. The next day put water and needles into a saucepan, boil, taking care that the water does not boil over or you'll lose the precious fragrant water, then strain the water into a container. You can then use it to add to a bath as and when you like.

Pine fresh salt steamer: Use pine needles to add extra fragrance to a steam clean facial treatment. For the facial, first put one teaspoon of natural sea salt (from most health food stores) into a bowl. If you can't get sea salt, then you can make a substitute by mixing together half a teaspoon of Epsom salts and half a teaspoon of table salt. Mix the salt in the bowl with two tablespoons of thick cream and just a few grains of fine oatmeal. Spread this mixture all over your face with your fingertips and then cover the mixture with a fine piece of gauze, which should be large enough to tie at the back of your head.

Now come the pine needles! Place a very large bowl on a solid surface about table height – a large baking bowl would do or a small washing up bowl. Fill the bowl with boiling water and add a cupful of fresh pine needles to the water. Then with the gauze secured behind your head, so that the salt mixture stays securely on your face, bend over the bowl of water. Cover your head and face with a large tea towel spreading this over the sides of the bowl as well. The steam should not escape: it is required to make the pores open and the salt mixture do its work. You'll probably only be able to stand the heat for about five minutes, so after that time remove the towel, then the gauze and rinse off the salt mixture. Be very careful indeed to get all the salt off your face or it will have a drying effect on your skin.

Pine and marigold: The pine water as described in the hint above, can be mixed with marigold for an even more cleansing bath. Make marigold liquid by boiling some marigold flowers and leaves in a pan. Allow to cool, then strain off the water and put it in a bottle.

Rose

Rose petal mask: This hint makes use of newly-fallen petals from your rose bushes. Gather fragrant rose petals from your garden and turn them into a face mask. Take a handful of petals and put them into a container. If you have lavender in the garden, then add some leaves from this too and about half a teaspoon of comfrey powder. Crush the petals with the back of a spoon to form a 'mush' and add enough hot water to make into a paste, then apply for your face. Leave for ten minutes, then rinse off.

Rosemary

Discourage dandruff: Dried rosemary, which is widely available, can be used to fight dandruff. Brew up a liquid by taking two tablespoons of dried rosemary and put it into two cupfuls of boiling water. Allow this to stand and when it is cool, strain the water off the herbs, put into a bottle, then use as a rinse, when you are next washing your hair.

Herbal hair brighteners: Two herbs from the kitchen garden, which make a splendid addition to a shampoo to add colour and lustre to your hair, are dried camomile and rosemary. For fair and blonde hair, bring 1 tablespoon dried camomile in 600 ml (1 pint) water to the boil, then simmer for five minutes, cool and strain before adding to the rinsing water. For dark hair use rosemary in the same way. These herb colour changes are effective if used on a regular basis and if you make a fairly strong brew. Camomile can lighten naturally fair hair by quite a few degrees and will add real brightness as well.

Rosewater

Safe skin softener: Rosewater is distilled from the leaves of roses and it has a mild toning effect. Use it to make your own inexpensive skin softening lotion which will be free of irritants. Mix rosewater with glycerine until you get the kind of consistency you like. This mixture can then be bottled and used on your face, neck or hands as you like.

Effective astringent: A very old recipe for an astringent to improve the texture of your skin and tighten greasy skin is made by mixing together two plant derivatives – rosewater and witchhazel. Take 175 ml (6 fl oz) rosewater and four tablespoons witchhazel. Mix them together thoroughly and store in a bottle or jar with a secure top. If you have very greasy skin, then you can change the quantities given to make a stronger astringent (use equal quantities of rosewater and witchhazel – 120 ml (4 fl oz) of each).

Rosewater for oily skins: Fragrant and mild rosewater can be combined with boracic acid to make an excellent lotion for treating greasy skin. Take a level teaspoon of boracic acid and add 175 ml

(6 fl oz) rosewater to it, mixing the two together. Put into a bottle or container and use it on your skin before applying your usual make-up and apply a little before going to bed at night. It is very mild and will not harm your skin.

Sensitive skin: All skins need toning, even sensitive ones, but it can be difficult to find a pack which doesn't irritate. Try this one. Mix one part calamine and one part magnesium together with rosewater to make a smooth paste. Spread over your face, leave for five minutes, then remove in the normal way with warm water.

Rose or orange tonic: Rosewater and orange flower water make good masks for dry skin. One part kaolin and one part magnesium should be mixed into a thin paste with either rosewater or orange flower water, then applied to your face and left on for about 15 minutes. Wash off with lots of warm water.

Rosewater tonic: Rosewater on its own can be used as a general purpose skin toner.

Saffron

For sunny highlights: You are probably more familiar with saffron in its powdered form but the plant can also be used to produce a natural hair colouring. For this you need the whole root of the plant (obtainable from herbalist shops) – don't try to use saffron powder. Bring it to the boil in a pan with some water, then simmer gently for one hour. Strain off the liquid into a bottle and apply it to your hair, as you would any other dye, using a small pad of cotton wool and leave it on for 10 to 15 minutes before rinsing off. The first time you use saffron you may not notice much difference but regular use should result in bright highlights. This is for fair-haired girls only, it is ineffective on brunettes.

Sage

Soften grey hair: A non-chemical treatment for grey hair can be made by boiling some sage leaves, straining off the liquid, then adding to it 600 ml (1 pint) strong tea. Apply to your hair and leave on for 10 minutes. If used regularly in this way, it will give a much browner appearance to your hair.

Soapwort

Herb shampoo: To make a herb shampoo, take 25 g (1 oz) of dried soapwort and boil it with 1 litre (1¾ pints) of water, allow to simmer for half an hour, then strain off the liquid through a piece of gauze and store in a bottle. Use as you would any other shampoo.

Sugar

All clean: Granulated sugar is a very good cleanser for hands if you've been doing some really dirty job and some of the dirt sticks stubbornly to your skin. Take a teaspoonful of sugar and put it into the palm of one hand, mix it with a few drops of oil (whatever you have in the house, even baby oil will do) and massage your fingers with the sugary mixture. You'll find them clean again in a jiffy.

Sunflower

A nourishing facial: Brewer's yeast and egg yolks make a nourishing facial, which can be used on all skin types. It freshens and stimulates the skin while lubricating it at the same time. Mix three teaspoons sunflower oil, two teaspoons of brewer's yeast (from shops stocking wine-making kits or from health food shops) and one egg yolk. Place in a bowl and mix into a smooth paste. Apply to your face and leave on for 20 minutes. Rinse off with warm water.

Tea

Teabags for tired eyes: Tea is well known for its reviving qualities. Cold used teabags (with the excess drips removed) make excellent pads for weary eyes. Just place one teabag on each closed eye, leave them there for ten or fifteen minutes.

Cold tea cure: If eyes are tired, any cold leftover tea can be used to soothe them. Pour the tea into a bowl and, with a piece of damp cotton wool, use the tea to bathe the eyes for several minutes. Finish off with a good splash of cold water, then pat dry.

Treat with tea: If you stay out too long in the summer sun and end up with burnt skin, which causes you discomfort, then a cup of cold tea will soothe it. Gently bathe the affected parts with the cold tea (use a piece of cotton wool dipped in it). For an even longer lasting effect, use the tea to make a cold compress and leave that on your skin until it begins to feel a little better.

Tonic for dark hair: An infusion of tea and herbs can be a tonic for dark hair. Take one teaspoon of tea and one teaspoon of dried sage. Put them into a 1 kilo (2 lb) jam jar and cover with boiling water. (To ensure that the jar does not crack when you pour in the boiling water, first warm the jar by putting it in the oven for a few minutes and stand a metal spoon in the jar, while you are pouring in the boiling water.) When the liquid is cold, strain it off into another container. To darken your hair you will have to rub this liquid into your hair and scalp at least twice a week. If you want the liquid to keep for more than a week or ten days add a tablespoon of vodka to the basic solution and put it into a bottle or jar which has a tightly fitting lid.

Wheatgerm

Nourishing special: Wheatgerm is good for any type of skin because it tones and nourishes. Take three tablespoons wheatgerm and one tablespoon peppermint extract, thoroughly mixed. It is a good idea to add extra moisture with two teaspoons of warm water (you can add a little more water if you feel the mix is just a little dry). This should give you a nice smooth paste, which can be spread over your face and left for 20 minutes before rinsing off with warm water.

Witchhazel

Freshen up: Witchhazel, distilled from tree bark, has astringent qualities which makes it useful for face packs and the same qualities can be used to good advantage on the hair for a quick shampoo. Put some witchhazel on a pad of cotton wool and rub over your hair. The witchhazel will absorb any excess greasiness and leave the hair fresh and ready to set or curl.

Grease remedy: If only part of your hair is rather greasy – say a fringe, and you don't want to shampoo your whole head of hair, then take a small pad of cotton wool, moisten it with witchhazel and rub it gently over the fringe. This will lift off the grease.

Witchhazel pack: Witchhazel can be combined with some other ingredients to make an excellent face pack for the normal skin type. Mix one part kaolin with one part Fuller's earth and sufficient witchhazel to combine them into a smooth paste. Apply to your face with your fingertips and leave on for 10 minutes before removing with lots of warm water.

Puffy eyes tonic: Witchhazel, first cooled (pop it into the freezer for a few minutes or plunge the bottle into a bowl of ice cold water with ice cubes floating in it) can be a wonderful tonic for puffy eyes. Just use the cooled liquid to saturate a couple of eye pads. Apply them and leave them on for 10 minutes or so while you relax.

Witchhazel pep up: Apply witchhazel before your moisturizer and foundation (not if you have a dry skin). This is excellent for oily or combination skins and good for drying up acne.

For tired eyes: If you are treating yourself to a face pack, then give your eyes a boost at the same time, soak two pads of cotton wool or gauze in witchhazel, place them over your closed eyes and sit back and relax.

Ylang Ylang oil

Voluptuous scent: Ylang Ylang oil is a lovely one hundred per cent natural oil, which is distilled from the flowers of a tree found in the Philippines. You don't have to go that far to get it though, it's generally available in the UK from most specialist health and beauty shops. It has a lovely voluptuous fragrance as well as very soothing properties for the skin. Put a little in your bath and it will soothe your senses and help beautify your skin.

HONEY

Smooth as honey mix: Take one tablespoon of honey and mix it with one tablespoon of top-of-the-milk, then apply it to your face. This is one pack which is purely for nourishing purposes and can be left on for as long as you like. Try to put it on just before having your bath, so that the steam can open your pores and let the honey soak in. Rinse off with warm water to get rid of all traces of stickiness. Pat dry with tissues.

Honey and fruit: A mixture that is especially good for mature skins and will put some softness into younger skins which have been overdried by wind or sun, can be made with a tablespoon of honey and a few drops of orange juice. Mix the two together well. Spread the mixture over your face (with this rich mask you can even cover the delicate skin areas around your eyes and lips). Leave it on for 20 minutes if possible, then remove with lots of warm water and a pad of cotton wool. Dry your skin thoroughly. If used regularly this treatment can stave off those nasty little lines which appear as we get older.

Honeyed egg compôte: A tablespoon of honey mixed with an egg white until frothy can be ideal for an oily or combination skin – you get the nourishing effect of the one ingredient plus the drying effect of the other. Apply to the face with your fingertips, leave for five minutes, then rinse off with warm water.

Honey and yogurt: If your skin is either dry or normal, then you want a mask which will give your skin a glow but not leave it feeling tight and stretched. This recipe is just right! Take half a standard carton of plain unsweetened yogurt and mix two teaspoons of honey into it. Smooth this mixture over your face (preferably after you've had a bath when the pores will be open) and relax for five minutes. Remove the mask mixture with a good dash of cold water. Finish off with a refreshing spray of ice cold mineral water before patting your skin dry with a towel or tissue.

HEALTH ON
THE SPOT

STRESS FACTORS

Stress is both good and bad. Think of it as an energy inside you which motivates you, protects you from danger and is something positive. Stress overload is when you have more than you can cope with, when your reactions to your environment have become frenetic, fraught or frightened. Stress is positive when your body is tense and alert but you know you are in control. You can learn to control stress and tension by becoming aware of your reactions to the pressures of life and the warning signals shown by your body. If you can't read the signals, or pay attention to them, you may find yourself tired, tense and even ill. So learn to make stress work **for** you not **against** you. Begin by recognizing stress-overload symptoms (see below), then teach yourself to relax both by 'letting go' and by suitable exercises.

Dealing with stress

Early warning signals: Your body reflects your emotional reaction to life. If you suffer from several of the following it's time to stop and take note of your lifestyle (see pages 203–5): clenched fists, hunched shoulders, head poked forwards, over-arched back, tongue on the roof of your mouth, constant frowning, nervous twitching, hair twiddling, shrill tone to your voice, foot flexed upwards when legs are crossed, foot kicking to and fro when legs are crossed, and nail biting. The sooner you are aware of these tensions in your body and act, the better. They are early warning signals that the amount of stress you are under is beginning to work against you. Each one of us has a different threshold of how much body tension we can cope with but if you have been suffering from these symptoms for more than a few weeks, then take action.

Second phase: The type of person you are – outward or inward going – will greatly influence how you react in the second phase of 'stress overload'. The key is to know yourself and if any of the symptoms below are severely exaggerated or out of character, then it is time to assess your life and find out what's going wrong. Symptoms: insomnia, irritability, loss of energy and stamina, lack of concentration, forgetfulness, inability to listen, drop in physical and mental performance, inability to cope with work leading to fatigue and exhaustion or hyper-aroused, over-excited, workaholic, unable to enjoy relaxation time through feelings of guilt.

A troubled shared is a trouble halved: No matter what your problem is, you can lighten the load by telling a friend or partner about your trouble. In this way you dispel any feelings you might have of isolation and it greatly helps to discuss which is the right course of action with someone else.

A chat with the doctor: Some illnesses are caused by stress, so it's sensible to cure the cause rather than the effect. Seek your doctor's advice if you have sustained evidence of the following: continual headaches, migraine, continual upset stomach, constipation or diarrhoea, light headedness, loss of appetite, over-eating, eczema.

Not to be ignored: It is easy to slip gradually into poor health. If you have any of the above symptoms try out the Positive Pointers below.

Positive pointers

Getting rid of the strain: Try to be conscious of how you feel mentally. Take immediate action if you feel uptight and trapped by telling somebody about it. Acknowledgement is sometimes a cure in itself.

Know your own pace: Are you a racehorse or a tortoise? In other words, do you work quickly or slowly? Being pushed to a pace beyond your ability will push you over the limit into the negative side of stress. Make sure you are working at a rate you can handle – at least for most of the time.

The pause that refreshes: Try to find time during each day for some day-dreaming and pleasant thoughts. There are so many good things in life worth thinking about.

The noise, the people!: Overcrowded streets, buses, trains, noise, all bombard your mind. If these things worry you, plan at least one quiet break during the day. Instead of going to a crowded coffee bar for lunch, take sandwiches and a vacuum flask and picnic in the park, or even an unoccupied office.

Thinking makes it so: Think on the positive side – what you **can** do as opposed to what you **can't**.

A question of balance: If you have a demanding family life as well as a demanding job, you could find yourself over-stretched. Don't try to be super-human. If it's vital to continue with your job, then you may need to spend money on help in the home; or your family may pitch in if they know you are reaching breaking point. An alternative may be a less demanding job until the children are older and off your hands.

All work and no play . . . : No matter how important your job is, make sure you are not taking your work and yourself too seriously. Make time to play and rest, then you will be more efficient and clear-headed at your work.

Passing it on: Learn to delegate when you are overloaded at work, but make sure the person to whom you are delegating wants the extra responsibility.

Positive outlook: Once you have covered all the possibilities of what could happen if you should fail, it does not mean that life becomes negative in its outlook. First of all, the reality of failing isn't as bad as it seems and secondly, there are always positive points within failure to be learnt, which will help you cope more successfully the second time round.

Turn off the T.V.: Sitting blankly in front of television night after night does not improve communications in a family, nor does it help someone suffering from stress. Problems should be discussed not pushed to one side in the hope they will go away.

One thing at a time: In order to stop your mind jumping from one thing to another, and throwing up different thoughts and worries, do one job at a time in order of priority, and make yourself do that job thoroughly.

What do you want?: Make sure the goal you are striving for is really your own and not imposed on you by friends or family.

Getting it off your chest: Bearing a grudge is a waste of your emotional energy. Better to have it out with the person concerned.

Dealing with the critics: Accept criticism if it's valid, forget it if it's not. Ultimately you only have to prove truths to yourself.

Dealing with self-criticism: Self-criticism can be very self-destructive. Without lowering your standards in life, try to be generous about human weaknesses. Learn to like yourself with your faults the same way you like a close friend with all his or hers.

Frustration and temper: Try pausing and breathing before you explode. This often has the effect of dispelling anger and will enable you to think logically as opposed to emotionally.

Financial pressure: If your financial commitments are too great and you are working purely for that end, seek help. Examine the ways you can cut down financially to relieve pressure. Talk to your bank manager – you'll find that he will be more than willing to give you expert advice.

Wasted energy: Do you rush around doing any job rather than the one that matters? Be conscious that this is a 'displacement activity', that what you are trying to do is avoid work, which is probably too much for you. Ask someone to help you so that you can clear the backlog and start afresh.

Housebound: Under-stress can be as debilitating as over-stress. If you are unable to get out of the house, explain to your partner that you need the odd evening free to go off and do the things that interest you. He or she will appreciate that you will feel much brighter during the week, if you can develop your own interests outside your family.

Self-massage

If you can't get to, or find, a masseuse try self-massage. One advantage of this method is that you can apply exactly the amount of pressure you want and, with practice, your fingers can learn to find the sensitive spots around your body. The disadvantage is that some of the areas are difficult to get to, such as shoulder blades. This can be overcome by using various aids such as towels, squash balls, tennis balls and loofahs (see below).

The tight head: Imagine that you are washing your hair and, using your fingertips make small friction movements all over your scalp. This is very effective first thing in the morning to get you going. Massage along the hair line all the way round the scalp to ease the tension over the scalp and forehead. Run your hands through your hair and then pull the hair away from the scalp tugging gently at the roots.

The taut neck and tense head: With your middle three fingers press behind the ears below the occiput bones (the two round knobs which stick out), then stroke down the neck.

Headaches: Remove any form of headache by massaging the sides of the forehead outwards and downwards taking the pressure away from the head.

Sides of the neck: The sides of the neck collect a lot of tension through lack of movement. Using your middle three fingers like pads, massage from just behind the ears down towards the shoulders. Make circular movements downwards too. Before massaging a really tight neck, have a warm shower and let the hot water run on the back of your neck.

Back of the neck: Place your right hand thumb and three fingers at the base of the skull. Now pinch the neck and slowly move down making slow pinching movements.

The face: Furrowed brows equal an anxious mind. Imagine someone is soothing your brow and gently stroke away the frown lines. Small circular movements with the pads of the fingers around the temples are very effective.

The eyes: Place the heels of your hands over your eyes. Press gently and pull away from the centre of your face. (Remember to remove contact lenses before doing this.) Using your three fingers as pads, make small circular movements following the bones around the eyes.

The nose: Massage up either side of the nose and across the cheek bones towards the ears to clear sinuses and assist breathing.

The jaw: Clenched teeth and anger can cause a lot of tension in your jaw. Release this by massaging at the articulation of your jaw. Press in with small circular movements. Also open your mouth wide, dropping your lower jaw right down and dropping your tongue to the bottom of your mouth.

The ears: A good relaxing movement for your ears, is to place your little finger into your ear, making sure your nail is short, and wiggle your finger about.

Shoulders and back: Place a tennis ball, or squash ball, between your back and a wall. Press yourself back against the ball and move around until the ball finds a tense spot on your back. Move the ball up around your shoulders too and down to your lower back. Move up and down over the spot you have identified by bending your knees.

Shoulders and neck: Turn your head to the left and right checking your range of movement. Place your right hand on your left shoulder and pick up the muscle rather like a cat picks up a kitten. Now rotate your shoulder back pressing in with your fingers quite firmly. Repeat on the other side. Turn your head from side to side again to register how much looser your neck now feels.

Feet: Massage the whole of your foot, kneading the soles, rubbing the ankles to improve circulation and stroking the foot for relaxation.

Beating the chill: During the cold weather circulation in hands and feet can be extremely poor, so massage your wrists and ankles to relieve this.

Bath time: When you have had a good soak for about 10 minutes, stand up in the bath and vigorously rub a loofah over your thighs, buttocks and backs of your legs. Sit down and then bend your right leg up, so that your foot is flat on the base of the bath. With your thumbs on the back of the calf and your fingers on the front of your leg massage the back of your leg, working up and down the calf. Repeat with left leg. This is very good for tired legs.

Help those thighs: The outsides of your thighs can become cold, so massage them with small pinching movements. Work down from the tops of your thighs and then up again. This helps to break up fat too. Another good form of thigh massage is to slap them vigorously all over, or use a hacking movement to work up and down your thighs.

Soothing moisturizer: After your bath, work in a thick moisturizing cream all over your body. Use gentle circular movements. This is very soothing before bedtime.

Away with hips: Take the rolling pin from the kitchen into the bathroom with you and roll it over your hips. Roll it up and down the sides and front of the thighs, just as you would roll out pastry. Do this for three minutes on each thigh.

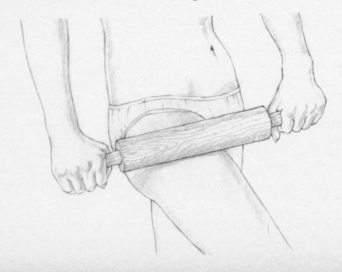

NO SMOKING

No smoking: If you smoke and have trouble breathing through bronchitis, coughs, colds, you know what to do, don't you! Giving up smoking is the same as putting yourself on a diet, you really have to want to give up for it to work. Discipline and willpower are needed. It is best to give up completely for this reason, as cutting down tests your discipline even more. Use every aid you can. Set yourself a goal or reward. Put the money you normally spend on cigarettes aside and at the end of the month treat yourself. Make sure you have support from your family and friends to help you when willpower is failing.

Smoking and pregnancy: If you are pregnant, you have the best incentive to give up smoking. Not only is your own body being damaged but your unborn child's lungs may suffer. It also reduces the amount of blood supply to the placenta, which in turn limits oxygen available which can lead to brain damage and growth retardation in the womb. Smoking also increases the risk of miscarriage. Plan to give up well in advance of conceiving, i.e. six months ahead, so your weight, too, can stabilize before you get pregnant.

A bad influence: Smoking is known to contribute to the main killers of western society: heart disease and cancer. It also contributes to chronic bronchitis and, through causing the coronary arteries to narrow, also influences blood pressure.

It's never too late: Here are a few hints to make the going easier.

- Possibly the best thing to remember is that your lungs are capable of quite a dramatic recovery and it is never too late to give up smoking.

- Initially cut down to 5 cigarettes a day, as the stage before giving up completely. Always leave long stubs. Buy mild brands and try not to inhale. Try nicotine gum.

- Sit in smokeless compartments in trains, planes, buses, cinemas, etc.

To help someone give up: There are various little things you can do to help someone else overcome the smoking habit:

- If you smoke, don't offer cigarettes to people giving up!

- Don't smoke in front of him/her.

- Give plenty of encouragement. Nicotine is a drug and there can be uncomfortable withdrawal symptoms, such as irritability, depression, weight gain, colds and sore throats. Try to be supportive.

SLEEP AND RELAXATION

Sound sleep helps you cope and live your life fully but there are sufficient myths around about how much sleep you do or don't need to make you into an insomniac just worrying about them! Recent research suggests that your brain needs sleep rather than your body and, provided you are in good health, your whole day will not be ruined if you don't get your standard eight hours or whatever.

If you have difficulty sleeping...

Are you an owl or a lark?: Try to establish whether you are an owl, that is you like staying up late at night and find yourself more lively in the evening, or a lark, in which case you love getting up early and find that you are at your most efficient during the early part of the day. If possible try to adjust your life to this routine. It is a myth that the hours before midnight provide more beneficial sleep than those after midnight.

Stop worrying: If you are in good health, do not worry if your sleep pattern changes for one or two nights. If it persists and may be caused by stress then try the relaxation tips given on page 214. Should your difficulty in sleeping continue, then see your doctor.

The bed: Do you have a bed that really suits you? It is quite surprising how little thought is given to this fundamental requirement for a good night's sleep. If you can afford it, invest in a really good quality bed which will provide the correct support. If your partner prefers a softer or firmer bed than you, different dual section beds are available. If your present bed is too soft (which may mean that it is the bed relaxing and not you) and your partner likes it that way, you can put a board under your half of the bed.

Movement in bed: Room to move in the bed is essential as none of us lies still all night. It is healthy and normal to constantly change position – maybe as many as 40 times a night – so you could easily be waking yourself up by moving against your partner. Either buy a larger bed or try twin beds which can be placed next to each other.

Change: Sleep needs may change with age. As you become older you may find that you need less. If you are in sound health there is no need to worry.

Wait until you are tired: Don't go to bed until you are tired. If you still can't sleep, then get up and read a book, not a thriller, or pursue a hobby. Only go back to bed when you begin to feel tired. If you still can't sleep just rest quietly. If you feel tired during the day, resist taking a cat nap. In this way you have more chance of resetting your body clock.

Unwinders: A warm bath or a soothing milk drink can help to induce sleep. Milk contains amino acids which are meant to assist with sleep. There are also plenty of herbal remedies, such as camomile tea, which are soothing.

Is it a crutch or a habit?: Ask yourself if you are using your insomnia to get attention. It is quite a hard question to reply to honestly. Try to think back when your sleeplessness started and make sure that it has not just become a habit. For example, you may have been ill and had to wake up to take medicine at night. Although you now no longer need it, you still wake up at the same time.

Coffee/tea/alcohol: The effects of caffeine can last up to 7 hours, so if you suffer from insomnia at the beginning of the night, it is inadvisable to drink coffee or tea after about 6 p.m. Alcohol, although it tends to make you feel relaxed to begin with, will often cause sleeplessness as it tends to excite the body later on.

Winding down: Winding down towards the end of the day is essential for sound sleep. This applies to all the family; children allowed to watch stimulating television programmes too late in the evening, can become over excited. The same can apply to adults who watch late night thrillers which make the mind work for hours afterwards. Soothing music is a much better idea.

No more work: Try not to take your work to bed with you. Read a good book instead.

Leave troubles behind: Try not to take troubles to bed with you. This can be difficult, but try to talk over a serious worry with your family or a good friend during the day (see page 203).

A secure feeling: Drowsiness comes with warmth and a sense of security. Make sure that you feel safe in your home, especially if you live alone. The telephone numbers of neighbours and people living in the same block of flats written on an easy-to-find pad can help. Obviously good locks on doors and windows are essential.

What to wear: Any clothing worn in bed should be loose and comfortable: no tight necks around night dresses for instance.

Make sure that your bed is warm and the coverings are lightweight. Electric blankets and duvets have revolutionized bed comfort. If you suffer from cold feet, use bedsocks.

Temperature: Make sure the temperature of your bedroom suits you. Too hot a room can be more uncomfortable than one that is too cold. Keep blankets handy or an extra cover in case you wake in the night and feel cold.

Say stop: If you are lying in bed and your mind is alert, jumping from one thing to another, say stop and either think of your breathing or concentrate on a prayer, poem or pleasant thought.

It's a yawn: Try inducing a yawn. Strangely enough, yawning can make you tired.

How do you sleep?: Observe yourself in bed. If you are tense with your teeth clenched and your fingers fisted, try pulling your shoulders down. Then go through the whole of your body, giving each part your attention and telling it to let go and relax.

On waking: When you wake up, try to recall how you are lying. If you are hunched up with your shoulders to your ears you are obviously tense. Stretch your body, telling each part to relax.

Bend and stretch: Stretching is a great form of relaxation; a few gentle stretching exercises done slowly and languidly before you go to sleep may help get rid of body-tension from the day.

Stop puffing: If you are a heavy smoker, it may be one of the reasons why you are not getting off to sleep. There is only one remedy – give it up.

Relaxation

Relaxation is not a state of collapse. It is not flopping in front of the television which, if done constantly, will strain your back, neck and shoulders and hinder your breathing. It is the ability to trust your body, to let go, to switch off – very difficult in our competitive society – and is a technique which, once learned, will greatly improve your health and the quality of your life.

Eyes: Sit back in your chair and close your eyes and imagine you are looking down either side of your nose. Now imagine you can no longer see out of the front of your eyes and only feel black velvet covering them. This greatly helps tired eyes and prevents headaches caused by eyestrain.

Rest your eyes: When you have a lot of desk work to do, give your eyes a rest by focusing on an object in the distance occasionally and then bring your attention back to the paper work.

Jaws: Grinding teeth and clenched jaws are a sure sign of tension. To understand how this affects your head, place your hands on your temples and then clench your jaws. You will feel your temples contract. To release this tension, drop your jaws relaxing the lower half of your face. Yawning or increasing the stretch by sticking out your tongue is also very beneficial.

Tongue and throat: Place your tongue behind your front teeth to relax it. Swallowing helps release tension in your throat.

The brow: Raise your eyebrows up as far as possible and then let them fall. This helps to relax your forehead.

The cheeks: Imagine you are shaving and pull your lips across your face to flatten the cheeks. This will improve the muscle tone of your face.

The head: To prevent tightness in the muscles of your head, which can sometimes be the cause of tension headaches, use the muscles of your head to try to pull your ears back and lift your eyebrows as well.

The neck: To help rid yourself of tension in your neck and upper back, tuck your chin in and take a good deep breath, then slowly lower your head drawing your chin in towards your chest. Hold the position for a short while, breathing well (see also self massage page 206).

Neck sides: Don't forget the sides of the neck, which can get very tight through lack of movement. Tuck the chin in and slowly let your left ear drop towards your left shoulder and repeat on the other side. If any of these exercises makes you feel like yawning, yawn away, it's a great way to release tension.

The mouth: For tight lips, purse your lips and then let them go or imagine the very beginnings of a smile.

The whole face: Screw your face up tightly towards the centre and then release it. Then open it right out as though you were screaming (without the noise!).

The hands: Shake your hands loosely from the wrists letting the fingers flap together. Then spread your fingers as far apart as possible, hold in that position and then release.

Shoulders: Circle your shoulders forwards and back imagining that your arms are very heavy at the sides of your body.

Arms: Let your arms hang at the sides of the body and then shake them loosely or lift your arms up to shoulder height and let them fall heavily against your body. Breathe in as you lift, out as you let them fall.

Thighs: Make sure that you don't sit all day with your thighs held tightly together. While you are sitting on a chair or stool you can open and close your thighs from time to time.

Ankles: Sit down and keeping your ankles loose rotate them inwards and outwards.

Feet: Take your shoes off whenever the occasion presents itself, to allow your feet to move. Pull your big toe and little toe away from each other. Shake your feet one at a time. Place a ball under each foot in turn and move it around.

Relaxation techniques and suitable exercises

Before choosing a relaxation technique, find out from your local library or bookshop the type of techniques available, and what each one has to offer. Yoga and Tai Chi, for example, hold a more physical approach whereas Autogenics and Meditation are less active and more mind oriented.

Exercises: Swimming and walking are the most relaxing forms of exercise as long as you go about them in a calm fashion and remember to breathe fully.

Relaxation classes: Relaxation taught by physiotherapists and relaxation teachers normally involves a series of loosening movements and deep relaxation lying on the floor. Enquire at your local library, community centres, health centres and hospitals for lists of courses in your area.

Relaxation and the sauna: The main aim of a sauna is to cleanse the skin deeply but because the warmth given out causes muscles to be released, many people find them extremely relaxing. There are also an equal number of people who find them claustrophobic, suffocating and not in the least relaxing; unfortunately there is no way to find out other than trying them out. Read the instructions carefully, so as to make it a pleasant experience.

When not to have a sauna: If you have heart trouble, chest problems, are in any way ill or off colour, have just had an alcoholic drink, or are already extremely hot after a game of squash, then do not have a sauna.

What to wear: Most people go into a sauna nude and take only a towel with them. If you prefer you can wear a bikini or briefs. It is better to wear nothing, so that the body is able to expel sweat easily. Metal clasps on bikinis or bra straps may also get too hot to be comfortable.

Wash first: The general procedure is to have a good shower before you go into a sauna to remove any superficial dirt. Then shower each time you come out, or, if there is a plunge pool and you like a strong contrast in temperature, jump in – but beware, they really are icy cold!

Oil: Rubbing oil on the body before you go into a sauna will make you sweat more and will also soften the skin.

Becoming accustomed: Get used to the temperature by sitting on the low shelf when you go in. Remember that heat rises and the top shelf may be too hot for you to begin with.

Temperature and time: The heat in the sauna can be pushed well over 93°C (200°F). Start off by just staying in for a few minutes and then increase the length of your stay to a maximum of 10 minutes. The usual is about five minutes. If you ever feel strange or off-colour leave the sauna immediately.

The most relaxing time: The most beneficial and relaxing time for a sauna is the evening when you have nothing else to do and can go home and go to bed.

Sensible slimming

There is one common denominator for all diets and that is discipline. Most diets work though many are not nutritionally sound. Yet they all work for one reason and one reason only – you lose weight by reducing your calorific intake. The reason why some diets seem more successful than others is perhaps because you like the type of food they specify or they suit you and your lifestyle. This way there is less tension imposed on you and you are more likely to succeed.

What diets don't do is consider why you are overweight, what will happen to you once the restriction is removed and how you can achieve a permanent weight loss. The quantity of books and magazines available on slimming is proof enough that the majority of slimmers are unsuccessful; five out of every six people who lose weight will regain it all within two years. However, before you become too disheartened, there are many things you can do both mentally and physically to help you succeed. It is only through getting to know yourself better that you can become the one out of the six to achieve permanent weight loss.

Am I overweight?: One simple way to decide whether or not you are overweight is to do the pinch test, see page 245. A mirror test will tell you whether you're in good shape. Take a look at the backs of your thighs and buttocks and your stomach. Look for lumps and bumps of flesh and any puckering of skin.

Determination is all: Do you really want to lose weight for good? If the answer is truly yes, then you can succeed. If you are half-hearted there is little chance of success. You have to be determined to survive the occasional failure.

Know yourself: Overweight is caused by one thing only – eating more than you need. Ask yourself why you are eating too much. Is it because you are tense, depressed, frustrated or lonely?

Emotions and appetite: Your appetite is emotional and will always reflect how you feel; your hunger is physiological. It is believed that overweight people never experience the hunger. Through habit and wrong training they eat in response to their emotional appetite, i.e. felt bored, ate. Felt angry, calmed down by eating.

You are in control: You must believe that you can succeed. The mere tension of being on a diet can make you crack, the desire to eat fighting your willpower which says you mustn't. Relaxation is an important part of dieting.

Temptation: An easy way to deal with the temptation to eat is to keep busy. When you want a bar of chocolate go for a walk instead. When you have succeeded once, it will be easier the second time temptation comes.

Think thin: We are what we think, by thinking thin you can establish thin habits. Make sure that you do not become obsessed and try to become too thin which is equally unattractive and unhealthy. It is generally true that people of normal weight only think of food when they are hungry; overweight people tend to think of it all the time.

If you fall: Remember that the odd failure will not ruin a month's diet. If you succumbed to the fattening pudding, ate the chocolate cake or finished off your child's tea as well as your own, do not give up completely. If you just resume the diet, in a few days you will continue to lose weight. After one failure you have to be on your guard and not allow yourself to tuck into another two bars of chocolate. Guilt feelings will soon pass if you stop yourself going on a binge.

Avoidance: Are you eating rather than getting down to the work on hand? If you are overloaded with work seek help. If you can't face the work, instead of reaching for the kettle and the biscuit tin, try writing to a friend or even yourself about your weight problems. You can learn a lot about yourself this way.

Delay reaction: If you are eating primarily because of your emotions try to delay your reactions. If your family is being particularly frustrating, go off and do a job in the house for a few minutes until you have calmed down. You are half way there, if you know why you are overeating.

Breaking habits: The week before you go on a diet, write down everything you eat at what time, how you eat, fast or slow, and why. This will help you to see your bad habits and be more prepared for them as they rear their ugly heads during the course of your diet. It will also greatly help you to achieve permanent weight loss.

Body clock: Do you eat because it's a certain time – such as 1 pm – even though you are not in the least bit hungry? Try to delay your meal by an hour, so that you experience true hunger.

Six o'clock blues: When you are tired your resistance is lowered. After work is a great time for giving into temptation and munching a snack. Go and lie down for half an hour, if you can, and wait for your evening meal.

Family and friends: Most of us diet to improve our appearance and not for health reasons. Being loved because we look good – and slender – is sold to us in most magazines. Make sure that you are getting love and support from your family and friends and masses of encouragement too before you embark on a diet. Let them know that you really are serious about losing weight.

Family and social pressure: One of the most common downfalls of dieting is social pressure. When you go out for a meal and fattening food or excess food is offered to you say a firm no, mean it, and stick to it. Be serious about your diet and your family will take you seriously too. Don't let them tell you that dieting makes you grumpy and they prefer you fat and jolly!

Confronting food: Watching someone devouring your favourite type of meal can be too much for even the greatest willpower. Avoid this if possible. Try to eat your meals alone, then join up with your family for after dinner tea or coffee.

Dieting aids: If your family is thin, or none of its members will go on a diet with you, try to team up with a friend or acquaintance who is dieting. Then you can compare progress. Another helpful approach is to join a weight-watchers group.

Slow change: It is far safer to change your eating pattern slowly and permanently than to go on a crash diet. A weight loss of one kilo (2 lb) a week is quite sufficient. During the first week of your diet you may lose much more, but this will be due to loss of water from your body.

Muscle waste: If you go on a crash diet **without** exercise, your muscles will waste and your metabolism will slow down because there is no food coming in for it to burn up. When you eat normally again, weight will return with a rush because there is less muscle available to help you burn up fat. So, no crash dieting and keep up these exercises.

The soundest diet in the world: The soundest diet is to increase your energy output by vigorous exercise and decrease your energy intake by cutting down on your quantity of food, then your body has to call upon its energy stores of fat and so you lose weight.

A true picture: Only weigh yourself **once a week at the same time of day** for a true picture of weight loss. Your weight is bound to fluctuate during the week and if you weigh too often you may become disheartened. The best time to weigh is first thing in the morning after you have been to the lavatory.

Regular routine: By getting into a regular exercise routine you will become more in touch with your body. Body fat is also reduced by consistent regular exercise as your muscles are trained to burn up fat efficiently.

Exercising working for you! Vigorous and moderate exercise makes you feel less hungry, whereas a gentle walk around the block will increase your appetite.

Slackness: Another reason why it is best to keep exercising is that as the pounds fall off, the tone of the body tends to become slack. Exercise improves body tone.

Fast results with aerobics: Jogging, running, ski-ing, dancing, cycling, skipping are all aerobic (that is, they require oxygen) exercises. The exercise period must last for a minimum of 12 minutes and take your heart rate up to 70–80% of its maximum (see page 279). In this way the metabolic rate is pushed up and even when you stop exercising the metabolism will remain at a higher level than normal for a long period afterwards, so helping you burn off more Calories.

When you are strong: Once you are used to dieting and feel confident and in control of your body, that is the time slowly to let yourself face your old habits and see how you handle them. A sign of success is when you can refuse the apple crumble!

Tips for the table

Water: Have a glass of water before your meal to help fill you up, plus at least eight glasses during the day.

Eat slowly: Chew each mouthful of food slowly, savouring its taste. Bolting your food down will make you overeat. Most of us eat too fast to experience any real satisfaction.

Music while you eat: Try to relax as you eat; if you are at home try playing gentle music during meal times.

Beating the sweet tooth: Sugar is not necessary, especially if you are dieting. Try to eliminate it completely. Use sweeteners if you have to, but you will find that after a week or so of denial you will soon cure your sweet tooth.

No snacks: Try not to eat snacks between meals. If you find this impossible, keep plenty of fresh vegetables and fruit ready chopped in plastic bags in the fridge. Carrots and new mushrooms are low on Calories.

Extend the gap: Allow yourself a period of at least four hours between meals. Some people prefer a lot of little meals as opposed to two main ones. It doesn't matter as long as you are watching what you are taking in, and how many Calories it contains. How much you ate at your last meal will affect how much you eat at the next, because you will have psychologically increased your appetite.

No magic: Grapefruit and lemons will not make you lose weight. The reason they are used so much in diets is because they are a low calorie food.

Main meal: Make lunchtime your main meal and eat a light salad at night. Meals eaten late at night overtax your system and make it more difficult for you to lose weight.

Main foods: The bulk of your food on a diet for life should be vegetables, salads, fruits, followed by a slice of bread per day (preferably wholemeal) and moderate amounts of protein, such as meat, fish, eggs. Naturally all this is relative to how much physical activity you do, and what age and sex you are.

Eliminating fats: Cut down on all dairy produce, use skimmed milk instead of ordinary milk. Try using yogurt instead of cream and low-calorie spreads instead of butter.

Bulk is vital: Bulky foods are essential for the health of your digestive system and your bowel. It is also far easier to diet if you feel satisfied and bulky foods will provide a satisfied feeling. They include wholemeal bread, bran, nuts, dried beans, certain fruits and vegetables and dried fruit.

No standing: Never eat standing up. Even if you are eating just a light snack, lay the table, sit down and eat slowly.

The right foods cooked in the wrong way: An easy slip-up is to have the right foods for the diet but to cook them in the wrong way. Pouring oil and butter over vegetables and salads for instance. Steam or boil vegetables, grill or boil meats and use lemon as salad dressing avoiding fats and oil as much as possible.

When eating out: When you are eating out and have no choice over the quantity of food brought to you, always leave something on your plate. The overweight person normally feels obliged, often through upbringing, to eat everything on his or her plate.

Helping yourself

How many units of energy do you need?: As a rough guide the average adult needs between 2,000–3,500 Calories a day. Women need less than men. If you do a lot of physical labour, be it exercise, gardening or cleaning the house, you will need more Calories than someone less active.

100 Calories: You only have to eat 100 Calories a day more than you require to gradually put on anything from 3–6 kg (6–12 lb) in a year. If you carry on eating more than you need without increasing your energy output by taking exercise, you will continue to put on weight. This might stabilize at 6 kg (12 lb) more than you used to be or increase even further. The time to take action is when you see the weight starting to go on, not when you have already put on a stone.

At work: Instead of going to the pub, wine bar or snack bar for lunch, see if there is a gym near your office. Take a packed lunch.

Refreshing break: Take a good walk in the park during your lunch hour – walk briskly, don't just stroll. In this way you increase the work of your heart and lungs, thereby improving your fitness level.

Forming good habits: Learn about nutrition and be aware of laying down good food habits for your children.

Shrinking appetite: After a long period dieting you won't be able to eat as much as you used to because your appetite will have decreased. Once you have reached this stage, take care never to overeat again.

Helpful hints for those on a diet away from home

Eating out: If you are on a Calorie controlled diet and are going out to eat in the evenings, cut down on your breakfast and lunch, so that you have a few Calories to play with by dinner.

Be prepared: Before you go out remind yourself of the foods you can eat. Grapefruit is on most menus; follow it with grilled fish or meat with a salad.

Take your own: If alcohol is taboo on your diet, take your own soft drink or fizzy water with you.

Helping: Helping your hostess serve the food is a good way to make sure that you are given a modest amount.

When out of your control: If you can't control the quantity of food you are given, leave some on your plate and explain that you are full. This works well and doesn't draw attention to the fact you are on a diet.

When all else fails: Place your hand over your plate and keep it there when your hostess refuses to believe that you have finished.

Advance warning: Phone your close friends in advance to let them know that you are on a diet; that you are really serious about it and would they help by giving you tiny amounts. Don't make them feel they should change their menu because of you – most meals contain some safe items. If not, eat like a bird!

Allies: Make your husband or partner your ally. Arrange beforehand that he or she will help you out of a difficulty if necessary. Make sure they back you up when your host tries to tell you that you can 'diet tomorrow'.

With the children at home: School holidays can be difficult for a mum on a diet, especially if your children like a proper afternoon tea with cakes and such. One solution is to introduce less fattening foods. It will do your children good too.

It is thought that . . . : The main reason why five out of six people put on weight after they stop dieting is that each body has a set point – say 66.5 kilos (9st 7lb) – of how much fat it should carry. Latest research suggests that the only effective way to reduce this set point is by exercise routine and your new eating pattern. The latter can be relaxed slightly once you no longer need to **lose** weight.

Nutrition

Balance: The key to a sound healthy diet is balance, variety and the right proportions of proteins, carbohydrates and fats containing their various vitamins and minerals.

Guideline: An easy guideline to follow is to make fruit and vegetables the bulk of your diet. Eat meat, fish and bread in moderation.

Proteins: Meat, fish and dairy produce, such as milk, eggs and cheese, are protein foods. The body needs between 40–80 grams of protein a day – that is 8–10% of your total intake of food. This will keep your body functioning well and allow for necessary tissue growth and repair. Excess of protein in your diet will turn to fat.

Vegetable proteins: Beans, soya, pulses and cereals are a good source of vegetable proteins which contain less fat than animal and dairy proteins. Nuts have a higher protein content but are, however, high in fat. Beans contain many more proteins than cereals. Vegetable proteins can provide you with sufficient proteins for all the body's needs and they do not contain saturated fat found in most meats and dairy foods. It is advisable to follow a vegetable protein chart (found in specialist books) if you are not eating any animal protein at all, so that you can achieve the right protein balance.

Carbohydrates: Refined, simple carbohydrates are found in sugar, starches, sweets, puddings and jams and should be reduced in your diet. Avoid sweetened fruit juices and try not to take sugar in tea or coffee. Sugar causes the body stress and has no nutritional value whatsoever. Complex carbohydrates found in fruits, vegetables, grain and pulses are essential for a healthy diet producing energy for the body and also fibre needed to keep your digestion and bowels working well. Complex carbohydrates should make up 70–80% of your total intake of food.

Fats: The same weight of fats will give you twice as much energy as the same weight of carbohydrates. You need relatively little fat in your diet – about 10% of your total intake of food – in order to get the fatty acids needed for the structuring of tissues. There are three types of fat. No fat is totally one category, but each type is predominantly saturated, polyunsaturated or monosaturated.

Polyunsaturated fats: Fish, game, soya, some margarines (only those marked 'high in polyunsaturates low in cholesterol') and vegetable oils such as sunflower, safflower, corn and sesame contain polyunsaturated fats.

Monosaturated fats: Chicken, turkey, nuts and olive oil contain monosaturated fats whose effects are neutral to the body. Olive oil, however, is more fattening than pure vegetable oils.

Saturated fats: If taken to excess, saturated fats are thought to cause the body harm as far as blood pressure and heart disease are concerned. They are found in beef, veal, lamb, pork, chocolate, butter, ice cream, whole milk, mayonnaise and palm and coconut oils.

However, do please remember: It is worth remembering that fats only do harm if taken in excess over long periods of time. Fats should not be totally eliminated from your diet, just reduced. Eating your favourite food, be it fattening, will not harm you, as long as you eat it occasionally and in moderation and it is not part of your everyday diet.

Vitamin and mineral supplements: If you are eating a well-balanced, fresh diet there is no need to take vitamin and mineral supplements. However, after sickness your doctor may prescribe them. If you are a strict vegetarian, then you may need them. If you do take vitamins, buy the cheapest around, preferably those containing folates (folic acid), which is important for the maturation of red blood cells.

Vitamins natural or chemical?: Vitamins are chemical entities, therefore, you will get the same benefits whether your vitamins come from food or from pills manufactured in a laboratory.

Shopping

Buy fresh: It is vital that fruit and vegetables should be bought fresh. If possible, buy and eat them within 24 hours.

Hidden sugar: Always read labels to check for ingredients, such as sugars, hidden in sauces.

Too much convenience: Make sure your larder is not made up totally of convenience foods.

Preparing foods

Trim off excess fat: Try to reduce fat before you cook by trimming off excess fat on joints and backs of chops. Also remove the skin from a chicken. Prick joints all over so that the fat can run out during cooking and avoid basting. Don't put joints or roasts straight in to a roasting pan. Use a grill to raise them off the pan's base, so they don't cook in their own fat or use a spit, so that the fat can drip off. Pour off excess oil from tinned foods.

Leave the skin on: Vegetables are best left with their skins on to get the maximum amount of fibre from them. Just scrub the skins to remove dirt.

Cooking foods

Avoid frying: When possible avoid frying as this raises the fat content of the food considerably. If you do fry, use non-stick pans and polyunsaturated oil and seal food quickly to reduce the amount of fat absorbed. Alternatively, use one of the spray-on oils which gives the pan just a light coating. Pour off any excess fat if you are going on to make casseroles and such. Allow stews and casseroles to cool, so that the fat will rise to the top and solidify and can be drained or skimmed.

Reduce salt: Excessive salt in your diet contributes to high blood pressure. It is also advisable for women to cut down on salt before a period, as due to the absorbency of salt, it increases water retention. So, cook vegetables and meats with a minimum of salt. Use unsalted butters. You can buy sodium-free salt from chemists and health food stores.

Steaming is best: Steam vegetables, do not overcook, and never boil them until they are soggy. Steaming is advisable as fewer vitamins are lost from the foods in this way. It also doesn't increase the calorific value of foods as much as, say, frying.

When eating: Trim excess fat off meat. Think before you add salt and try not to use it just out of habit. Use skimmed milk rather than full cream. Your stomach needs three hours between meals to digest food well.

WHICH DIET?

All protein diet: This consists of lean meats, eggs, fish and poultry with little or no vegetables or fruits. While such a diet will produce a quick weight loss, it is not nutritionally sound and should not be undertaken for long periods. The lack of carbohydrates, which produce energy, may make you feel cold and tired.

All fruit diet: This consists of eating different types of fruit in unlimited quantities and is not nutritionally sound. It will also not help you control your eating pattern, if you eat whenever you like. Eating fruit constantly for more than two weeks may also cause diarrhoea, and dizziness. Treat fruit diets as cleansers for the body for short periods only (one or two days at a time).

Low carbohydrate diet: On this diet carbohydrates are restricted but not completely eliminated. High in fat and protein, it results in quick weight loss. While such a diet is sensible because it eliminates refined carbohydrates, it is not sound because of its increase in fats and lack of fibre. It is to be avoided by anyone with high blood pressure or a family history of heart disease.

Vegetarian diet: This form of diet eliminates animal protein contained in meat, poultry or fish. Provided milk and eggs are included with the vegetables and fruit, the diet is balanced. The strict vegetarian, who won't eat any animal product, has to be careful that he or she is getting enough B vitamins. Vitamin B12 is found only in animal protein. This diet is high in fibre but is inadvisable if you are pregnant.

Fibre diet: This consists of fruits, nuts, vegetables, wholegrains, brown rice, wholemeal bread and pasta. All these foods contain fibre, which is not digested in your body and passes through without contributing Calories. It also contains vegetable protein, which provides protein without fat. A good diet if you want to reduce your blood pressure and eliminate fat from your diet.

A balanced diet: Bearing in mind that the majority of your total intake per day (80%) should be fruit and vegetables, eat meat and fish in moderation (8–10%) and dairy products, eggs and cheese also sparingly (10%).
 Start the day with a light carbohydrate breakfast of a bowl of muesli, with fruit either mixed in or separately and a slice of wholemeal bread. For lunch, keep to 50 g (2 oz) of protein – meats or cheeses with a fresh raw salad, fruit for dessert. At supper watch your intake of protein and fill up with vegetables, potatoes, rice, pasta and again fruit for dessert. If you follow this guide, then the occasional excess of fats or sugar will not have a dramatic effect on your body.

Calorie requirements

Women: Adults need between 2000–2500 Calories a day. The higher your energy output, the greater number of Calories you need, unless you are on a diet, of course. If you take no exercise at all and lead a fairly sedentary life, keep to 2000 Calories a day. As you get older (60+), you will need fewer Calories – about 1500–2000 Calories a day depending on your weight and height.

Men: Adults need between 2500–3500 Calories a day. If your energy output is high, if you are a manual labourer for instance, you will need more Calories. As you get older (60+) you will need fewer Calories – roughly 2000 Calories a day.

Exercise is energy/Calories are energy: By exercising you can use up between 250–900 Calories per hour in the following sports: running, jogging, skipping, squash, swimming, cycling, ski-ing, dancing, tennis, riding, golf, aerobic exercise, badminton, netball. The more demanding and strenuous the sport is, the more Calories it will burn up.

Walking: If you are unable to play any sport, walking will burn up 100–250 Calories per hour depending on the pace.

How active are you? If you want to establish how active a life you lead, use a pedometer to see how much walking and moving around you do during the day. Attach it to a waist band or to trousers above your hip bone.

Better eating

Coffee: As coffee is a drug, it should be treated as such. It affects the central nervous system and if taken to excess will make you feel jittery. It destroys Vitamin C in your body, so try to limit yourself to two cups a day. Better still, use decaffeinated coffee or dandelion coffee especially at night.

Tea: Although tea contains slightly less caffeine than coffee, if taken to excess it, too, will make you feel jittery. It's a good idea to use herbal teas as substitutes. Tea, like coffee and alcohol, destroys Vitamin C in your body.

Milk: Whole milk contains saturated fat, so try to substitute with skimmed milk.

Cream: As cream contains saturated fat, it's best to use single cream rather than double. Better still, substitute with yogurt.

Cheese: Try to keep to the low fat cheeses like cottage cheese, Edam, Camembert and Ricotta.

Salt: Salt blunts your taste buds and increases your blood pressure, so substitute with herbs or use a sodium free salt.

Flour: Plain flour is a refined carbohydrate, use wholemeal flour or cornflour instead.

Eggs: As eggs contain cholesterol, have no more than three a week, if you are of normal weight. They are good for you so should not be omitted from your diet. (They are a nerve food containing thiamin and riboflavin. These vitamins are essential for nerve health and repair. Eggs are also one of the best sources of protein.)

Butter: Substitute a low fat spread or low cholesterol margarine for butter, which is a standard fat. If you are using butter, then use unsalted. A low fat spread contains more water and less fat.

Sugar: Your body does not need refined sugar, so try to eliminate it completely from your diet as it causes the body stress. Eat fruits or vegetables, which contain nature's natural sugar, fructose, rather than cakes and sweets. Honey and black molasses are also refined sugar and while honey contains some nutrients, it is best taken in moderation. They are certainly not health foods.

Alcohol: In moderation alcohol is fine but try to keep to the lower calorie drinks, such as the dry white wines. Remember that a woman's threshold is lower than a man's and her liver is more likely to be affected by alcohol. One glass of wine a day won't do you any harm.

Fruit squashes: It's better to drink carton orange and fruit juices rather than fruit squashes which have little nutritional value and contain sugar. Invest in a juicer or a squeezer and make your own.

Vegetable oils: Check that your vegetable oil is fully polyunsaturated. When the label just says vegetable oil, the bottle will contain a higher level of saturated fat. Get into the habit of reading labels.

Meat: If you eat a lot of meat, try to stick to the monosaturated meats, (see list on page 226) as opposed to the saturated.

Margarines: Not all margarines are polyunsaturated. Hard margarines contain more saturated fat but so do some of the soft margarines. Read the labels to check the proportions and look for the words 'low in cholesterol'.

Gravy: Avoid making gravy from the fat of the roast. Even if you try to drain most of it off the gravy will still have a high fat content. Use powdered gravies or stock cubes.

Wholemeal bread: Though all bread is nutritious, wholemeal bread has three times the fibre. Check that your loaf is really wholemeal and not just coloured with caramel.

HEALTH ON THE RUN

EXERCISE FOR PLEASURE

What is fast being forgotten in this fitness conscious age is that exercise is for pleasure and relaxation. It should never become another of life's burdens which you feel you ought to do. Should this happen, you will only begrudge the time it takes, possibly dislike the effort it demands and, more often than not, give it up pretty quickly. There are fitness fanatics, who push themselves to exhaustion, no matter what the cost, forgetting that exercise should be enjoyed. However, if you regard it as a treat, think carefully about a routine that suits you and your lifestyle, then you will receive all the benefits that exercise has to offer.

It is important to know the various qualities of exercise in order to decide what you need. They are strength, flexibility, stamina and balance.

Strength: The muscles of your body should be strong in order to support your body. Weak muscles cause joints to take too much strain. To develop muscle strength and build up muscle power exercise regularly three times a week.

Exercises to give you strength: Plan some weight-lifting and/or some keep-fit exercises. Developing muscle strength is relative to how strong/weak the various parts of your body are to begin with. Weights will increase strength and can be used to strengthen individual parts of your body. Weight training is graded and you choose the weights suitable for your sex, age and body type. Keep-fit exercises are given on television; you can buy books on the subject or join a keep-fit class.

Flexibility: This is the ability to move your muscles and joints through their full range. When muscles lose their elasticity this has a detrimental effect on the joints of your body.

Exercises to give you flexibility: Join yoga and/or keep-fit classes. If this is not possible, exercise at home. It is important to stretch all your limbs to keep them supple. Stretching is a simple exercise which practically everyone is capable of doing. Begin with a long, slow stretch of each limb. Hold every stretch you do for at least 30 seconds. Do this at least three times a week. After any series of exercises where you contract your muscles, remember to stretch them afterwards.

Stamina: To cope with your daily life you need stamina, which comes through increasing the performance of your heart and lungs through aerobic exercise (see Aerobic classes page 250).

Exercises to increase stamina: Jogging, running, swimming, fast walking, skipping, cross-country running, ski-ing, aerobic exercise classes, will all increase your stamina.

Balance: The complex process of subtly moving your body to adjust itself to maintain a position is called balance. A body is never static. Like any other exercise, the more you practise balance, the more it will improve. Being able to find your balance quickly gives you the assurance to move around with confidence – especially as you get older. It is a vital part of being fit.

Exercise to improve balance: A simple everyday exercise is to stand with your feet and ankles together, pelvis in balance (see Perfect posture page 245) and your spine stretched. Go up on to the balls of your feet, pulling up the front of your thighs. When you feel steady, keep your shoulders down and take your hands above your head and balance. When you can balance confidently, look around you. We depend a great deal on vision for our balance but it should really be a sense inside our body. Try this near a wall first for moral support!

Be calm: In order to balance well you have to breathe well, be calm and concentrate on what you are doing. As soon as your mind becomes unsure and wavers, your body will lose its balance.

Total fitness: For total fitness you must have a combination of strength, endurance, flexibility and stamina. For instance, you may be able to play a demanding game of tennis, yet find it impossible to stay in a stretching yoga position for one minute. This means you are not completely fit!

To bear in mind

Body shape: It is not true that you have to work your body violently to get into shape. Gentle, graded exercise and body alignment greatly improve body shape.

Forcing: If you force your body to do what it doesn't want to do (such as the splits when it's not ready for them) you will only be met with resistance. Give your body time to adapt, then you won't become disheartened. It will come faster if you don't fight it.

No end-gaining: While you are exercising, concentrate on the stage you are at rather than anticipate the final stage. You will derive more satisfaction this way. Eventually, when you can cope with the final stage of the exercise, it will be more precise and the benefits will be greater.

Precision: Precision in exercise pulls the muscles of your body back into their correct alignment. If you ever become bored with the exercise, think 'How precisely am I doing this?' and you will alleviate the boredom.

Rest: Pauses between exercises should be taken, especially if you are a beginner.

Overdoing it: Enthusiasm, or a sudden urge to get fit, can lead people to overdo exercise. Never push yourself to exhaustion. The older you are, the longer you should give yourself to get fit.

Aches and pains: Pain is a warning signal from the body and should be heeded. However, there is bound to be some resistance from your muscles when you first start to exercise, so listen to your body. Work slowly at first so that you have time to learn the difference between the unpleasantness, which has to be gone through to overcome stiffness, and the danger signs of pain telling you to stop. If you feel a sharp pain during exercise stop immediately. If it persists consult your doctor. Pain may occur during exercise but it may not necessarily be caused by exercise. It should always be treated as a warning signal.

Alternatives: If, through injury or ill-health, you are told to stop exercising by your doctor, ask if you can do another sport. If you were told not to run because of poor knees, perhaps swimming would be a safe alternative.

In tune: You will only get fit if you are in tune with your body and your capabilities. Doing too little, or too much, will not increase fitness.

Fanatics: Once you reach a maximum of four hours strong exercise a week, there are no fitness benefits in extending this time. The good effects stabilize. If you overdo things you may injure yourself.

In the cold: Avoid alcohol before exercising at all times but particularly when exercising outdoors in cold weather. Alcohol causes the blood vessels to dilate and the body loses heat. It will, therefore, be harder to warm up with exercise.

In the heat: The body heats up during exercise, so remember to wear suitable clothing, which will allow your body to cool (see What to Wear page 243). In excessive heat you lose water and salt, so drink water before and after your exercise period. Avoid exercising in very hot sun.

Exercise and saunas: Do not raise your body temperature further by going into a sauna, if you are already very hot from exercising.

Before and during your exercise routine: Check your posture. Your body should be in the correct alignment for exercise to be of real benefit and for the health of your body (see Posture page 245).

Awareness: As you exercise, be aware of how your body is moving. Try to become aware of this in your everyday life too. Just living can be an exercise, if you are conscious of your body and give yourself the amount of movement a healthy body demands.

Stillness: Feel the stillness between your movements; it is as important to know when to conserve energy as when to use it.

Body habits: Your body will assume the posture of the action it does the most. For example, a writer may be hunched over his desk day after day and develop rounded shoulders. Try to be aware of your body habits caused by your lifestyle,' so that you can compensate for them when you exercise.

When to be cautious

If you are pregnant: Check with your doctor that it is alright for you to continue your normal exercise routine. You can keep to the same system as long as you don't push yourself too much or do anything that is too strenuous.

Dieting or fasting: It is inadvisable to exercise if you are fasting, as it will sap you of the little energy you have. It's best not to go on a crash diet anyway but certainly don't combine it with strenuous exercise or you may feel faint. On a balanced diet, which reduces your calorific intake to 1000 Calories a day, you should be able to exercise as normal and it will greatly benefit your diet.

Back problems: Don't avoid exercise if you have a bad back but proceed with caution and under the guidance of someone who really knows about backs. Consult your doctor if you have severe back trouble and get advice before you start exercising.

Knee problems: If you ever feel pain in your knee cap and it persists stop exercising at once and seek medical advice. If your knees are weak strengthen the muscles (quadriceps) above your knees (see Thighs page 260). Avoid strong kicking movements or deep knee bends.

When not to exercise

Not well: If you feel very tired or ill, have a temperature, or have eaten a large meal within the last hour, you should not exercise.

After an operation: Seek medical advice on the right kind of exercise to help recovery after an operation or injury.

Heavy periods: Moderate exercise may greatly relieve the discomfort of a bad heavy period, but hardworking or aerobics classes usually prove too much at this time.

Exercises to avoid (if you're unfit)

Sit ups: If you lie on the floor on your back, your legs straight and raise your trunk up to a right angle with your legs, this exercise mainly works your hip flexors and not your tummy. It can cause strain to the lower back or hernias internally and should only be done if you have cast iron stomach muscles.

Double leg raising: If you lie on the floor on your back lifting your legs straight into the air, you are working your hip flexors mainly and not your tummy. This strains the lower back, stretches your tummy muscles and can put too much pressure on your pelvic floor. Lower back ache and hernias can also occur. (See Isometric exercises page 250.)

Exercises to treat with caution

Push away from the walls: This exercise consists of placing your hands flat on the wall, legs 60 cm/2 ft away, and pressing up into the wall. Do not do it if you have severe round shoulders and a rounded back, as it strengthens the chest, triceps and front shoulder muscles and will pull your shoulders forward even more.

Head circling: Never circle your head fully; for example never drop your head forward and then roll it full circle over your right shoulder across the back then over your left shoulder to the front. This has a pepper grinder effect to the joints in the neck and can cause wear and tear and will most probably give you a stiff neck.

Touching your toes: It is always better to let gravity help you to touch your toes slowly instead of vigorous bouncing movements which can overstretch the spine and hamstrings. Don't bounce down from a standing position with your legs straight and your knees locked.

Knee bends and squats: When bending your knees, or squatting with a straight back, watch for weak knees which tend to fall in as you bend your legs and can cause strain to the ligaments of your knee. Avoid strong kicking movements.

Back bends: If you already suffer from lordosis (an inward curve of the spine) exercises bending the spine backwards will shorten the lower back muscles even more. Avoid also if you are overweight or pregnant.

Bicycling: A bicycling exercise, with your legs up in the air, your weight resting on your neck, shoulders and upper back, can cause strain to these areas. Bicycling is best done on the real thing or on an exercise bike.

Exercise on your own

Aids to help you: If possible work with a tape or a book or watching a television programme, if the time suits you. Most of the television programmes now have books which go along with the classes. You have to learn about body awareness when you exercise on your own, so concentrate on how it feels as you do the exercise and remember to be conscious of your whole body, even though you may be working with only part of it. (See Exercise aids, page 270.)

Disadvantages: It can be difficult to keep up enthusiasm when working on your own. It takes time to know if you are doing an exercise correctly. Videos and tapes, though extremely good, may become boring and not cater for your specific needs. (Separate tapes are required for backs, necks etc.)

A different style: If you can afford it, move on to a different style of exercise tape. This is provided your first tape gave you a good foundation in how to move your body.

Working together

There are quite a few exercises which are better if you can do them with the help of a friend. If you have a weak back, a hand placed on it will increase your understanding of where you should be trying to lift or push in. You can also use your partner's hands to act as weights creating resistance for you to work against.

Shoulders: Ask your friend/partner to stand behind you to check that your shoulders are the same height. If one is higher than the other ask him/her to press the higher shoulder down with you as you do the shoulder exercises (see Shoulder section, page 254).

Back: Sit on the floor, the soles of your feet together, your legs bent and hold your ankles. Ask your friend/partner to help you lift your back by pushing your back in gently where it is rounded. (The spine normally protrudes in areas of weakness, see Backache, page 264.) If your helper makes long strokes up either side of your spine, this will help you to understand how to lengthen and lift it.

Back and thighs: Sit on the floor facing your partner, both of you with your legs apart. Put the soles of your feet against your partner's feet. Hold hands. Try to lift yourself out of your hips (so that the distance between your ribcage and your hips increases and the breastbone lifts up). Let your partner pull you forward gently and then you pull him/her towards you.

Thighs: Lie on your back with a cushion underneath your bottom. Bring your legs towards your chest, straighten them up in the air and then take them wide apart. Your partner should then place his/her hands on your inside calves to create resistance as you try to bring your thighs together. This will strengthen your inner thigh muscles.

Abdomen: Lie on your back with your hands at your sides, knees bent and breathe in. As you breathe out, do a pelvic tilt (see page 247) pressing the back of your waist into the floor. Ask your partner to hold your hands as you pull forward.

Back: Lie on your front and stretch your arms out on either side away from your body (like a bird spreads its wings). Ask your partner to hold on to your feet as you take a good deep breath in and lift your head, chest and arms off the floor.

Backs of calves: Stand feet together, arm's length away from your partner and hold hands. Both of you should now bend your knees and crouch down as far as you can, keeping your heels in contact with the floor.

That competitive spirit: A word of warning – working together with other people can lead to a strong element of competition. Watch that you don't overdo it. If your body is not ready, you may well strain it.

WHAT TO WEAR

In the gym

Leotard and tights: Make sure that your leotard and tights are long enough in the body and legs so that you can stretch. Check that your leotard is not tight around your neck. Cotton is better than lycra as it absorbs sweat. Wool is good for a top covering as it is warm but porous and can still insulate when wet. Nylon doesn't let sweat evaporate.

Shorts and T-shirts: It is better to wear loose shorts and T-shirts for yoga. If you go up into a shoulder stand you can then hold on to the skin of your back and your hands are less likely to slip.

Leg warmers: If worn over the whole leg, and not around the ankles, they are excellent for keeping out the cold.

Sweat suits: These suits will help you warm up but they will not help you lose weight. They have also been blamed for giving people rheumatism. If you are using a sweat suit make sure you take it off immediately you have finished exercising and dry yourself well with a towel.

In and outside the gym

Track suits: A track suit is the best way to keep warm in the winter. If you are running, jogging, or doing an aerobics class, wear a T-shirt underneath so that you can strip off the top when you have warmed up. Replace the track suit top as you cool down.

Bare foot: To exercise the feet, do not wear any shoes, tights or socks at home around the house. Walking barefoot over pebble beaches is also good exercise.

Shoes: For jogging, running and aerobics, wear the proper shoes. Tennis shoes won't do! Make sure that the back of the shoe doesn't have a flap, as this will cut into the back of your heel.

Bras: A good supportive bra is essential for exercising and running. Make sure it fits round the ribcage as well as the chest (see Chapter 4 Sizing up, page 140).

Gloves and hats: It is important to keep your hands and head warm when you are exercising outside in winter, otherwise a lot of your body heat will be lost.

Don't restrict movement: Whatever you are wearing there should be no restriction to your movement, such as tight waist bands which hinder good breathing.

General guide: The more active you become, the less clothing you will need. If you wear too much clothing, your body can't get rid of the heat. Make sure you are as warm as possible when you start and replace clothing for relaxation afterwards as your body temperature drops rapidly when you stop exercising.

FROM
UNFIT TO FIT

How to tell if you are:

Unfit: Any exertion will leave you puffed and exhausted and you lack energy. You need strengthening exercises and stamina.

Stiff and tight: Your body will have lost its flexibility, joints will have lost their full movement. You need stretching exercises.

Loose and flabby: Your body will have lost its muscle tone. The tone of your muscles is to do with the capability of your muscles to stretch to their full size and also with the strength of the muscles. You need strengthening and stretching exercises.

Fat lies on top of muscles: Do the 'pinch test' to check the flab – take hold of the flesh at the sides of your ribs, at the bottom of your ribcage. If there is more than 2.5 cm (1 inch), you need to lose weight and tone up.

Clumsy: You will have lost good co-ordination of your body. Agility and balance are needed combined with stretching and strengthening.

Groundhog: You will find it difficult to leap or do small jumps. You need exercises for agility, stamina and strength in the legs.

Weak: You will find it difficult even to lift a light load. You need strengthening exercises.

Giddy: You will be unable to hold yourself still on your toes and on one leg. You need balancing exercises (see Balance section, page 235).

Tense: You will feel uptight and short of breath. You need relaxing, stretching exercises with a slow rhythm.

Perfect posture

Perfect posture, or correct body alignment, is the foundation of any good exercise programme. If you are exercising to improve your shape, improving your posture will produce immediate results. It will also enhance any exercise from running to jazz ballet, as your spine is the central axis of movement in your body, which is only able to work properly in the correct position.

Perfect posture: Stand sideways on to a mirror and imagine a plumb line hung from the middle of your ear straight down to the floor. The imaginary line should run slightly in front of the tips of your shoulders, through the centre of your hip bone and slightly to the front of the centre of your knee and down through your ankle.

Benefits: Good posture helps to prevent back problems, neck problems and knee problems. It also aids digestion and breathing and will help prevent over-tiredness at the end of the day.

High heel test: Stand in front of a mirror naked, sideways on, with your shoes off. Look at your posture. Now put on a pair of high heel shoes and see what happens. Your body weight will be pushed forward with all your weight pushed into the arches and on to the balls of your feet. Your bosom will be thrown forward and your buttocks thrown backwards. Your body will be under strain to stay upright. Obviously low heels are better for good posture. Avoid changing constantly from high to low.

Shoulder bag test: Your shoulders are designed to slope down at the ends. Wearing shoulder bags causes the shoulders to hunch to keep the bag from falling off completely. This posture then becomes normal and neck and upper back problems may occur. Change the shoulder you hang your bag regularly or, better still, wear the shoulder strap across your chest.

The right way to stand – from head to toe

Head: Feel that your head is being pulled up from the crown.

Chin: Your chin should be at a right angle to your neck.

Neck: Your neck lengthens as you correct your chin position.

Shoulders: Your shoulders should be down away from the ears.

Arms: Arms hang loosely. If your shoulders are pulled down evenly, your hands will be at the same level on each thigh.

Ribs: Your rib cage should be raised slightly to assist good breathing.

Pelvis: Your pelvis should be tilted up in the front, which allows your tummy to flatten and your back to lengthen. The buttocks will then be able to tuck under.

Feet: Your feet should be slightly turned out, standing hip-width apart. You should feel your weight evenly distributed between the balls of your feet and your heels.

Extra exercises for posture

To prevent round shoulders: This exercise can be done sitting or standing. Lift your shoulders up towards your ears. Without arching the lower part of your back, squeeze your shoulder blades together. Hold for a count of four. Release and pull your shoulders well down.

To re-centre your pelvis and correct a sway back: A sway back is one with an inward curvature at the lower end of the spine. To correct this, stand against a wall with your feet slightly away from it. Tilt your pelvis to flatten the back of your waist against the wall. Register this feeling and repeat.

To strengthen the muscles of your back and help correct a sway back: Lie on your back with your knees bent up and your feet flat on the floor. Do a pelvic tilt, so that the back of your waist presses into the floor. Lift one leg up and bend it into your chest and hold. When you change legs, see if you can hold the pelvic tilt position.

To strengthen neck, shoulder girdle, back: Lie on your front. Place your arms down by your hips. Breathe in and, as you breathe out, lift your head and shoulders off the floor. Hold for a count of four and release. Repeat four times.

Plus: Do all the exercises (see pages 254–260) for shoulders, back, buttocks and stomach. The buttocks and stomach exercise will help strengthen your pelvic corset (i.e. the abdominal muscles, which run down the body from the ribs to the pelvis, across the front of the body and diagonally across the body round to your back, corseting the waist) which carries your spine.

Weight and posture: Being overweight causes immense strain on your back. Imagine carrying a sack of potatoes round your middle every day and you will see the effect overweight can have. The best remedy is to lose weight and begin a gentle exercise routine to strengthen your back.

Pregnancy and posture: Perfect posture should be practised all the time to help prevent backache during pregnancy. It will also help you get your muscles back into shape after the birth.

Body types – which are you?

Endomorph: These are large framed, prone to weight gain but not necessarily strong and muscular. (Measurements are for females only.) Wrists 16 cm (6¼ inches +), hipbone to hipbone 25 cm (10 inches +), ankles 22 cm (8¾ inches). Aerobic exercise (see page 250) is suitable to keep weight down.

Mesomorphs: These are medium framed, not prone to weight gain, muscular and strong. General fitness training needed (see section on 'What each exercise can give you', page 250). Wrists 14.5–16 cm (5¾–6¼ inches), hip to hip 21–25 cm (8¼–10 inches), ankles 20.5–22 cm (8–8¾ inches) – for females.

Ectomorphs: These are small framed, either tall or short. Not at all prone to weight gain and find it difficult to put on muscle. Muscle strengthening exercises needed and relaxation. Wrists 14.5 cm (5¾ inches) or less, ankles 20.5 cm (8 inches) or less, hip to hip 21 cm (8¼ inches) or less – for females.

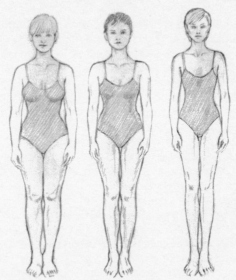

Mixture: Most of us are a bit of a mixture. Use the measurements of wrists, ankles and pelvic girdle to make an assessment.

A good finish to your exercise

At the end: It is important to make sure that you don't keep tension in any area once you've finished exercising it. Do the complementary opposite action (e.g. a stretch after a long contraction) to the exercise you've just done in order to relax muscles after working hard.

At the end of your exercise class: To reap the benefits of your exercise period, lie on the floor stretched out and just close your eyes and centre your attention again and do some good breathing.

When relaxation is difficult: If it is impossible for you to do any form of relaxation, do some slow stretches, rocking movements on the spine or curl up into a little ball.

Rocking the spine: Lie on your back, squeeze your legs into your chest and hold on to your knees. Tuck your head in by your knees and gently rock forwards and back.

The ball: Kneel up and then rest the weight of your bottom back on your heels, breathe in and lift your ribs away from your hips. As you breathe out bend forwards and tuck your head in towards your knees, so that the top of your head is flat on the ground. Pull your shoulders down away from your ears, and your arms backwards and let your hands relax on the floor behind you, palms facing upwards.

The roll: Lying on your side along your arm, your body in a straight line, very slowly let your head fall back and roll on to the floor followed by your body. It is a floppy movement and important to let your head go first.

What each exercise can give you

Aerobic classes: These classes improve stamina and endurance by working the heart and lungs at your individual training level (see page 279) for 12–15 minutes constantly. They are more about maintaining fitness than getting fit. There must be a warm-up and warm down from the constant movement and agility and stretching should be included in the class.

Ballet: This works on co-ordination, balance, strength, endurance, agility, suppleness and will work the heart and lungs if done vigorously for long enough. An advanced class would make you fit if done regularly.

Cycling: This provides strengthening exercise for your legs and will build up stamina if done vigorously. It is best combined with stretching exercises as your legs tend to become tight.

Dance: The pleasant movements of dance assist agility, endurance, stretch, balance and stamina if done for a long period. It's a fun way to get fit.

Exercise classes: A good exercise class should offer you suppleness, balance, agility, flexibility, stamina, starting you off gently and building up to a good level of fitness.

Isometric exercises: These are holding exercises done against resistance and can be quite strenuous. They are for strengthening the body within a limited range only and should be combined within an exercise class. (They are not suitable for people with high blood pressure or the older person.)

Jogging and running: These are not all round exercise though they will make you fit by improving your stamina and breathing capacity. They build up the leg muscles. They are both best combined with stretching exercises.

Swimming: This is a good all round exercise and will stretch the body, provided the strokes are done properly. It is both relaxing and can improve stamina if done strongly and regularly. It is a good exercise for training up to a good level of fitness. It is also marvellous if you are pregnant.

Squash: This enjoyable game develops strength, stamina and agility. In order for it to really make you fit, it has to be played three times a week. Playing squash just once a week, if you are unfit, will only strain your body and can be dangerous if you are heavily overweight. It should be combined with stretching exercises to warm-up and cool down.

Tennis: This is a good exercise for working your heart and lungs in moderation and strengthening the muscles of arms and legs. It is best combined with stretching exercises.

Tai Chi: This is an ancient Chinese exercise system devised to strengthen and harmonize the body. It works on flexibility, balance, breathing. It also calms the mind.

Walking: If you walk hard and long, this exercise will build up stamina. Other benefits are that it strengthens legs and is relaxing.

Yoga: Yoga is an ancient practice of exercise, set postures, breathing techniques and meditation. You can take from yoga what you want, using it, for example, purely for exercise without going into meditation. It brings suppleness to your body and strength from sustaining the postures. It also calms your mind and aids breathing and works on balance. Yoga experts say that it does work the heart and lungs and helps endurance.

ESSENTIAL EXERCISE

It is essential to have a good understanding of basic exercise and how to work correctly before going on to the various styles and methods. Knowing how to work your body properly leaves you free to enjoy the movement without the worries of injury.

When possible: Try to use the following exercises during your daily life. This will bring faster results.

The neck: The muscles of your neck need to be strong and flexible to support your head and allow sufficient movement. Most of us, through misuse, carry our heads incorrectly, causing strain to our necks. This leads to loss of movement. The other disadvantage is that if your neck and shoulders are tight at the start of your exercise routine, and you don't loosen them, they will become tighter and you will leave the class feeling worse instead of better.

Please note: Movement in the neck should start at the atlas, which is the indentation just below the base of your skull and the start of your neck spine. When you bend your neck try to think of this point.

Before you start: Tuck your chin in a little, thinking of the back of the neck lengthening and the head lifting up from the crown, then pull your shoulders down. If you find this difficult, imagine you are carrying a heavy suitcase in each hand and pull down again. Release and begin your neck exercises.

The stretch: Sit down and make sure that your spine is lifted and your shoulders are down. Clasp your hands on the big knob at the back of your head and tuck in your chin. Breathe in and, as you breathe out, slowly lower your chin to the chest, letting the elbows fall to the sides of your face. (If your elbows stick out in the air, you know you have not let go properly.)

For your neck

Strength: With the back of your neck long and your chin well tucked in, clasp your hands on the knob at the back of your head. Gently pull your hands forward and push your head back at the same time. Hold for a count of three and release. This will help to get rid of double chins. Repeat up to four times.

Stretch: Turn your head to your right shoulder. Lifting your shoulder slightly, kiss the shoulder. Repeat on the other side.

Loosen: Turn your head and look over your right shoulder, use your eyes and try to see the far corner behind you. Then turn your head the other way.

Anywhere/anytime stretch: With the back of your neck long and your chin tucked in, clasp your hands on the base of the skull with your thumbs running down the neck. Try to pull your skull up out of your neck with your hands. This helps keep the neck free from tension through lengthening the muscles at the back of the neck, which tend to shorten during the day, through body postures adopted.

For your shoulders

Your shoulders play a vital part in your health and the look of your spine (see Posture page 245). Round shoulders and tight chests will also affect the look of your neck and suggest that you are depressed or afraid.

Before you start:　Look at your shoulders in the mirror. Is one shoulder higher than the other? During the exercises, try to become aware of the balance of your shoulders and if one of them happens to be higher than the other, pull it down more.

The stretch:　Sit on a stool or hard chair and let your body slump. Fold your arms in front of you and then lift your arms pulling your elbows away from your body.

Strength:　Lift your arms up at the sides of your body to shoulder height and make a loose fist with both hands. Pull your shoulder blades together; keep them there, then press your arms back in small further movements. Do not arch your back and keep your arms up at shoulder height throughout. Work up to 12 repetitions.

Loosen:　With both arms hanging at your sides, swing your right arm in a full circle past your ear and back several times. Do the same with your left arm. Then both arms together. The swings

don't necessarily have to be in just one direction; experiment across your body too.

Squeeze: Circle your shoulders back and, as you do so, squeeze your shoulder blades together. This area of your back should become nice and warm, thus helping the muscles to relax.

Warning: Shoulder joints are easily dislocated. If you wish to swing a child round in the park, remember to hold him/her under the armpits, not by the hands.

For your arms, wrists and hands

Arms and hands are continually being bent. For this reason, especially in women, the back of the upper arm loses muscle tone as it is forever lengthened. Likewise the hands are seldom given a good stretch. Remember that the joints in your hands are as important as the joints of your knees and should be stretched frequently.

The stretch: Sit or stand with your arms by your sides with the palms of your hands facing towards your body. Lift up your arms and at the same time flex your hands forwards and back. When you reach shoulder height, hold and then lower with the same action of the wrists and hands.

Strength: Sit or stand with your arms by the sides of your body. Rotate your hands and arms inwards, so that the backs of your hands face forwards. Clench your fists loosely. Then straighten the arms, pushing them back until you feel a good squeeze in the back of the upper arm. Repeat several times strongly.

Squeeze: Sit and, with your wrists resting on your thighs, clench your hands and then stretch the fingers wide apart.

Loosen: Stand or sit and lift your arms away from the sides of your body and rotate your arms, thumb towards the back of the room and then towards the front.

Anywhere/anytime loosener: Stand and, with your arms by your sides, drop your hands and wrists and let them go limp and then give your whole arms and hands a good shake. Repeat several times. When you stop you should notice that your fingers are tingling.

For your face

Have you ever wondered why men tend to have better muscle tone on their faces than women? One theory is that because they shave every morning, they exercise their facial muscles. Believe it or not, because of our natural expressions, be it constantly frowning, squinting, smiling or pursing our lips, our facial muscles benefit from a good squeeze and stretch.

Shaving: Imagine you are shaving; purse your lips and flatten your cheek to the right and then to the left, thinking of your lips trying to touch your ear.

Squeezing out: Screw your face up tightly towards the centre, then open it up wide, lifting your eyebrows, opening your mouth, eyes and eyelids as far as possible. (See Chapter 7 The whole face page 215.)

Sucking in: Suck your cheeks in and then release and repeat.

Drop your jaw: Drop open your jaw and, keeping it open, move your chin towards the right and then the left in a sliding action.

Circles: Purse your lips and then circle them to the right keeping them pursed and then to the left.

For your abdomen

The muscles of the abdomen lose their strength for a number of reasons: bad posture – everytime you slouch the muscles of the abdomen lengthen – pregnancy, overweight and operations.

Important re-training: Two important points to remember in re-training your muscles are: breathe **out** as you do any exercise, pulling your abdominal muscles in. Do not overstrain, as this is counter productive.

For weak abdominal muscles: Lie on your back, bend your knees, your feet flat on the floor, your arms at your sides. Breathe in and, as you breathe out, press your waist into the floor and lift your head and shoulders sliding hands forwards towards your knees. Work up to 12 slow repetitions.

The diagonal muscle strengthener: Lie on your back as above. Breathe in, and, as you breathe out, lift your head and shoulders twisting towards the right, stretching past the outside of your right knee with your left hand. Repeat on the left. Work up to six repeats on each side.

The side muscles strengthener: Lie on your back with your hands touching your thighs. Breathe in, and, as you breathe out, lift your head and shoulders slightly off the floor pressing your waist down at the same time. Slide your right hand down towards your right knee and then the left hand down towards your left knee. Repeat four times. Have a rest and then repeat the whole sequence. Work up to 12 repetitions.

Care of your back

The way we live contributes greatly to the health of our backs. To prevent wear and tear on your spine, the muscles of your back need to be kept strong, long and supple and be helped not hindered by the muscles of your abdomen. (See page 245 for correct standing position.)

Stretch: Standing, take your weight on to your left foot and lift your right knee up to your chest holding underneath the knee and at the same time, bend your spine and take your head down to your right knee. Repeat the movement on the other side.

Strengthen: Sit sideways on to a mirror with your legs straight out in front of you. Place your hands behind your buttocks. Push down on your hands as you lift the spine and the breastbone and straighten the back. Hold for a short while.

Different ways: You can work on your back in different ways. Try sitting as above but with your legs bent and the soles of your feet together, or with your legs straight out taken apart, so you get a good stretch on the inside of the legs.

Lengthen: Standing with your legs apart, clasp your hands behind you on your bottom. Bend forwards from the hips, bending the knees a little and lift your arms up behind you pulling towards your head.

Loosen: Stand with your legs wide apart. Stretch your arms out to shoulder level. Keep your hips facing forward and twist your upper body round to the right and then twist to the left. (Spot something on the wall behind you to prevent dizziness.)

Anywhere/anytime exercises:

Sitting: Whenever you can remember, just sit up tall and try to keep your spine lengthened for as long as possible. The stronger your muscles become the less tired your back will feel.

Bracing: Brace your abdominal muscles on an out breath.

Working your pelvis

Movement of the pelvis greatly contributes to health and a good posture. Correct placement of the pelvis is essential for good pelvic mobility, which is important in childbirth and lovemaking.

Standing: (See exercise to re-centre pelvis in extra posture exercises page 247.)

Strengthen tummy and lengthen back: Lie on your back with your legs hip width apart, knees bent, feet flat on the floor. Breathe in and, as you breathe out, push the back of your waist into the floor and pull in your abdominal muscles. Don't let your buttocks lift off the floor but squeeze them tightly.

For your buttocks

Buttocks spread easily through continued sitting and are also prone to collecting fat. The buttock muscles are large and need exercising strongly to maintain good tone.

Squeeze: Sitting on a sturdy chair, feel your two sitting bones (see page 272) and lift your spine. Push your thighs into the chair so that your buttocks clench tightly together. Hold the position for a count of six and do faster movements as well.

Strengthener: Sitting on a sturdy chair, roll your pelvis back and lift your legs off the floor. Turn your legs out from your hips. Clench your buttocks strongly several times.

Anywhere/anytime exercises: Do the squeeze exercise if sitting. If standing, clench your buttocks together and release.

For your thighs

Apart from the look of thighs, which are often mis-shapen through incorrect use, it is vital to have healthy thighs to protect the whole knee joint.

Toning: One of the best toning exercises for your thighs is walking, so go for a walk as regularly as possible.

Strengthen: (Not to be done if you have knee trouble.) Sitting on a sturdy chair, roll your pelvis back and lift up your right leg turning it out from your hip. Bend your leg at the knee and push your heel

away from you sharply, so that your thigh wobbles. Repeat several times until thigh begins to tire. Repeat with your left leg.

Stretch: Lying on your back with a cushion under your pelvis, bend your legs towards your chest, then take them straight up, so that they are at a right angle to your body. Let them drop apart. (Your abdominal muscles should not bulge in this position.) Keep your back pressed into the floor throughout.

Squeeze: Lie on your back with your legs bent, feet on the floor. Place a cushion between your thighs. Squeeze your legs together several times, slowly and then quickly.

Anywhere/anytime exercises: Stand with your feet apart. Try to squeeze your legs together but do not allow your feet to move. Then try to push your thighs apart without your feet moving.

For your ankles and feet

Ankles and feet need to be flexible and strong to keep the balance of the body sound. Unhealthy feet strain backs and necks.

Strengthen: With your feet together, go up on to the balls of your feet and then come half way down and push up again several times. Try to keep ankles together. (If you like, rest your fingertips lightly on a wall to help you balance.)

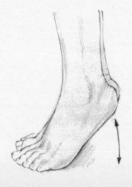

Loosen: Sit, stand, or lie with your feet up a wall. Rotate your feet outwards and inwards, flex them up and down, and then shake them loosely.

Squeeze: Squeeze the balls of your feet tightly with your toes and then spread your toes wide apart.

Strengthen feet: Stand and press your toes into the floor, so the soles of the feet lift. Repeat several times.

Strengthen ankles: Sit down and lift your big toes up towards the inside of your calves. Keep your heel on the floor, then move your little toes up towards the outside of your calves. Repeat several times until your ankles and calves begin to tire.

Stretch: Stand and lift one leg off the floor slightly, point your toes and then pull up towards the front of your leg, pushing away with your heel.

Stretch again: Stand, hands supported in front. Take a step forwards with your right foot. Bend your right leg, take your weight on to it and push your knee out over the little toe. Stretch your left leg behind and try to push the heel on to the floor. Repeat by stepping forward with your left foot.

At home: Try picking up objects like pencils with your feet. Place a towel or tea cloth over a book ('phone books are good) and try to lift the towel off the book.

FOR ACHES AND PAINS

Headaches

Many headaches and migraines can be eased and prevented by keeping your neck and shoulders loose. Do the movements suggested below preferably several times during the day to achieve the maximum effect.

The likely causes: Do you hold your neck on one side, causing strain, or stick your chin in the air or hunch your shoulders? Do you always turn round, using your whole body, so losing mobility in your neck muscles? Become aware of such body habits, so that you can break yourself of them.

Anywhere/anytime exercises: Without bending your neck forwards or sideways, and looking straight ahead imagine that you are drawing a circle in the air with your nose. Do this both to right and left.

Exercises that will help: Lie on your tummy on the floor, your arms clasped on your bottom with your elbows bent. Raise head and shoulders from floor. Breathe in, breathe out as you nod your head forwards drawing in your chin. Squeeze your upper arms and shoulder blades together at the same time. Breathe in raising your head and releasing your arms. Repeat the nod and squeeze three times and then lower your head and shoulders to the floor. Repeat the sequence up to four times.

Backache

After headaches, pain in the back, usually the lower back, is man's most intractable complaint. Exercising your back will improve the strength and health of your back, preventing strain due to weak muscles or wrong usage.

The likely causes: Do you cross your legs straining an already weak back? Do you stand bearing your weight on one leg only? Do you stand badly? Become aware of how you sit and stand.

Exercises that will help: For your lower back, lie on your front with a cushion under your pelvis. Bend both the lower parts of your legs up at the back, so they are vertical. Move your legs a hip width apart. Lift your right, then left, thigh off the cushion slowly.

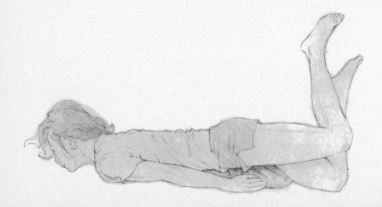

Before you get up: Lie on your back with your legs straight. Lift your right hip up towards your right ribcage at the same time pushing your left foot away from you. Then reverse the action. Repeat several times changing sides smoothly.

Spine: Stretch out your spine. Hanging from wall bars in a gym or from a door at home will give your spine a good stretch and alleviate backache caused by compression (an inward curvature of the spine can cause extra pressure on the vertebrae of the lower back). Put a box or stool by the door, so that you can stop when you want. Simply hold on to the top of the door or the wall bars and hang. Do not do this if you have any problems with shoulder joints.

Period pains

Most movement will benefit period pains as long as you don't feel sick. Avoid any violent exercise.

Exercises that will help: Sit on the floor with the soles of your feet together and your back straight against a wall if necessary. Hold on to your ankles and try to lift your chest out of your abdomen. Then push your thighs down towards the floor.

Tired aching legs

The way you stand and sit will affect how tired your legs feel. Do the thigh exercises given below to improve their strength as well as the foot and ankle exercises given in various sections of this chapter.

The likely cause: Do you sit with your legs crossed? This impairs circulation in the thighs and makes them feel tense and tired.

Anywhere/anytime exercises: When sitting, straighten your legs along the floor and push your heels away as you pull your toes towards you.

An exercise that will help: Lie on the floor with your bottom near the wall, squeeze your legs into your chest and then take them up the wall and lie there for a while. You can do the same exercise with your legs over a chair.

Aching feet

Feet take a lot of battering from the way we walk and the shoes we put them into, particularly high heels. If you tense your feet and curl your toes up in your shoes, this may make your feet ache.

An exercise that will help: Swimming is a good exercise for tense feet and ankles, as they get a good working in the water.

Anywhere/anytime exercises: Take your shoes off and wiggle your toes. Reach down and pull your big toe away from the other toes and rotate it fully both ways. Repeat with the other foot.

Varicose veins

Varicose veins can be helped by good muscle tone in the calf. Muscles need to be strong to help support the veins and loss of tone can contribute to varicose veins. Also remember, never stand when you can sit, preferably with your feet up. The following exercises are to strengthen weak veins and prevent varicose veins.

An exercise that will help: Stand with your fingertips touching a wall or chair and with your feet together. Raise on to the balls of your feet, then bring heels half way down towards the floor and push up again. Repeat until your calves begin to tire.

Anywhere/anytime exercises: Walking creates a strong pumping action in the leg muscles which helps the blood upwards through the veins. That's why standing still is not good for varicose veins as the strong pumping action is not taking place.

20 MINUTES A DAY

(See Posture page 245 for correct standing position)

Neck – 2 minutes: Drop your head forward and roll it slowly towards your right shoulder, then back across your chest towards your left shoulder.

Shoulders and arms – 2 minutes: Standing correctly, lift your right arm up brushing past your ear and back in a large circle. Repeat the same movement with your other arm and then do the exercise with both arms.

Upper back – 2 minutes: Lift your shoulders up towards your ears, then pull them back, squeezing into your upper back and then pull them down.

Spine – 2 minutes: Lift your leg, placing your hands under your knee, at the same time round your spine and take your head down towards your knee. Repeat with your other leg.

Waist, spine, back – 2 minutes: Stand with legs wide apart, hands on your chest with your upper arms close to your body. Keeping your hips forward, twist round to the back of the room to your right and then to the left.

Lower back – 2 minutes: Lift your right hip up towards the right ribcage, then transfer your weight on to your right leg and lift up your left hip. Repeat several times.

Waist – 2 minutes: Stand with legs apart and your hips square to the front. Stretch your right arm over your head towards your left, your elbow in line with your ear. Repeat the same action on your left side. Repeat slowly and quickly several times.

Pelvis – 2 minutes: Legs apart, bend a little at the knees. Now imagine that you are belly dancing and roll your pelvis in a large circle to the right and then to the left.

Legs – 2 minutes: Stand with your feet together, hands on hips and your hips square to the front. Lunge your right leg forward in a very large step, pressing left heel downwards behind you. Bring your feet together. Repeat several times with alternate legs.

Ankles – 2 minutes: Holding on to a support, if need be, lift your right leg off the floor and rotate the ankle outwards and inwards. Repeat with your left leg.

During the day: Everyday increase your heart rate to 120 beats (see page 278) if you are in good health by running upstairs. Getting yourself puffed exercises your heart which needs the exertion to keep it healthy and strong.

Day to day posture

The way you sit, stand, lie and walk affects your back and your body shape. Try to observe these basic principles.

Check bad habits when standing: Watch out for the following bad habits and correct them. Do you stand on one hip? This often develops from the habit of carrying young babies on one hip? Do your knees knock and does your bottom stick out?

Sitting: Make sure that your spine is well supported when sitting. Pull your shoulders down as you lift your spine and lengthen the back of your neck.

Check bad habits when sitting: Do you slump in your chair with your head disappearing in your chest and your shoulders practically touching your ears? Do you sit with arms crossed tightly in front of your chest pulling your shoulders forwards? Do you cross your legs which can strain your lower back and stretch your buttocks? Is the hollow in your back unsupported?

Lying: Try to keep your spine long and straight when you are lying down. It depends upon what condition your back is in as to the position you should lie in. Lying on your side with your knees slightly bent is safe for most people. If your problem is neck tension, lie on your back with just a small pillow at the base of your skull. If you have a sway back place a cushion under your thighs.

Check bad habits: Do you have a sway back and sleep face down, causing your back to overarch? Sleeping face down when you have neck tension, will cause strain and can create it in the first instance.

EXERCISE AIDS

There are many aids in your own home and at the gym to make exercise easier and more effective for you.

Mats: It is useful to have a mat to help cushion your body during exercise. There are some good Yoga mats available, which will not slip on polished surfaces.

Blankets: You can use blankets to cushion your body during exercise. Fold them and use as a pad to sit on when you are doing back exercises on the floor. Cover yourself with a blanket during relaxation, since your body loses heat as it relaxes.

Cushions: Make sure that cushions are sufficiently firm to support your body well and large enough to sit on comfortably. Use a cushion in back control exercises. Sit on the edge of the cushion so that it tips your pelvis forward.

Towels: Roll a large bathroom towel and lie on it when you relax placing it so that it runs down the whole length of your spine. This will help your chest to open and to get rid of the forward pull of your shoulders.

Tennis balls: Playing with a ball under each foot before your exercise routine will stretch and release the muscles of your ankles and the backs of your legs.

Belts: Ropes or belts are useful for stretching the backs of your legs and helping you to lift your back during back control exercises. Sit on the floor with your legs stretched straight in front of you, put the belt round the balls of your feet and try to straighten your back. (This is also the best way to judge the length of the belt needed.)

Broomsticks: You, or your teacher, can use a broomstick to help you develop body awareness. To test the position of your spine, place a broomstick against it and sense how swayed or straight your back is. Alternatively, hold a broomstick between your legs in front of you close to your body, during the back control exercises, to help you lift your chest as you straighten your back.

Mirrors: When you are starting to exercise, mirrors can be helpful. Do all your back exercises sideways on to a mirror, so that you can see your back. Eventually you have to be able to feel the correct position from the inside of your body, so do not rely on mirrors.

You are never too old

As you get older your body loses its flexibility. To keep your normal range of movement you need to exercise. This does not mean vigorously (though people jog well into their seventies) but gentle, loosening and strengthening exercises to prevent your body becoming stiff and your muscles deteriorating. Many people associate old age with lack of movement, so they just don't move. There is no sense behind this. Your muscles need to move to be healthy and they are never too old to benefit from movement.

Gentle exercises

Neck: Do all the exercises in the neck section (see page 253).

Shoulders: Lift them up as high as you can towards your ears and let them fall slowly pulling them towards your toes. Don't jerk.

Waist: Sit on a sturdy chair, keep your hips square to your front. Twist round to your right and reach across your body; let the back hand hold the far leg of your chair behind. Take a good deep breath in and, as you breathe out, try to twist a little more, remembering to turn the neck as well. Draw the chin in slightly, so the back of the neck lengthens. Repeat twisting to the left.

Shoulders: Lift your arms a little way from your body and then rotate your thumbs and hands as much as possible, so that your arms rotate in your shoulder joints as much as possible. Repeat slowly and more quickly.

Arms: Stretch your arms down firmly at your sides, stretching out the fingers as well. Relax and repeat.

Pelvis/lower back: Sit on a chair on your two sitting bones (these are the two knobbly bones you can feel in the bottom, which form the base of the pelvis) and lift your spine. Place your hands on your hips and roll your pelvis forward, breathe out as you roll it back, so that the pubic bone moves upwards.

Thighs: Squeeze your legs tightly together and release. Add a cushion between your legs and squeeze again to make the exercise stronger. (See Thigh section, page 260.)

Ankles: Sit on a sturdy chair. Cross your legs and rotate your upper ankle outwards and inwards. Repeat the same movement on your other ankle.

Feet: Sit down. Pull your toes back towards the fronts of your shins, then stretch them out, pointing your toes. Then give each foot a really good shake.

Skipping

If you are agile and have no problem joints, skipping is a very easy and convenient way to get fit. You can skip inside or out, provided you have enough space, and you can choose the time of day to suit you. If you maintain the exercise for more than 12 minutes it will be aerobic, thus increasing the fitness of your heart and lungs and you will build up body strength by endurance.

The right way to skip: Start off in the correct standing position and just jog through the skips. A helpful tip is to count the number of skips you do. This helps concentration and coordination. Build up slowly; for a minute the first day, depending on your level of fitness. Remember to skip backwards as well as forwards, so that your shoulders are pulled back occasionally.

Jumping rope: This is for the very energetic. Progress slowly to this stage after you have mastered skipping, as it is more tiring. Jump the rope with your legs together and remember to bend your knees as you hit the ground to lessen the impact. Your heels should also touch the ground to prevent damage to your calf muscles.

Before skipping: (See warm up exercises especially the calf stretch page 277.)

Check your rope: Make sure that your rope is long and heavy enough.

JOGGING AND RUNNING

The right way: Good posture is important so you don't create unnecessary tensions in your body. Think of your spine being long, keep your shoulders down and your pelvis centred. Watch the position of your knees as you run and don't allow them to fall in. Pad through from the heels to the balls of the feet. The heel must come down completely every time your foot hits the floor in

order for you to use your legs properly and to prevent too much strain being taken by your calves or spine. Use supports for weak ankles or knees and warm up thoroughly first.

See your doctor: If you are over 30, or haven't exercised for some time, or have a history of heart trouble and high blood pressure, or you are overweight, have a check up with your doctor and ask if jogging/running is suitable for you.

Fit fast: Jogging and running are for getting fit fast. They are aerobic exercises (see Aerobics and Swimming, pages 250 and 251).

Physical benefits: Physical fitness, improved circulation and breathing capacity, improvement in look of skin and tone of body are the benefits from jogging and running.

Mental benefits: Jogging and running relieve anxiety, depression, fatigue and build up confidence, satisfaction and contentment.

Slimming: Running and jogging use up fat stores in the body for energy thus decreasing body fat and changing it to lean muscle. You lose inches, if not weight, as muscle weighs more than fat.

Training effect: In order to increase fitness, you have to train. Aerobic exercises are the most suitable and should be done three to four times a week for a minimum of twenty minutes.

How much should you do?: It all depends on your level of fitness. If you are very unfit, then a walk in the park four times a week will make you fitter. It is best if you are thinking of taking up jogging seriously to talk to a qualified instructor. Always give yourself time to build up.

Build up slowly: To begin with walk for 3 metres/3 yards then jog for 3 metres/3 yards. Then each time you go out for a run decrease the time spent walking.

The harder it becomes: The fitter you are, the harder it is to raise that level of fitness. Increasing distance and lessening time is the usual way.

Is it safe? Jogging and running are safe as long as you prepare your body first and don't overdo it. You should be able to speak easily as you run without gasping for breath.

If you overdo it?: If you are running, jogging or in an aerobic class and you feel yourself gasping for breath, you have over-exerted yourself and created an oxygen debt. You need to slow down to pay off the debt and then maintain a comfortable pace.

Warm up: (see below.) Warming up your body before you start is essential to prepare your heart for the extra work. This will prevent muscles tearing.

Cool down: (see next page.) It is very important to cool down after jogging and running to allow your heart to readjust to its normal rhythm. This prevents strain and the muscles of your body becoming stiff. Stopping suddenly can make you feel dizzy.

Break in point: After between five and ten minutes your hand should begin to feel warm as your circulation starts to work faster. After 10–15 minutes you should feel that there is a slight slackening of effort and the rhythm of the exercise takes over.

Breathing: Pay attention to your breathing and try to get it going in a good rhythm as you run.

Fuel: If you are a serious runner/jogger you will need to take in a lot of carbohydrates. Consult a book on nutrition for a suitable diet.

Jogging in town: If you can't find a park and you are jogging by the kerb, remember to wear bright colours. White/yellow are good for early morning and dusk. You can buy orange bands to wear on arms. Always run with the traffic coming towards you.

Warm up

Walk, then jog on the spot: Stretching becomes easier once you have warmed up the circulation by first walking and then jogging on the spot. Remember to use the whole of your foot and keep your ankles loose.

Stretching up: Standing with your legs apart, pelvis centred, lift your arms up above your head keeping your shoulders down. Reach up stretching the sides of the body.

Touching your toes: Stand with your feet a hip width apart and bend your knees slightly as you bend from your hips to touch your toes. Breathe in and come up. Repeat several times. Combine stretching up and touching the toes breathing out as you go down and in as you come up.

Side bends: Stand with legs wide apart, hands on your hips and bend from side to side. Repeat with your arms stretched upwards.

Prepare your calves: Lunge on to your right leg taking the left way back behind you along the floor. Press the heel of your left leg into the floor. Hold the stretch for a count of five at least. Repeat with the other leg.

Take time: The older you are, the longer your body needs to stretch, so give yourself enough time – a good 10 minutes at least.

Twists: With legs wide apart, hands on your shoulders, twist from side to side several times.

Off you go: Start off slowly. If you just run off in a sprint and have to stop, the exercise is anaerobic, which means it doesn't improve the fitness of the heart and lungs.

Cool down

First of all: Decrease the pace of your run or jog then jog on the spot for a short while.

Touch your toes: The same exercise as in the warm-up but keep bouncing.

Stretch out the legs: Crouch down, placing your hands, palms down, on either side of your feet. Bounce on the balls of your feet, then put your heels down as you try to straighten your legs. Repeat several times.

Hang and swing: With your legs wide apart, bend forwards from your hips; take a good deep breath in and make sure your neck is relaxed. Swing to the right and left and bounce loosely towards each foot in between. Note: With knees bent, take a good deep breath in, then uncurl your back from the hips as you come up from bending forwards and finally lift your head. Hanging forward rests the heart.

Your pulse

Taking your pulse is the simplest way to assess your current level of fitness.

Average heart rates: For women it's between 75–90, for men it's between 70–85.

Taking your pulse: You can take your pulse on your wrist or on the carotid artery at the neck. The carotid artery is at the upper side of the neck, up towards the jawbone.

Wrist: Turn the palm of your hand upwards. Firmly place your three middle fingers towards the outside edge of your wrist and feel for your pulse.

Carotid: Lift your right arm to shoulder height and bend it so that the fingers point towards the neck. Place the middle three fingers on to the carotid artery and press gently.

Fitness check: Time your pulse rate before, during and after exercise to check your fitness level.

Finding your resting pulse rate: Use a clock with a second hand and count the number of times your pulse beats in six seconds. Multiply by 10. If, say, you counted eight beats in six seconds simply add a 0 and you have your resting pulse which is 80. Take your pulse at the beginning of your aerobic exercise to find your resting pulse.

Monitoring your pulse: This should be done 10 minutes in to the exercise, if you can, and at the end, when you stop your aerobic exercise. While you are working, your pulse rate should be in its training zone which is 70–75% of its maximum (see below).

How do you find your maximum pulse rate?: To find your maximum pulse rate, if you are unfit, you take your age away from 200, 220 if you are already fit. Say you are 30 years old – your maximum pulse rate if you are unfit would be 170. In aerobic exercise you only ever take your heart rate up to 70–75% of that maximum. If you are over 40 begin by only taking it to 60% of your maximum.

First time: To begin with don't let your heart rate go above 120 beats.

High blood pressure – caution: Exercise must only be taken in moderation, though it is extremely good for you as it encourages blood vessels to relax and dilate. Avoid sudden vigorous exercise.

Exercise in the pool

Benefits: Less strain is inflicted on your body. The water creates resistance for you to work against and it can be both relaxing and stimulating.

Before you jump in: Your shoulders and arms should be loose and flexible. Rotate your shoulders forwards and back. Let your arms hang heavily by your sides and give them a good shake.

Warm up: Do jumping jacks, that is jumping up and down and opening and closing your legs and arms at the same time, to warm up.

Swings: Hold on to the side of the pool, swing your leg forward as far as you can and then backwards. Repeat on the other side.

Rotations: Feet and ankles need to be strong for swimming. Stand sideways on to the edge of the pool; lift your right leg off the bottom of the pool and circle your ankle out and in. Repeat with your left leg.

Tone: Pool exercising is especially good for your bustline working the pectoral muscles of the chest.

Squeeze: Face the edge of the pool and hold on at arm's length. Lift your body so that you are floating on your front. Squeeze your legs into your chest while trying to keep yourself up in the water.

Stretch: Face the edge of the pool. Hold on at arm's length and lift your feet on to the wall. Push your feet into the wall as you try to straighten your legs.

Strain: If you have any neck tension, swim sidestroke or breaststroke with your head turned to one side for air. Lifting your head out of the water on a tight neck can add more tension.

Stretch and relax: Swimming is about stretching the body through the water which brings with it relaxation. Think of your strokes being long and make your breathing deep and rhythmic to benefit from this type of exercise.

INDEX

A

Abdomen, exercises for
the 242, 257–8
Accessories 145–52,
(xii), (xiii), (xv)
Acne 27, 76
Aerobics 221, 235, 248,
250
Aerosol mouth
fresheners 62
Age spots 36
Alcohol
diet and 231
effects of 212
exercising and 237
Allergies 31
Almond, beauty aids
with 174
Angelica for spots
186–7
Ankles
exercises for the 261–
2, 268, 272
relaxing the 215
swollen 43
thick 42–3, 126
Anti-perspirants 156,
157, 160
Appetite, loss of 203
Apple, beauty aids with
174
Arms. *See also* Elbows,
Hands
exercises for the
255–6, 267, 272
goose pimples on
the 46
relaxing the 215

shaving under 45,
157
Astringent lotions 59,
114, 160
Autogenics 216
Avocado, beauty aids
with 175

B

B vitamins 229
Back, exercises for the
241, 242, 258–9, 267,
268
Back problems 238
Backache relief 56,
264–5
Balance, to improve 235
Ballet 250
Bare foot exercise 244
Barrier cream 35, 164
Basil 187
Bath cubes 50
Bath oils and emulsions
50
Bath salts 50
Baths, bathing
after your bath 51–2
before your bath 51
cool summer 154–5
mock sauna 54
mock Turkish 53–4
preparations and
paraphernalia 50–1
quickie 54
saunas 52–3
Beans as source of
protein 225
Beauty kit 112–14

Beauty spots 32, 169
Bed, types of 211
Belts 145–6; from
scarves 149
Bi-focals and eye make-
up 10
Bikini 142, 143
Bikini hair 44
Birth marks 31, 77
Black molasses 231
Blackberry, beauty aids
with 176
Bleaching unwanted
hair 24, 44
Blemished skin 27
cleansing 67
covering 76–7
Blemishes 31–2, 76–7;
on legs 126
Blow drying hair 19–20
Blushers 89–92, 102,
104, 105, 161, 169, (ii)
Body brushes 51
Body lotion 52
Body shampoo 55
Body types 248
Boots, choice and care
of 126, 128–9
Bras 140–2, 244
Brown rice 229
Bruises 31, 184
Brushes for make-up
112, 169
Bubble baths 50
Bulky foods 222
Bunions 34
Butter in diet 222, 231
Buttermilk, beauty aids

using 179
Buttocks, exercises for
the 259–60

C

Caffeine, effects of 212
Calories 223, 230
Calves, exercises for
the 41, 242
Camomile tea 171, 212
Candlelight, make-up
for 105
Carbohydrates 225–6;
diet low in 229
Carrot facial 183
Chapped
hands 164
legs 165
lips 162
Cheeks 214. See also
Blushers
Cheese in diet 229, 231
Chilblains 164
Chloasma 31
Circulation 36, 39, 163,
207
Clay masks 59, 60
Cleansers, cleansing
26–9, 58–60, 113
Cleansing preparations
for ageing skin 67–8
for blemished skin 67
for combination skin
66
for dry sensitive skin
67
for dry skin 64–6
for the face 58–60
for the hair 61
for the hands 60–1
for the mouth 62
for normal skin 66–7
for travelling 68
for young skins 64
Cleansing massage 29
Cleansing tissues 58
Clothes. See also
Underwear
antique or
secondhand 134–5

basics to build on
118–19, (xi), (xii)
care of 122–3
colours, colour co-
ordination 119–21,
(xiv), (xv)
for travelling 137,
138
for winter 165
mixing and
matching patterns
and plains 121, (xvi)
packing 136–9
pressing 130
right, for your size
and shape 123–4
shopping wisely for
131–5
slimming tricks
with 125–6
trying on 132
wardrobe
organization 121–3
Coffee 212, 230
Coffee beans as hair
colourant 188
Cologne stick 155, 160
Complexion milks 58
Compressed powder
68, 82, 84, 115, 116
Concentration, lack of
203
Constipation 203
Contact lenses and eye
make-up 10, 100
Corns 34
Cosmetic sponge 80
Cotton-tipped sticks 169
Cream
beauty aids with 179
in diet 222, 231
Crêpey throat 30
Cucumber, beauty aids
with 183–4
Curly hair 17
Cuticle care 35
Cycling 221, 250

D

Dairy products 229;

as beauty aids 179–
80
Dancing 221, 250
Dandelion coffee 230
Dandruff 15, 61, 195
Decaffeinated coffee
230
Deep breathing 171,
172
Dehydrated skin, to
avoid 27
Dental check-ups 23
Dental floss 23
Deodorant talc 157
Deodorants 45, 156–7
Depilatories 23, 45
Diarrhoea 203, 229
Diets, dieting 217–24
away from home
224–5
balanced 229
exercise and 220,
221, 238
types of 228–9
Disapproval lines 30
Disco lights, make-up
for 106
Double chin 102
Down on arms 45
Dry shampoos 62, 168,
192–3

E

Earache 24
Ears
cleaning the 24
pierced 25–6
pressurization and
the 24
relaxing movements
for the 207
shapes 25
swimming and the 24
Earth-based face masks
59, 60
Eating habits and
weight loss 218–23
Eau de cologne 155
Ectomorphs 248
Eczema 203

Eggs
  beauty aids with 181–2
  in diet 222, 228, 229, 231
Elbows 46–7
Elderberry, beauty aids with 176
Electrolysis 23, 45
Endomorphs 248
Energy
  loss of 203
  wasted 205
Enlarged pores 59
Evening bags 146
Exercise, exercising
  after 249–50
  aids to 240, 270–1
  benefits of 250–1
  caution with 239–40
  dieting and 220, 221, 238
  for aches and pains 263–7
  for each part of the body 252–62, 267–8
  for posture 247–8, 268–9
  gentle 271–3
  types of 250–1
  what to wear for 243–4
  with a friend 240–2
Eye make-up 12–13, 93–100, (ii–viii);
  removal of 57, 94
Eyebrow pencil 13, 96, 113, 114, 116
Eyebrow pinching 9
Eyebrows
  closing in wide-apart 13
  gleaming 172
  relaxing exercise for the 214
  smoothing and shaping 98
  speedy make-up for 169

tweezing the 13
Eyelash curlers 98, 169
Eyelashes 97–9
  curling 98, 169
  dyeing 169
  false 99–100, 112
  separating 99
  thickening 98
Eyeliner pencils 10, 95, 115, 116, 169, (iv)
Eyes, See also Eye
  make-up, Glasses
  brightening the whites 94
  dark rings under the 8, 174
  hair colour to enhance (i)
  puffiness 8, 167, 180, 199
  massaging away tension 207, 214
  sparkling 9
  wrinkles and lines round the 8–9, 30, 32–3
Eyeshadow 113, 114, 169, (iv–viii)
  blending your own 95
  highlighters and 89
  skin type and 12
  water repellent 161

F

Face. See also Skin care
  cleansing the 26–9
  cleansing
    preparations for the 56, 58–60, 63–9
  exercises for the 256–7
  foundations for the 76–83
  highlighters for the 88–9
  instant face lift 166
  last minute face-savers 172
  make-up see

Foundations, lipstick etc.
  massage for the 29–30
  powdering the 82, 83–4
  relaxation techniques for the 214–5
  self-massage for stress signs 206–7
  shaping with make-up 101–5
  summer make-up 160–1
  winter make-up 162–3
Face-bronzer 161
Face masks 27, 59–60, 167
Face shape
  choosing glasses for 9–10
  choosing hats for 151–2
  hair style and 18–19
Facial cleansing pads 83, 115
Facial hair 23–4
Fading cream 77
Fake tan 108–11
False eyelashes 99–100, 112
Fashion see Clothes
Fasting 238
Fats in diet 222, 226, 229
Feet. See also Toe nails
  aching 33, 266
  care of 33–4
  care of in winter 165
  choice of shoes and boots 126, 128–9
  corns 34
  exercises for the 34, 261–2, 273
  infections of the 34
  keeping cool in heat 160
  massage for the 34, 207

pedicure routine 34
relaxing movements for the 215
Fibre diet 229
Financial pressure, stress caused by 205
Finger nails
applying and removing nail polish 106–8, (x)
care of 36–8
don'ts for 38
first aid for 35
manicure routine 38
Fish in diet 222, 226, 228, 229
Flour in diet 231
Foam baths 50
Food and slimming 217–27
Foot bath 165
Forgetfulness, stress as cause of 203
Foundations 76–7, 114, 168
application of 79–83
colour of 78–9
Freckles 32, 77, 160, 179
Friction mitt 163
Friction rub 172
Friction straps 51
Frown lines 30
Fructose 231
Fruit 222, 227, 229
beauty aids using 174–8
diets 229
squashes 231

G

Gel-based face masks 60
Gel foundations 111, 161
Glasses
bi-focals 10
coloured frames 10
eye make-up and 10, 100, (iii)

shape of, for your face 9–10
shape of, for your nose 11
Gloves 164, 165, 244
Gold highlighter 161
Goose pimples
on arms 46
on legs 39
Gravy-making for dieters 232
Gums, care of 22–3

H

Hair, hair care
blow drying 19–20
brushes and combs 14, 15
brushing 14, 168
climate and 21–2
colour 15, (i)
conditioner 15
coping with in emergencies 168
curly 17
face shape and 18–19
finger drying 21
fringes 18
growth 16
henna 187–8
in hot weather 158–60
in winter 165
on holiday 20–2
pageboy style 20
partings 18
scalp massage 14
shampoos 14–15, 61–2
split ends 14
sticking up, to deal with 166
styling 17
Hair, unwanted
facial 23–4
on legs 44–5
underarm 45, 157
Hand cream 36
Handbags 145, 146
Hands. See also Finger

nails
age spots on the 36
care of in winter 164
cleansers for the 60–1
exercises for the 36, 255
first aid for the 35
improving circulation of the 36
keeping cool in heat 160
relaxing movements for the 215
Hangnails 37
Hats 145, 150–2, 244
Head
massage for a tense 206
relaxing techniques for the 214
Headaches 203
exercises for 263
massaging away 206
Henna 187–8
Herb and plant beauty aids 186–99
High blood pressure 228, 229, 251, 279
High-cheekboned look 101
Highlighters 88–9, 161, (ii)
Hips, massage for 208
Honey
as sleep inducer 171
facials with 200
in diets 231

I

Ingrown toenails 34
Insomnia 203, 212
Instant tan 108–10
Irritability from stress 203
Isometric exercises 250

J

Jaw, jaw-line
  ageing and the 31
  minimizing a heavy 104
  playing down a square 101
  relieving tension in the 207, 214
  widening the 101
Jewellery
  as fashion accessory 146–7
  for holidays 138
  keeping safe 122
  old 135
  packing 137
Jogging 221, 235, 251, 274–8
Jumping rope 273

K

Keep-fit exercises 234, 235
Keep-fit routines, speedy 171
Khanga 144
Knees
  massage for fleshy 41
  problems of the 238
  smooth 41

L

Lace 135
Lavender, beauty aids with 188–9
Leek treatment for bruises 184
Leg warmers 243
Legs. See also Ankles, Knees, Thighs
  all-round beauty treatment for 39
  bare 160
  clothes and your 126, (xi)
  exercises for the 265, 268
  heavy or slight calves 41

improving
  circulation in 39
  massage for the 208
  removing hair on the 44–5
  rough skin and goose pimples on the 39
  thread veins 39
  varicose veins 41–2
  winter care of 165
Lemon, beauty aids with 177; for freckles 32
Leotard for exercising 243
Light
  and eyes 8
  and make-up 105–6
Light headedness 203
Lines on the face 8, 9, 22, 30–1, 32–3
Lip gloss 85, 113, 114, 172; substitute for 112
Lip pencils 85, 114
Lips
  chapped 162
Lipstick 22, 85–8, 113, 114, 115, 116
  colour matching with clothes (xiv)
  repairing broken 112
  shaping lips with (ix)
Liquid soap 59
Loofahs 51
Lordosis 240
Luggage 136
Lying down correctly 269

M

Make-up see Eye make-up, Face, Foundations, Lipsticks etc.
Make-up kits 112–15

Margarines 226, 232
Marigold as hair colourant 190
Mascara 113, 114, 161
  to apply 98, 100, 169
  to remove 99
Massage
  cleansing 29
  in-depth facial 29–30
  self, to relieve stress 206–8
Massage gloves 51
Meat in diet 222, 226, 228, 229; to cook 223, 227
Medicated shampoos 61
Meditation 216, 251
Mesomorphs 248
Midriff, to minimize 47–8
Migraine 203, 263
Milk
  beauty aids with 180
  in diet 229, 231
Mineral supplements 226
Mineral water sprays 28, 82, 114
Moisturizers 27, 77, 79, 113, 114
Moles 32
Monosaturated fats 226, 232
Mouth. See also Lipstick
  care of teeth and gums 22–3
  cleansing preparations for the 62
  counteracting droopy corners of the 22
  emphasizing the 88
  relaxing the 215
Mouth washes 62
Mud packs 60
Muscle strength 234
Muscle waste 220

N

Nail polish 114
to apply and remove
106–8, (x)
to thin 112
Nails see Finger nails,
Toe nails
Neck
care of the 31, 32
exercises for the 252–
3, 267, 271
foundation for the 81
massage for a taut
206
relaxing the 214
short or long, clothes
for 125, 126
Neon lights, make-up
for 106
Nettle lotion 190
Nose
choosing glasses to
go with shape of
11
foundation on the 80
massage for sinus
trouble 207
red 163, 166
shape and make-up
102–4
Nose-to-mouth lines 22,
32
Nutrition 225–7
Nuts in diet 222, 225,
226, 229

O

Oatmeal beauty aids
190–2
Oil shampoos 61
Olive oil 184–5, 226
Onion juice for itchy feet
185
Orange flower cleanser
192
Orris dry shampoo
192–3
Overeating 203
Overweightness 218, 248
'pinch test' for 245

P

Packing 136–9
Pear-shaped, clothes
for the 124
Pelvic exercises 247,
259, 268, 272
Peppermint and plant-
oil massage 193
Peppermint tea 171
Perfumes
care of 74
choosing 70–1
making go further
72–3
matching up fabrics
and 74
strength of 70
types of 69–70
using 71–2
Period pains, relief from
239, 265
Perspiration 156–8
Petite, clothes for the
124
Pierced ears 25–6
Pillow creases 166
Pine needles, beauty
aids with 193–4
Pipe cleaner hair
curlers 168
Plant and herb beauty
aids 186–99
Polarized lenses 12
Polyunsaturated fats
226, 232
Pool exercising 280
Pore and cleansing
grains 59
Positive thinking 204
Posture 245–7, 268–9
clothes and 123
exercises for 247–8
Potato eye freshener
185
Poultry in diet 226, 227,
228
Powder blushers 89, 91,
113, 115
Powder, powdering the
face 82, 83–4, (ii)

Powder puffs 116
Pregnancy
exercises and 238
hairdos for 18
posture and 248
smoking and 209
varicose veins in 42
Pressing clothes 130
Protein diet 228
Proteins 222, 225
Puffy eyes 8, 167, 180
Pulse rate 278–9
Pumice stone 33, 44

R

Raspberry, beauty aids
with 178
Relaxation techniques
213–17
'Rolling' lotions 61
Rose petal mask 194
Rosemary, hair
preparations with 195
Rosewater 114, 195–6
Round shoulders, to
prevent 247
Rubber-based face
masks 60
Running 221, 235, 251,
274–8

S

Sable brush for make-
up 169
Saffron highlights 196
Sage treatment for grey
hair 196
Salads in diet 222, 223,
229
Sales, shopping in the
133–4
Salt in diet 228, 231
Saturated fats 226
Saunas 52–3, 237
mock 54
relaxation and 216–17
Scalp massage 14
Scars 77, 126
Scarves 139, 148–50,
(xiii)

belts made with 149
turbans from 148
ways to trim 148–9
Sea salt body rub down 46
Self-criticism, dealing with 205
Self-massage for stress 206–8
Shampoos 14, 15, 61, 64
dry 62, 168, 192-3
Shaving
legs 44
underarms 45, 157
Shawls 135, 148
Shirt, ways to wear a classic 147
Shoes, choice and care of 126, 128–9, 145, (xi)
for exercising 244
Shopping
for clothes 131–5
for food 227
Shorts for exercising 243
Shoulder bags 146
Shoulders
easing tension in 207, 215
exercises for the 241, 254, 267, 271, 272
preventing round 247
Showers 54–5
Sinuses, to clear 207
Sitting correctly 269
Ski-ing 221, 235
Skimmed milk in diet 222, 228, 231
Skin, skin care
acne 27, 76
ageing process and 30–1
banishing blemishes 31–2, 76–7
cleansing the 26–9
cleansing
preparations for ageing 67–8
cleansing

preparations for blemished 67
cleansing
preparations for combination 66
cleansing
preparations for dry 64–6
cleansing
preparations for dry sensitive 67
cleansing
preparations for normal 66–7
cleansing
preparations for young 63–4
deep cleansing 29
eye make-up and skin type 12–13
foundation
preparations 76–83
hair colour and skin tone (i)
improving rough or scaly 54
moisturizers 27, 77, 79, 113, 114
preparing for sun-bathing 110
protecting from cold 162–3
protecting from heat 160–1
soap and water washing 28
tonics and fresheners 59, 160
types of 26–7
Skipping 221, 235, 273
Sleep, aids to 171, 210–13
Sleepers for pierced ears 25
Slimming and eating sensibly 217–32. See also Diets, Nutrition
Sloughing cleansers 58
Smoking, to give up 209–10

Smudgeproof mascara 161
Soap and water washing 28
Soaps 59
Soapwort herb shampoo 197
Sodium-free salt 228
Soya vegetable protein 225, 226
Spectacles see Glasses
Spine, exercise for the 267, 268
Spots 27, 32, 67. See also Acne
Squash 251
Stamina 235
improving 250–5
loss of 203
Stockings 127, (xi)
Stress 202–8
and body odour 158
Stretch marks 48
Stretching exercises 213, 235, 251
for ankles and feet 262
for arms, wrists and hands 255
for the back 258
for the neck 253
for the shoulders 254
for the thighs 261
Suede shoes 129
Sugar in diet 222, 226, 227, 229, 231
Sugar hand cleanser 197
Summer beauty routine 156–61
Sunbathing, preparing skin for 110
Sunflower facial 197
Sunglasses 11–12, 138
for children 12
Sunscreeners 109, 111
Sway back 247, 270
Sweat suits 243
Swimming and pool

exercising 235, 237, 251, 280
Swimwear 138, 142–4

T

T-shirts 243, (xi)
Tai Chi 215, 251
Talcum powder 50, 52
Tall, clothes for the 124
Tan, to keep a 110–11. See also Fake tan
Tea 212, 230
  beauty aids using 197–8
Teeth, care of 22–3
Tennis 251
Tension 9, 172, 202. See Stress
Thermal underwear 165
Thighs
  clothes for heavy 126
  exercises for the 241, 260–1, 272
  massage for the 40, 208
  relaxing the 215
Thread veins 39
Throat
  crêpey 30
  relaxing the 214
Tights 127, (xi)
  for exercising 243
Toe nails 34, 160
  ingrown 34
Toilet waters 155
Tomato treatment for the arms 185
Toning lotions 64, 114
Tooth picks 23
Toothbrush, care of 23
Toothpastes and powders 62
Top heavy, clothes for the 124
Topless bathing 142
Track suits 243
Translucent powder 84, 113, 114, 161
Transparent powder 84

Tweezers 13
Tweezing
  eyebrows 13
  unwanted hair 24

U

Underarm hair 45, 157
Under-stress 205
Underwear 139–42
  for winter 165
Unfit, how to tell if you are 244–5

V

Varicose veins 41–2, 126, 266–7
Vegetable oil treatment 185–6
Vegetable oils 226, 232
Vegetable proteins 225, 229
Vegetables
  beauty aids using 183–6
  in diet 222, 223, 227, 229
Vegetarian diet 229
Vitamin A 46
Vitamin B 229
Vitamin C 230
Vitamin supplements 226

W

Waist, exercises for the 268, 272
Walking as exercise 235, 251
Walnut as hair colourant 186
Warts 32
Wash-off creams 58
Water
  and the face 28
  importance of drinking plenty of 27, 221
Waterproof cosmetics 57, 161
Waterproof mascara 99, 161

Wax-based face masks 60
Waxing away unwanted hair 23, 44
Weight-lifting exercises 234
Wheatgerm facial 198
Wholemeal bread 222, 229, 232
Winding down routines 212
Winter beauty routine 162–6
Witchhazel 114, 195, 198–9
Wrinkles 8, 9
  egg treatment for 181–2
Wrists, exercises for the 255

Y

Ylang ylang oil 199
Yoga 215, 235, 251
Yogurt
  in diet 222, 231
  toner 180